MW01090027

"Rick Ridder takes us on a hilarious ride along the campaign trail, from the Iowa caucuses to Italian hill towns. Along the way, he introduces us to every kind of candidate and campaign, from the earnest but misguided to the wildly undisciplined. Beneath the humor, Rick shares savvy and practical observations from the real world of politics."

—ROSE KAPOLCZYNSKI,
long-time California political consultant and
campaign manager for Barbara Boxer's campaigns

"There is no doubt that Rick knows the rules of the road when it comes to campaigns. Anyone looking to work in politics should take Rick's advice: work hard, ask questions, and don't be afraid to say 'yes, I'll get in my car and drive through the night for the next job'—you never know where you'll end up."

—STEPHANIE SCHRIOCK,
president of EMILY's List

"Rick Ridder is one of the most experienced and wryly thoughtful campaign operatives in the world and this book is both insightful and hilarious!"

—GOVERNOR HOWARD DEAN

"There are so many fascinating elements to campaigns that the public never hears about. Incredible characters, plots, drama. Rick Ridder has seen and done it all. In the United States and around the world, Rick has compiled his stories into a riveting book that tells all and reveals what it is really like to be in the back room when the political deals are being cut."

—MARK McKINNON,
co-founder of No Labels,
co-creator and co-host of *The Circus*

"A political insider's rollicking tales—wise, funny and insightful."

—MERYL GORDON,
author of *New York Times* bestseller *Mrs. Astor's Regrets*

*[Handwritten inscription:]* To Colin wonderful for you to come and to enjoy campaigns ints 4497!

# LOOKING FOR
# VOTES IN ALL THE
# WRONG PLACES

*[signature]*

# LOOKING FOR VOTES IN ALL THE WRONG PLACES

## TALES AND RULES FROM
## THE CAMPAIGN TRAIL

## RICK RIDDER

radius book group

Distributed by Radius Book Group
An Imprint of Diversion Publishing Corp.
443 Park Avenue South, Suite 1008
New York, New York 10016
www.DiversionBooks.com

Portions of Chapter 7 were originally published in *Campaigns & Elections* in July, 2013.
Portions of Chapter 8 were published by the *Denver Post* in March, 6, 2015.
Portions of Chapter 13 were originally published in *Campaigns & Elections* in July, 1992.
Portions of the chapter "A Few Musings at the End" were published previously by
RealClearPolitics, December 8, 2014.

For more information, email info@diversionbooks.com

First edition: November 2016
eBook ISBN: 978-1-68230-798-4
Paperback ISBN: 978-1-68230-799-1

For Joe Napolitan, Bill Daly, Matt Reese, and Jean Westwood
—mentors who let me learn by making my own mistakes.

*Change is inevitable—except from a vending machine.*
Robert C. Gallagher

# THE GENESIS OF THIS BOOK

My entry into political campaigning, and into associating myself with a political party, began at a young age. I remember it clearly.

Late fall, 1956. I was accompanying my mother to a meeting of the Fairfax County Democrats at Franklin Sherman Elementary School in McLean, Virginia. As she pulled her vehicle—a Nash Rambler—toward the sidewalk to park, she told me, "Sit in the car. Quietly."

I protested. "Can I come with you?"

She reiterated. "Better you wait in the car. I won't be long."

I reiterated. "Can't I come with you?"

She gave in. (If only all my arguments ended with such a quick victory.) "Okay, you can get out of the car, if you promise to stay nearby." She reached to the floor mats and collected a sheaf of papers. "And hand these to the people going into the building."

"What are they?"

"They are papers telling people to vote for Adlai Stevenson for President." She opened the door to let me out of the car.

"Okay," I said jumping down to the sidewalk. "Is Daddy for him, too?"

"No, he's for General Eisenhower." She handed me the leaflets.

I stiffened and, chest protruding, announced, "Well, I want to be like Daddy."

My mother was always open-minded. "That's fine," she said, reaching for the leaflets. "But then you can't hand these out for Adlai Stevenson. And you will have to stay in the car. Quietly."

"I can't be like Daddy and hand these to the people?" I asked.

"No, you can't!" responded my mother with a stare.

Lesson one: Politics is about forcing choices.

I chose automobile liberation and so, at age three, became a Democrat and a political operative. Later in my organizing career, I wondered what was written on those leaflets and why I was handing them to people entering a Democratic Party meeting where, presumably, all of the participants already supported Stevenson. Wouldn't it have been wiser to send me to a street corner to target swing voters?

This misdirection of resources may explain why my efforts on behalf of Stevenson did not result in victory. He lost—as have many of the candidates, causes, parties, and wannabes on whose behalf I have labored.

This book started as a reaction to one of those campaigns—a campaign during which staff and consultants enjoyed way too much laughter and conviviality along the way to a monumental loss. After a brief recap of our polling—we were never going to win, as our polling had shown us from start to finish—and a few more beers, wines, and whiskeys, one of our younger team members asked me, "As the old curmudgeon among us, what were campaigns like before cellphones, computers, Facebook, micro-targeting, online advertising, and text messaging?"

I resisted the opportunity to add microbrews to his list of nouveau campaign accoutrements. Further, I elected not to tell the assemblage that I was a key member of the Adlai Stevenson team. But I did accept the challenge of describing what campaigning was like back when many of us owned only twelve-inch black-and-white TVs. I began by recounting a few war stories from the 1972 presidential campaign of George McGovern, which had taken place before the birth of every other person in the room. When I finished, our campaign field director, who had been schooled in the Obama voter contact program, commented, "I can't believe your McGovern door-to-door effort was so extensive and detailed. By the way, you should write this down."

I didn't immediately commit to his suggestion, but I did try to explain that strategy had not changed a great deal since 1972; it was the tools of the trade that had changed significantly, even as the purpose remained the same. For instance, we now have computers to track voters, which as a friend once said, "is a really, really fast way to track and sort 3 x 5 cards that have voter data."

The stories that night did not end with the McGovern campaign, nor did my political life—although it took a bit of a detour post 1972. After I worked on the McGovern campaign, I was a college student, graduate student, doctoral student, law student, sportswriter, music critic, minor-league gambler on baseball games, radio and television producer, newscaster, disc jockey, ski instructor, and Boston cab driver. I had some notable successes, but finding a career path was not one of them. At best, I was headed toward becoming an academic specialist in media law who could produce rock-and-roll and country music recordings. That was an eclectic skill set, but one for which there was zero demand in the job market. Moreover, it did not seem to satisfy some more grandiose instinct I possessed to effect societal change.

That instinct, along with a distrust of excessive state police power, probably stemmed from my one week as a fifteen-year-old McCarthy for President volunteer at the 1968 Democratic convention in Chicago. I watched from our hotel hallway as cops beat and pulled my fellow coworkers from their rooms on the 15th floor. This was only hours after the cops had bloodied demonstrators in Grant Park in what was later called a police riot. Yes, teenagers are impressionable.

In 1980, I gave up my job as a broadcast producer, which had netted me an offer to get in on the ground floor of a new cable network known as the Entertainment and Sports Programming Network (ESPN). I declined, saying I didn't want to produce demolition derbies. Of course, many of my friends say that is precisely what I have been doing for the past thirty-plus years as a campaign consultant.

Instead of ESPN, I went to work for two months for Senator Gary Hart, whom I had met in the McGovern campaign eight years earlier. Then, forgoing my Ph.D., I spent nearly a year working for Ralph Nader as one of Nader's Raiders on media and telecommunications issues, before returning to Colorado to work for Governor Dick Lamm's re-election campaign.

It was after that campaign that my life's calling crystallized. When I returned to my home in Washington from the Lamm campaign, I was twenty-nine, married, and had one son. One evening as he prepared himself a martini, my father, in his upper-crust, cultured tone, asked me, "Now, just what the hell do you plan to do with your life?"

In Colorado, I had worked with Matt Reese, a highly regarded political consultant, and I thought that a career advising political candidates and campaigns was at least worth investigating. So I told my father, "I want to be a political consultant."

"You want to be what?" He dropped an olive into his drink.

"A political consultant," I repeated, proud that I had found some occupational ambition—at least for the immediate moment.

"What exactly is a political consultant?" he asked. Although he had been a national political reporter for forty years, covering numerous political campaigns, the precise term wasn't that familiar to him.

I was in trouble at that point. I saw what was coming. The old White House journalist was going to fire questions at me as if I were a press secretary trying to obfuscate the details of an incipient scandal. "Well, um . . ." I said, ". . . a political consultant gives advice on strategy and tactics in campaigns."

"How many of these *political consultants* are there?"

"I dunno. Maybe forty or fifty. Not a lot."

He put down his martini. "If there are only forty or fifty, then it can't be a position in high demand. I'd imagine you'd have to be extremely skilled in that occupation, yes?"

"Yeah but it's a growing field. There were only a few consultants a decade ago."

I actually had no idea how many political consultants existed in 1972, so "a few" seemed like a good number.

"A few? Is that ten, twenty, three, four?"

In the years to come, I would adapt his line of questioning into the maxim, "If you can't count it, it didn't happen."

"I don't know how many," I conceded. But there's a book called *The New Kingmakers* that details about ten of them."

My father picked up his glass, took a sip, and smiled, "Okay, so just how, then, do you become a political consultant?"

"I guess . . . you get a lot of jobs in campaigns, so you get good at it," I answered.

My father clearly recognized my discomfort in trying to explain my career path and offered me a drink. "Then I suppose you ought to go out and actually find campaign jobs before you become a political consultant," he reasoned, handing me a Scotch.

I agreed.

Within six months, I was back working on campaigns. Within five years, I had my first client as a consultant. Thirty years later, I am still involved in campaigns on a daily basis. With my wife, Joannie Braden, I run a political consulting firm, Ridder/Braden, Inc., aka RBI Strategies and Research. Our clients have almost always been Democrats, environmental groups, or those on the center-left, speaking in international terms.

Although we are mostly consultants to Democrats and progressives, that doesn't mean we don't work with Republicans or conservatives. Ballot initiatives, such as those for LGBT rights and marijuana legalization, have given us an opportunity to work with those who, in most cases, we try to defeat. Generally, though, we have turned down entreaties from oil and gas companies, mining companies, and conservative groups and organizations.

Over my forty years of working as a field organizer, campaign manager, and consultant, I developed or followed a few rules of the road. Like all rules, often they are not applicable, often not appropriate, and often should be disregarded. Indeed, some long-established rules are not such a good idea. Many of the stories I tell are sterling examples of the over-zealous application of cornerstone rules.

The rules in the following pages should not be seen as the only political campaign rules to follow. There exist numerous campaign management books and manuals, and every campaign operative has his or her own dictums. I even have a few more than I list here. But I selected these rules because they add focus and flavor to a good story, even as they provide guidance to the novice and perhaps even the veteran political organizer or consultant.

There is no specific hierarchy of importance in the rules presented here. Obviously, though, as with all things in life, some are just more important than others. You will figure out which ones are key after you fail to heed them.

Using these rules as my touchstones, I recount some tales from my forty years of campaign organizing and consulting. Like almost all tales, they tend to grow taller with age, increased blood-alcohol level, and THC level, but they always rest on a residue of the truth as best I can recall it. I have changed some names, identifying details and geographic locations because certain fine people I mention need not be further haunted by their pasts. In the same spirit, I certainly hope that any surveyor of my life would be kind enough not to attribute some of my antics to me. I have retained other names because acknowledging these familiar personalities might give us a better understanding of our heroes and villains, and my clients. And in a couple of cases, certain stories include composites of actions of more than one individual to provide a better lesson and, frankly, a better story.

And—oh, yeah—about my mother's telling me her meeting would "not last long," Lesson Two from that first political engagement is that there is no such thing as a short political meeting.

# RULE #1

## KNOW YOUR POSITIVES AND NEGATIVES.

Good candidates know their positives. They (or their staff) highlight the inspiring elements in their biographies, the aspects that illustrate their values and capabilities. Good candidates also know their negatives. They (or their staff) avoid situations in which the less attractive parts of their background, character, romantic history, libido, or food issues might come to the fore. I've seen candidates cancel events because former lovers would be attending; others have refused to campaign in rural areas during ragweed outbreaks. One rumored Lothario refused to be photographed in any form of an embrace with any female not his wife. These candidates had made the proper self-assessment of their weaknesses and then acted accordingly.

If they are unsure of their advantages and limitations, candidates should not tread into self-perceived areas of expertise without first consulting staff and/or experts who must dissuade them from doing or saying something likely to cause them embarrassment. But when it comes to assessing their personal vulnerabilities, candidates rarely consult wiser heads. So, not surprisingly, most candidates are not good candidates.

• • •

It was a beautiful night for baseball at Coors Field. A warm breeze was blowing across center field. The sun was setting behind the Rocky Mountains as the Colorado Rockies were set to host the Los Angeles Dodgers.

My wife Joannie and I arrived early. We settled into our seats, beers in hand, and were writing the starting line-ups into our scorecards when we looked onto the field and saw a familiar figure heading toward the microphone.

"What's the congressman doing down on the field?" I asked. Before Joannie could respond, we heard the announcer say, "Ladies and gentleman. To honor America, please rise, remove your caps, and join a member of the United States Congress to sing our national anthem."

I had heard that the guy enjoyed singing. There were insider stories that his staff would block time for him to attend rehearsals of his church choir, even during campaign season. I was unaware, however, that he harbored ambitions as a soloist.

"Who put this on his schedule?" I wondered aloud to my wife—but we both knew: he'd probably arranged it without telling his staff because they certainly would have told him to forget the whole idea.

The congressman strode to the microphone at home plate, and began—a capella. In other words, he was out there all alone. Vocally naked.

Now, I believe that if Rex Harrison could carry a tune in *My Fair Lady* anyone can sing a song—as long as it's not "The Star Spangled Banner." A friend of mine who is a music teacher argues that "no one but a trained professional can sing our national anthem properly because the melody demands the vocal capacity of a boy soprano combined with that of an operatic baritone."

The congressman proved my friend correct. As he was not a trained professional, he could reach neither the highs nor the lows, but rather was simply flat and strained.

It also was clear early in the rendition that he had no clue as to the sound system's time delay. As he took a long pause after "O, say can you see"—long enough to order and pay for a hot dog and a beer if the concession stand was only slightly mobbed—the guy sitting behind me said, "Oh, shit. Has he forgotten the words?"

Which is exactly the impression you want to leave when you're a United States representative: that you don't know the words to our national anthem. Next thing you know, people will think you're a secret member of the Communist Party.

Finally, he came to "O'er the land of the free . . . and the home of the brave," which had the tonal qualities of a jumpy chainsaw.

I heard again from the guy behind me, "Who was that guy?"

"A congressman," the man's friend said.

"Jesus. No wonder the country's such a mess."

• • •

Ralph Cheever had a clear idea of what his assets were and had the pedigree to prove it. He was convinced that his work in the animal kingdom made him not only qualified for the office of state legislator but a stone-cold lock to win it.

Cheever showed up at our office one bright June day in the late 1980s. We were consultants to the Colorado Democratic Party at the time, with the responsibility of working with candidates aspiring to the Colorado State House. Ralph came highly recommended by one of the state's leading lobbyists. At first glance, he appeared to be an excellent candidate to run against a long-time Republican incumbent.

We told him our first job would be to conduct a poll for him.

"What district are you running in?" we asked.

"House District Fifty-five. I live in Cañon City and have worked that area all my life."

"That's a pretty rural area," I pointed out, "covering a lot of territory, probably a hundred miles from one end to the other. So you've worked that area? That's great. Doing what?"

"I've been a part-time rancher. Run a small cow-calf operation."

"That's good for that district."

And it was. It was manly, down-home, authentic, Western. But Cheever's opponent had represented that area for decades and he had the manly, Western thing going as well.

"What makes you think you can beat the incumbent?" I asked.

"Everyone knows me."

"Everyone?"

"Yep. Everyone."

"Fantastic."

I didn't live in the district, but if "everyone" knew him you'd think I'd have at least *heard of* him. I hadn't.

"How do people know you?"

"Well, Rick, I *am* a rancher, it's true. But that's not my *real* job. Everyone knows me for my *real* job."

"Your *real* job. Which is . . ."

"I am an internationally recognized cat judge."

"An internationally recognized . . . what?"

"I am a cat judge. I fly all over the world to judge cats. Last week, I was in Japan."

"Japan, wow."

"They love cats in Japan."

"I'm sure they do. You make a living doing this?"

"People know me all over the world for it."

"All over the world—that's great. How about within House District Fifty-five ?"

"You bet. Let me show you a newspaper article."

He took out his wallet, pulled from it a yellowed newspaper clipping, and unfolded it. It was on the seventh of its nine lives.

He handed me the clipping. It was from the *Cañon City Record*, two years previously. There, on Page 5, was an article on Ralph Cheever's exploits as a world-renowned cat judge.

At least I knew he wasn't just messing with me.

"This is great," I said. "Any other press?"

"Sure. There's the KRKZ radio interview."

"Fabulous. When was that?"

"About a year ago."

A two-year-old newspaper clipping. A year-old radio interview. This avalanche of media exposure made me curious.

"Just what do you judge these cats on? Their purring capabilities? Their prowess as mouse catchers?" I resisted the urge to blurt out, *Their ability to stay alive in an alley?*

This got him started on a monologue describing the criteria used to judge feline flawlessness: what to look for in the hair, the eyes, the "representation of the breed," and the "composure." It was like Billy Beane, of *Moneyball*, waxing grandiloquent on the intricacies of the OBP.

*Gotta hand it to the guy*, I thought, *he really knows his cats.* I didn't have the guts to tell him that I hate cats. I am so allergic to cats that the local clinic makes me their regular guinea pig when they test asthma medicines. They simply put me in a room with cat hair, then see if the medicine saves my life. So far, they've all worked.

Ralph could have gone on for hours. In fact, it seemed as though he'd been speaking for days when I finally interrupted him with the ultimate candidate-stumper: "So why do you want to be in the legislature?"

"Oh, that's easy. Because I will bring my experience as an impartial judge of cats to a partisan environment. I will use my cat-judging talent and skill to bring us together."

My God, what a beautiful idea. Why hadn't I thought of it before? Maybe because I'd met the dogs in the state legislature.

"Tell you what," I said. "In your poll, we'll test the following factors: your name ID, the cat judging, the ranching, and your reason for running. Let's see what we get and we'll take it from there. Okay?"

In the few minutes remaining, we turned to the issues of the day: education funding, transportation, and balancing the state budget. He knew less about these issues than he did about feline finery.

"I'll look to my friend Wally to tell me how to vote on those issues," he said, referring to the lobbyist who had recommended him to the chairman of the Colorado Democratic Party.

We fielded the poll. Ralph Cheever began the campaign down thirty points against his opponent: 50 percent to 20 percent. His name ID was at 8 percent. (I guess "Everyone knows me" had been a slight exaggeration.) Twelve percent of voters found his status as an "internationally recognized cat judge" to be a "very" or "somewhat" convincing reason to vote for him. His ranching background, on the other hand, scored 65 percent "very" convincing. As for the *raison d'etre* of his candidacy? Well, somewhere in HD 55, there were two people out of the 300 sampled who found the impartiality of a cat judge to be the key to ending partisan division in the legislature. The other 298 were not convinced. We advised Cheever to replace "cat judge" with "rancher" as the lead element in his biography.

He didn't. Late in the fall I saw a brochure in which he included his feline judging capabilities as a qualification for office—on the line above rancher.

He lost.

# RULE #2

## KNOW WHY YOU ARE RUNNING FOR OFFICE.

Traditionalists and campaign consultants argue that the most important ingredient in the campaign stew is "the rationale." A candidate's rationale has a great deal to do with winning the office, so he or she must come up with something more compelling than just Sir Edmund Hillary's, "Because it's there." I've heard candidates who, when asked why they're seeking a particular office, say, "It's an open seat. Why wouldn't I go for it?" Causes? Issues? People? Commitment? Nope. Just unabashed, unadulterated, unapologetic ambition—and nothing more.

Prior to running for office, candidates need to identify their goals. It's a standard question consultants ask potential candidates: "If you are elected, what is the first thing you want to do as senator/congressman/assemblyman/ chairwoman of the mosquito control board?"

A candidate for the Tennessee legislature, speaking to a crowd of supporters, answered this important question with a lofty avowal: "First, I think I want to get sworn in." He quickly followed this up with an even braver declaration: "After that, I want to get on a committee."

No doubt impressed by this man's bedrock convictions and deep understanding of the public weal, the audience wanted to learn more about his goals should he be elected to do the people's business. "What will you do about unemployment and education here?" asked one voter.

His answer displayed every ounce of his political courage: "Oh, I don't know. I guess I'll have to ask the leadership what they want me to do."

Seeing how well the candidate had prepared to seek the public's trust, his campaign manager forbade him from making any more public appearances.

It didn't help. He lost.

By contrast, some candidates do have an issue at the centerpiece of their campaign—a cause to which they are devoted and upon which they promise immediate and sustained action once they take office.

Of course, the issue may not have anything to do with the office to which the candidate aspires.

In a precursor to twenty-first-century airline fees, there was a time when many establishments charged patrons a dime or, later, a quarter, to use a toilet. March Fong Eu ran to be secretary of state for the State of California on the elevating platform of banning pay toilets. As you may have guessed, the Office of Secretary of State of the State of California has no jurisdiction over pay toilets. It's normally concerned with corporate registration and election oversight. Toilets form no part of its portfolio. But her position on the issue demonstrated Eu's values, her dedication to the proposition that we all are endowed by our Creator with certain inalienable rights—among them, life, liberty, and going to the bathroom for free.

Lo and behold, the platform proved to be a winner. Even more amazingly, Secretary of State March Fong Eu burst the boundaries of her office by cutting a deal with the legislature to ban this scourge.

# RULE #3

# KNOW YOUR AUDIENCE.

"All for one and one for all" was a hell of a mantra for guys with capes and curls and cutlasses, but it is lousy campaign strategy. There is not one candidate (except, perhaps, Fidel Castro) who can successfully appeal to everyone. So, "divide and conquer" is a far better modus operandi for a candidate. It is called targeting. But you need to know whom to divide and whom to conquer.

I have watched as numerous candidates have tried to appeal to their target audience through the donning of hats (cowboy hats, in particular), ties, sports team apparel, barn coats (almost always right out of the box from LL Bean), and even snowshoes. It doesn't generally work, as voters' bullshit meters redline.

Every once in awhile, though, a candidate's instincts *are* far better than the wisdom of his or her advisors. The candidate is acutely aware of his or her own deficiencies and tries to minimize or work around them. It is rare, but it does happen.

• • •

One mid-summer morning in 1986, I had strong suspicions that my candidate was about to be divided and conquered. He was completely unaccepting of his deficiencies—in other words, he had no idea how to appeal to a certain important segment of the campaign funding community.

Ben Nighthorse Campbell, candidate for the United States House of Representatives, sat in the passenger seat while I, his campaign strategist, drove him to the Wellshire Inn in Denver for the first of several fundraising meetings that day: a breakfast buffet with leaders of Colorado's Jewish community. (In case you're wondering why I was working for a Republican, I wasn't—Campbell was a Democrat then.) During the ride, I quizzed him a bit, attempting to confirm that he was prepared for the day's schedule. A Colorado state representative, Campbell lacked broad familiarity with federal issues. He knew agriculture inside out, but not much else in any detail. Yet, if someone briefing him could break an issue down to its most basic elements, he could not only grasp the issue but could talk about it with ease and conviction.

I was worried, however, about the "Israel issue." It wasn't a topic you could narrow down to a couple of sentences. Too much history. Too much animosity. Too much to grasp for any human being who hadn't studied the issue for a decade or two. And the group we were meeting at breakfast would be key to our fundraising. Without them, we'd be riding off into the sunset on Election Night.

"So, do you want to talk about the Arab-Israeli conflict before we go into the meeting?" I asked.

"No," he responded as he sipped his cup of coffee.

"You sure? There are lot of ins and outs and we don't want to screw this meeting up."

"No. I got it. I know what I want to say."

"Well . . . you want to give me a hint? Just so we're on the same page?"

"No. You'll be okay."

"Me? I'm not worried about *me*. How about the campaign?"

"Don't worry. I got it."

But I did worry as we walked into the small conference room with the buffet breakfast. I knew this crowd, and simple answers and pledges of allegiance to Israel were not going to be sufficient, especially for an American Indian from the western part of the state, with few Jews in his state house district, with no history of activism in the Jewish community, and who was challenging an incumbent member of Congress. Plus, he wore a ponytail easily.

After the attendees had filled their plates, they settled into their seats around the table. The convener, who had been active in Democratic and Jewish politics for thirty years, asked Ben to "tell everyone a little about yourself." Ben said he had been an orphan and a judo champion. He'd carried the flag in the closing ceremonies at the 1960 Olympics. He'd been a rancher and a jeweler.

"So," the leader said directly, "what do you know about Israel and our issues?"

I started to drink my coffee in large gulps.

"When I was on the U.S. judo team," Campbell began, "we traveled to over 50 nations. Nowhere were we better received than in Israel. They were always friendly, always welcoming."

The people around the table nodded ever so slightly. I could see that they weren't impressed. I was about to speak up, to try to rescue my candidate, when he started speaking again.

"Look. My people are tribes. Your people are a tribe. My people live on reservations. Your people live on a reservation. Let me tell you, I know how important those reservations are. If you protect my tribes and their reservations, I will do everything I can to protect your tribe and your reservation."

Never previously and never since have I seen checkbooks emerge so quickly and with such verbal enthusiasm.

"There's more where that comes from!"

"What exactly is the federal contribution limit?"

"Let me call Washington for you, to make sure the Israel PACs give the max."

"When can you go to California, New York, or Miami? I've got good connections with money people there."

The leader of the group ended the meeting with the words, "There will be no more questions. You all know what needs to be done."

• • •

It was the spring of 1988, April to be exact, but given the poll results, it was definitely still winter for Al Gore in the New York presidential primary. The latest polls showed Gore losing to Michael Dukakis by nearly 30 points in this make-or-break state for the Gore campaign.

But the candidate seemed to be enjoying his recent endorsement by the estimable Mayor Ed Koch of New York City. It had given the youthful senator from Tennessee cred with the Jewish community, though it came with some significant downsides, because Koch was caught in a verbal battle with another candidate—the Reverend Jesse Jackson. Koch kept reminding primary voters of Jackson's 1984 remark in which the reverend referred to New York as "Hymietown." Jackson had repeatedly apologized for the remark, but Koch would not forgive or forget.

The New York press, looking for any intrigue in a primary in which one candidate was clearly going to defeat both Jackson and Gore, began to focus on the Jackson-Koch battle and, by association, the tension between Gore and Jackson. It was easy to set up the battle lines: white southerner vs. urban black man.

On the Sunday before the primary, as Gore's newly named national field director (a gig that would last two weeks), I was assigned to ride with Gore in his vehicle and staff him at events. I was happy for a chance to get to know the candidate, but mostly I was glad to evacuate the rat-infested (no joke) state campaign headquarters.

Some of the worst campaign headquarters in politics are presidential primary headquarters. What type of landlord is likely to offer a six-week lease (with no possibility of renewal) on a 4000-square-foot office space with twenty-four-hour security and access?

I joined Gore at a rally in the Bronx, intended to focus on federal efforts to reduce drug use and crime in declining neighborhoods. It was attended largely by neighborhood drug dealers. There may have been more people with beepers there than Gore supporters. Nobody really cared about the size or the nature of the crowd, because this 10:30 a.m. event was organized for the purpose of coverage on the noon news with the lead, "Candidate Gore Outlines His Drug Policy." Gore wanted to demonstrate that he knew and understood the needs of urban America.

After the event, I hopped into the limo with the candidate, seizing my chance to speak with him and brief him on the next event. We talked about mutual friends and family connections. He wanted to know my thoughts on the Bronx anti-drug rally.

"It wasn't well attended," I told him, "but I think it was good for the noon news."

He nodded, then peered for long minutes out the window at the East River before asking, "What are we doing next?"

"Well," I said, "we're meeting Mayor Koch in Little Italy for a walk through the streets, and then on to a few restaurants in the area."

"Is there a policy angle to this?"

"No. No, this is quite literally a meet and greet through Little Italy. "

"A Joe DiMaggio crowd, I bet," he said.

"Rocky Marciano, too," I said.

"Well, just get me to the restaurants as fast as you can."

We junctioned with the mayor's motorcade on the FDR drive and the two limos moved through the city streets very rapidly, hoping to reach Little Italy at 12:05, just as the churches concluded Sunday mass and the worshippers exited onto the streets.

If the Gore Advance team had failed to turn out a crowd in the Bronx at 10:30 a.m. on a Sunday, they truly succeeded in Little Italy. Parishioners streaming out of the churches were elbow-to-elbow with people heading to restaurants for Sunday lunch. Hundreds of them thronged every block. As we approached the corner where Koch and Gore would start their midday walk, the streets became increasingly jammed, and Gore's back increasingly stiffened. His eyes became larger and larger. His face was taut. This clearly wasn't his hometown of Carthage, Tennessee, or Nashville, or even Washington, DC. This was New York City at its most buoyant and intense.

Koch, in the front limo, barely waited for his vehicle to come to a full stop before opening the car door, leaping onto the sidewalk, and screaming toward the masses, "Hey, everybody! It's Ed Koch!" Then, he immediately turned to our vehicle and pointed at Al Gore, who was trying to find a way to disappear through the back seat into the trunk, and screamed again, "WITH AL GORE!!"

Gore turned to me, his eyes the size of salad plates, and asked, "Now, what do I do?"

"Get the hell out of the car. "

He looked at Koch, turned to stare at me for a half a second, took a deep breath, opened the car door, and waded into the crowd with Koch leading the way. As Koch shook hands and smiled at everyone who approached, Gore's hands remained in his pockets.

I told the Advance team to get the two pols to the restaurants as quickly as possible, but it seemed Koch knew every person in the crowd. Every person was met with a, "How am I doing? Meet my friend and the next president, Al Gore." Gore would then weakly put his hand out and nod hello.

We passed the churches and finally reached the restaurants, coffee shops, Italian grocery stores, and pizza shops, where Koch introduced Gore to all manner of Italian food and drink. It took Gore about three minutes to realize that this was a food tour, not a mega meet-and-greet with 10,000 uninterested voters—and once he figured that out, his demeanor completely changed. He ate and drank everything put in his way: calzones, cannoli, ravioli, red wine, Moretti beer. At one point, one of the Koch staff accompanying us sidled up to me and advised, "Tell him to slow it down. We have at least five more locations on this stop. Is the food that bad at the Waldorf Astoria?"

I informed him that as far as I knew the food at the campaign's hotel was satisfactory. It was simply that Senator Gore had a substantial appetite and was behaving as if this were a Tennessee political barbeque, where it is *de rigueur* to have something in your mouth at all times, whether tobacco, food, toothpick, or drink.

After the last stop on the Italian cornucopia tour, where he pointed out to me a signed picture of Joe DiMaggio, we returned to the Waldorf for candidate "downtime" and a change of shirts. After a few hours, we were off to Rockaway for an evening event and dance at a community senior center in a Jewish neighborhood. As we drove through Queens, he asked, "What is this stop?"

"A senior group at a community center. Jewish. Meet and greet. Stump speech and Q&A. Probably all about Israel."

"Foreign policy questions? That will be good," he said, smiling as he pulled his foreign policy briefing book from his briefcase.

The ladies—70 percent of those at the community center were women—"ooh'ed" and "aah'ed" as the just-turned-forty, dashingly handsome senator entered the community center. He moved quietly and easily through the crowd, carefully stepping around the wheel chairs and walkers, asking their names, the names and ages of their children, their grandchildren, and, in many cases, their departed husbands. When it came time to dance to a boombox with a cassette tape consisting almost entirely of music of the Rat Pack, he took time to partner with as many of the widows as possible. He didn't ask for their votes. Instead, he asked, "Would you care to dance with me?"

I'd have had more than enough for dinner at the Waldorf Astoria if I'd gotten a dollar from every women who whispered to me, "He reminds me so much of John Kennedy."

When they stopped the music, Gore talked about why he was running, but also—most important—his commitment to Israel. He fielded questions, most of which came from the males in the audience, deftly and confidently. He handled well the issue of Jewish settlements on the West Bank, offending only a few in the crowd. Then came questions about Medicare, Social Security, medical costs, veterans' benefits, and the inevitable question about Ed Koch's relationship with Jesse Jackson, to which he simply responded, "I respect both gentlemen."

After my third attempt to cut him off by giving him the hand across the throat sign, he thanked everyone, worked the crowd one more time, and left. As a result of his masterful performance, we clearly had eighty committed for the '88 campaign, and perhaps a handful who would be still alive for his 2000 run.

We returned to the limo and headed back to the Waldorf, which was more than 45 minutes away. As we were driving back, the car phone—cutting-edge technology at the time—rang. The Advance man in the front seat answered, turned to Gore, and said, "It's the Reverend, Senator." He handed the handset to Gore.

I pulled out my notepad to record anything the senator might say to Reverend Jackson during these purportedly tense times between these two Democractic presidential contenders. Words said by Gore on this call might be distorted later. I wanted to make sure the campaign had Gore's comments. Here are my notes from the Gore side of the conversation:

> *Hi Jesse . . . what's going on? I am coming back from a Rockaway Jewish community center event. You? . . .Bronx? I was there this morning . . . . So, what's up? . . . I am not sure what can be done. Do you have any ideas? That's good, that's good. When can that happen? . . . He is a great candidate . . . . What? He can't announce the switch until June? Better late than never . . . . Have you talked to the principals? . . . The family is good with it? . . . So we will be all set for the fall? This should give us a good chance to win a few more . . . . Right, right. This will be a good answer to our linebacking now that Youseff has left. UVA, right? . . . Perhaps we can beat Landon and*

*Prep now with this new transfer and a couple of the juniors stepping up . . . .*
*Wonderful. Could be a good year for St. Albans football. Good idea . . . .*
*Talk tomorrow? . . . If not Tuesday. Bye.*

Al Gore lost the New York primary, receiving only 10 percent of the vote, and dropped out of the presidential race two days later. Jesse Jackson also lost, although he got 37 percent of the vote and stayed in the race right up to the Democratic convention.

St. Albans School in Washington, D.C., from which Gore had graduated high school and where Jackson's son had starred in football, had a very successful football season in the fall of 1988. The team secured a spot in its league championship, at which point it lost. Despite the loss, the team certainly provided a very positive mutual comfort zone for two prominent Democrats.

# RULE #4

# PERSONAL INTEGRITY IS NOT NECESSARILY A QUALIFICATION FOR OFFICE.

Parents and teachers will tell you that you should never tell a lie. Never, ever. And we in the politics business pass that time-honored wisdom on to our clients. "Come clean," we say. "Honesty is the best policy. The cover-up is worse than the crime."

Except we don't mean it—not always, anyway. There are times in politics when, as a candidate or a political consultant, truth is the last thing you want.

Lying is good. Lying is fine. Lying is strategic. Lying—sometimes—is the only way to win an election.

I'm not talking about "spinning" or "strategic admissions." I'm not talking about splitting hairs or emphasizing a nuance or glossing over another. I'm not talking about telling a half-truth or even an incomplete truth. People expect that kind of truth-twisting from politicians. The good ones hone it to a fine art:

"I never said we should raise taxes. I said we should seek revenue enhancements."

"I served in the Vietnam *era*—I didn't say I served in Vietnam."

"Healthcare mandates are an infringement on freedom—but not in individual states."

No, I'm talking about good old, straight-out lying—no shame, no compunction. I'm talking about willful and direct efforts to deceive voters about one's true values, attitudes, and past. I'm talking about I-am-not-a-crook lying, I-did-not-have-sexual-relations-with-that-woman lying, we-know -there-are-weapons-of-mass-destruction lying.

The first time I saw the need for the lie, the whole lie, and nothing but the lie was when I worked for a woman who was running for statewide office. The candidate was born in the midwest but her nasal accent betrayed the land where she was raised: Long Island, Noo Yawk.

However, she wasn't running in the midwest or Noo Yawk. She was running in the Old South.

It was mid-August and my second day on the job as campaign manager. Although we were down by more than twenty-five points, I felt certain I could find a path to victory. Our candidate was a smart former legislator with a couple of good ideas about the economy and the military. If we could build her "positives" a bit and then attack the incumbent for being "out of touch" with the values of the state's voters, we could close the gap. The key was to beef up those positives so our campaign would be credible when we attacked the incumbent.

That was the plan.

Then I learned of her unfortunate addiction to truth—truth told to any listener at any time, especially if the listener happened to carry the job title of "journalist."

One lovely late-summer afternoon in the 1980s—I suppose there was a smell of honeysuckle somewhere, although not in the campaign headquarters—the phone rang. It was the campaign's press secretary, who was out on the hustings with the candidate.

"Hey, how's it going out there?" I said, my voice full of good cheer, hoping that he wanted to relay a great, human moment that had just occurred: our candidate making a deep connection with an ordinary voter, all captured by cameras.

"We've got trouble."

*Trouble? Ha! I am an accomplished political operative. With me in charge, any problem can be "spun" or "nuanced."*

"What kind of trouble?" I said.

"Well, you know we were at a tobacco sale barn, right?"

*Did she acknowledge she wants a dollar-a-pack tax on cigarettes?* I thought. *That's not a problem. That's fantastic. Great stuff. Straight talk delivered in the belly of the beast.*

"Yep, a sale barn."

"Well, after the stump speech, reporters asked questions."

"Reporters are prone to do that. So?"

"So, the first question was, 'What do you like about this state?'"

"Jesus, what a softball."

"Yeah, yeah. She said something like 'the mountains, the opportunities, the families, the pride, the patriotism. No problem."

"So what's the problem?"

"The next question."

"Which was?"

"What *don't* you like about the state?'"

"Another softball," I replied. "I'm sure she answered by talking about the need for better schools. And about how it's time we had more money for highway improvements, not an incumbent who has spent so many years in the state capital that he's out of touch with the needs of the average voter in this, the finest state in the finest nation on the face of the Earth."

"That's not what she said."

*How bad could it be? How could you possibly fuck that one up?*

"What did she say?"

"She said, and I quote, 'I hate southern accents.'"

"No, she didn't."

"Yes, she did."

"Did she also say that she hates grits, barbecue, and Stonewall Fucking Jackson?"

"No, that's all. I didn't let her take any more questions."

"What's our response?"

At that moment, the phones in the office lit up like the place had just won first prize in the power company's contest for Home with Gaudiest Holiday Lighting. The press was onto the story.

In the twenty-five years since, I've run this situation by dozens of the most capable spinners in the world—Democratic and Republican communications pros, the best of the best. I've asked them, "What is the right response to that comment?" Among the suggestions was this from a former White House press secretary: "She said 'axes,' not 'accents.' She hates 'southern axes.' The Second Amendment to the Constitution clearly ensures the right to bear Southern axes.'"

Believe it or not, that was the most hopeful suggestion.

In the days before cellphones, it would often take hours before campaign staff could reach a candidate. In this case, it took six. "So," I said when I finally got hold of her, "that comment about the accents . . ." I tried to remain calm. ". . . Do you think that maybe you should not have, um, insulted, um, every single person whose vote you're asking for?"

"Look, all I did was tell the truth," she told me. "I can't stand Southern accents. Did you want me to lie?"

"Let me think about that for a minute . . . Okay, I've decided. YES! LIE! OF COURSE! LIE! This isn't about 'fessing up to your father that you chopped down the cherry tree. You're not a saint refusing to renounce your faith as you're being burned at the stake. You're trashing the way everyone talks in the part of the USA you want to represent!"

In my prayers that night, I had only one entreaty to God: that the comment had not been preserved on audiotape. If it was only in print, we could say that she was misquoted. We could accuse the press of misrepresentation and bias. Silently, I made this deal with God: *You grant me this one favor and I'll swear off drugs, sex, cigarettes, gambling, fatty foods, driving above the speed limit, and parking in handicapped zones. Just this one favor, Lord. I'll never ask for anything again.*

God didn't take the deal.

I woke to the sound of my candidate's words blaring through the speaker of my clock radio. Loud and clear. No mistaking that she had said she hates southern accents—not axes, not axles, but accents. And her words were uttered with an especially heavy dose of Long Island.

If the truth sets you free, then we were in free-fall. We moved to damage-control mode, seeking to get beyond Accentgate by depicting the candidate's comments as an aberration and a distraction, kept alive by her opponent, while she wanted to talk about the needs of the working people of the state. We put her on the road to the outer counties, where reporters were unlikely to follow her and report any denunciations of motherhood and apple pie. Slowly, we brought her back to the state's media centers. Things were going well. Maybe there really was life after death.

Then I went with her to our nation's capital to raise some national money.

Our day in Washington ended with a fundraising dinner at the home of an ex-congressman, hosted by his wife. The event was priced at $250 a plate.

The evening was sparsely attended—we'd come a long way for a few thousand bucks. But so what? She was rubbing elbows with official Washington.

As we were leaving the site of the event, I heard a reporter ask the candidate, "How did the fundraiser go?"

*Another softball.*

"I wouldn't go to a fundraiser like that!" said the Queen of Candor. "Imagine paying $250 for cold chicken and a side of beans. Beans! I just don't know how the hostess thought that was all right."

I thought of going back inside and drinking some more, but instead, settled for crying myself to sleep in my hotel room.

The following day, after my candidate's show of ingratitude appeared in a major state daily, I received a call from the ex-congressman whose wife had hosted the soirée with the cold chicken and beans. Mrs. ex-congressman was demanding an apology. Mr. ex-congressman was also not the happiest person in the District of Columbia that day. I called the candidate to ask her to please call the hostess and make nice.

"Um, she threw you a party . . ." I began. "She . . . raised money for you. She, um, did you a favor."

"Look, what I said was the truth. I would never pay to attend a dinner like that."

She never apologized to the ex-congressman's wife or the ex-congressman. She did, however, call the journalist to thank her for the "nice" article.

Ah, you say, these are just a few of the expectable "campaign gaffes" that typically occur in the heat of a hotly contested campaign. She was tired. Some things just popped out. She didn't intend for them to sound the way they did. Or, you say, maybe she was just trying to leaven a long, serious campaign with a few morsels of "tongue-in-cheek" humor that no one appreciated. No. This candidate had a penchant for true confessions. There were numerous other moments of killer truth during the course of the campaign, forcing the press secretary and me and everyone else on the sinking ship to humble ourselves by trying to massage her comments until they came plausibly within the orbit of modern American political thinking.

In the midst of all of this honesty, we took a poll. Here's what the pollster told us: "Maybe, just maybe, with the best political advertising of the decade, ten million dollars, and your opponent being caught in Lafayette Park at 2 a.m. with a hooker and a dime bag—maybe then you might just have a ghost of a chance. But probably not."

Everyone needs a title and record to hold. Mine is Campaign Manager for the Worst Democratic Defeat in This Particular State Since Reconstruction.

Sometimes honesty is not the best policy.

## RULE #5

# THERE IS GOOD PRESS AND THERE IS BAD PRESS. THE FORMER RARELY HAPPENS. THE LATTER ALWAYS HAPPENS. BETTER TO HAVE NO PRESS.

The media have a nasty tendency to report precisely what you don't want them to report, despite your valiant efforts to present the story in your favor. You may be able to direct their investigation to some degree, but all you'll end up with, if you're lucky, is a story that turns out not as awful as it might have been.

So my practice is this. Don't try to control or spin the press. Maybe it's better to say little or nothing. Silence can be a savior.

• • •

"Holy Mary, Mother of GOD!"

Shouting from the office next door, Luther Symons had reason to be perturbed. Our senior associate and self-titled Master of Medical Marijuana, Luther, was the staff member in charge of overseeing all elements of our firm's effort in 2000 to legalize medical marijuana in Colorado. As one of America's longest-living people with AIDS, Luther had fought hard to bring the issue to the ballot. He had taken to heart all the arguments in favor of legalization. He'd talked to the cancer and glaucoma patients who relied on their then-illegal pot to ease their pain. And, in spite of his personal stake in the matter, he was a political pro, able to assess a situation rationally and take action accordingly.

However, now he was suffering from acute paranoia, tinged with rage, shaded with anxiety.

His state was fully justified by events that had taken place two years earlier. In 1998, medical marijuana (MMJ) proponents had submitted to Colorado's secretary of state 130,000 signatures calling for the question of MMJ's legalization to be placed on that fall's general election ballot as a citizen's initiative. About three weeks after the submission, on the final day for qualification, the secretary's office announced that of the 120,000 signatures she'd received, not enough were valid to win a spot on the ballot. According to the secretary of state, we were 2,000 valid signatures short.

But the team hadn't submitted 120,000. It had submitted 130,000. Luther spent days and days and even nights trying to figure out the 10,000-signature discrepancy between those submitted and those reported by the secretary, but he could not resolve the problem in time for election day. The campaign was certain that we had sufficient valid signatures—even with only the 120,000 that the secretary of state admitted to receiving—and that she was illegally disqualifying us.

A judge agreed, but too late. In late October, the judge overruled the secretary of state and placed the medical marijuana initiative on the Fall 2000 ballot. In 1998, however, Colorado voters did not get to vote on MMJ.

What happened to those 10,000 signatures? The mystery simmered for seven months and resulted in what became urban myth. According to the oft-told story, the secretary of state keeled over and died at her desk. While the medical staff and her office staff were hauling her out of the office, they found under her desk two boxes of petitions containing more than 10,000 signatures in favor of MMJ legalization.

In truth, she died at home and it was her successor who found the boxes under the desk—but regardless of how they were found, it's clear that the secretary of state had tried to undermine the medical marijuana campaign.

Even though the judge ordered MMJ onto the ballot for 2000, the case of the missing signatures had supplied additional proof to everyone in the MMJ community of a nefarious conspiracy to deny patient access to MMJ despite, as polling repeatedly showed, significant voter support. Of course, we all know that conspiracy theories are crazy and wrong. Except when they're not.

When Luther blurted out his appeal to the Blessed Virgin, we took note. Unlike most of us, who often applied such exclamations to words or antics of elected officials, law-enforcement personnel, and even our own supporters, Luther had remained focused and calm through most of the craziness of the MMJ campaign. But he finally became unnerved by the last category: our own supporters.

"We've got ourselves a Pogo," Luther told me as I walked into his office in response to his outburst. This internal shorthand referred to the immortal words from the comic strip *Pogo*: "We have met the enemy and he is us." Most often, a Pogo was some ardent supporter of an endeavor—precisely the kind of person for whom strategy and tactics to win a campaign are secondary to the righteousness of the cause—who has some stupid idea. The energy and commitment of these people make them indispensable to a campaign, but as political professionals, we would just as soon bar them from any campaign activities.

"What is it this time?" I asked.

"They want to put out a press release about how there are doctors and nurses supporting the medical marijuana initiative."

"Jesus," I said, adding Holy Mary's son to Luther's exclamation. "That could get press." Press was the last thing we wanted at this point.

But, you ask, don't you *always* want press coverage of your candidate or cause? Especially if the press will be covering a group of experts touting him, her, or it?

The answer: nope, uh-uh, wrong, *nein, nyet, non,* fuhgeddaboudit.

During this MMJ campaign there were hundreds of volunteers and true believers who, whenever they had a vision or an epiphany or a revelation in the proximity of a journalist, felt they should share it. They were certain that in relating their vision or epiphany or revelation, they would be speaking for the campaign.

We, on the other hand, did not want anyone sharing his or her spiritual experiences on behalf of the campaign. Spiritual experiences are fine when you're in church or at the ashram or in the desert or going through a car wash—but not when you're trying to assemble fifty-percent-plus-one to approve a controversial ballot initiative. Accordingly, we tried to keep these true-believing troops corralled and on message. But there was a strong strain of independence among the MMJ supporters, and no campaign management team was going to direct or control their communications efforts short of imprisoning them.

The good news is that most of the time, the efforts of these missionaries of truth were foolhardy and ill-conceived, so the press ignored them. The bad news for us was that this idea about supportive nurses and friendly doctors was sufficiently compelling to actually become a story.

"It was Jonathan," said Luther. "You know, the only straight one." (Because of marijuana's pain-killing properties, nearly all of the campaign activists were gay and HIV positive, or were close to someone who was.)

I remembered Jonathan from fuck-ups in the past. "Have you explained the campaign strategy to him?"

Luther sighed. "Yes, but I'll try again. Ridder, you really don't pay me enough."

He picked up the phone and dialed. I heard only Luther's side of the conversation.

"That's right, we *don't* want you to put out a press release on this. I've explained this before. We don't want any press coverage. . . . No, *no* coverage. None. Zero. Zip. . . . Yes, I understand that this press conference would tell undecided voters that we have support from members of the medical community, but. . . . Yes, yes, generally it is a good idea. . . . NO! Not this time. We don't want to get our message out. . . . Remember, the more people know about this initiative the less they like it. . . . No, these people are not 'persuadable'—they just don't like it. Period. No press. Got it? . . . Yes, I know that the polling indicates we have about 55 percent support, and about 45 percent against it. It also says there are almost no undecided voters. When we do the polls, if we read the respondents' arguments for this initiative, we actually lose support. . . . I have no doubt that all the people you know are for it. But there are 750,000 in the state who aren't. . . . I know they are not your friends, but unfortunately, friendship with you is not a requirement for voting in the State of Colorado. . . . WHAT? You've already sent it out? Who approved that? . . . You thought it was a good idea? What did it say? . . . *Jesus H. Christ!* Hang on. I need to talk to Rick."

He put Jonathan on hold and turned to me.

"Get this, Ridder. He's announced a news conference tomorrow with three doctors and three nurses."

"We need to kill the story," I shot back. "Has he spoken with Roche?"

The appropriately named Julie Roche was our official campaign manager and the only person authorized to speak on the record. She was also the *only* official campaign employee, and she took most of her direction from Luther or me as the lead strategists.

Luther asked Jonathan. No, he hadn't spoken with Julie.

This was rogue behavior with potentially major ramifications. We told him to call back in fifteen minutes while we got Julie on the speakerphone.

"Delay it," she said. "I can get the press to wait. But we are going to have to do the press conference eventually because, if we don't, Jonathan and his gang will do it on *their* terms, on *their* timetable, with *their* speakers. So, when do we do it?"

I saw the wisdom in her plan. I had always feared the scenario of a pro-pot press conference featuring Ziggy Marley, Hunter S. Thompson, and a rapper to be named later, occurring amidst a pungent haze of marijuana smoke and a pile of Twinkie wrappers. So we needed to give the activists a news story or they'd go ahead and create their own.

But, when to hold a press conference? There were no good days, just days that might be less rotten than others by virtue of the low likelihood of attracting any, you know, *press*.

We considered various dates: the Bush-Gore debates? No good. Colorado was not in play and the media around here might want a local story to balance the national story. Columbus Day? Nope. There was always a parade and always a demonstration against the parade by the Native-American community. We didn't want to be the subject of TV stories that began, "In another controversial issue, supporters of medical marijuana today . . ." We tried to anticipate when campaigns for other initiatives might hold *their* major press conferences; perhaps if we held ours the same day it would be buried. But we quickly disposed of that idea, realizing that if this was our only news event, it would draw coverage no matter what the other initiatives did.

Then Luther said, "I've got it. The day before election day! Traditionally, there's a news blackout on that Monday—it's all soft stories about 'getting ready for the voting.' They don't cover hard stories the day before the election. That's it! If we hold it, they will NOT come."

It was a brilliant plan as long as we could keep the activists from going rogue. At every campaign steering committee meeting, composed of some of the most well intentioned and jacked up MMJ activists in the state,

Julie promised the members, "Yes, we will do it. We will have that press conference. Next week."

We put next week off until there were no more next weeks. Finally, as the campaign's ultimate weekend approached, we scheduled the conference for the day before the election. Our diabolical scheme was in place.

We did everything we could to make sure that our activists thought we were working our hardest to ensure the event's success. We told them we were using our special, super-secret connections to make sure that the editor of the *Denver Post* would be alerted. We showed them phone logs of calls to TV news stations. Julie even went on a major news-radio station to announce the event.

What we didn't tell them was that we were breaking just about every rule in press relations. We sent the notification on Saturday at 7 p.m., to make sure that no one besides the weekend copy person and the guy who delivered coffee would receive it. We made no follow-up calls. We set the event for 8 a.m. on a Monday, when no reporters could possibly be available. And we held it outside in early November—in Colorado—when frost is a certainty and snow a distinct possibility. And that radio show? Julie was interviewed at 6 a.m. on a Sunday morning.

Monday came. Our three doctors and three nurses arrived promptly at 7:45. Our steering committee was there five minutes later, along with a lone radio reporter from public radio who grabbed a cup of the complimentary coffee. I was pleased. Luther was pleased. Julie was pleased.

Score: Professionals 1, Activists 0.

And then the TV trucks came. First, Channel 4. Then Channel 7. Then Channel 9. Even Channel 31.

The guy from Channel 9, number one in the market, greeted me. "What a great idea, holding this event at this hour. I can still get it on the morning news, and then the noon, the five o'clock, the six o'clock, and the ten."

"But," said I, "I thought you guys had an embargo on election news on the Monday before the election."

"Yeah, we generally do, but there's nothing going on here with the presidential. Besides, this is too good. Doctors, nurses, and dope—it's fantastic. The polls have it close, right?"

"Right. Right. Close. Yeah." *What could possibly have gone wrong? Our plan was so perfect. What had we missed?* "By the way, how did you learn about it?" I asked.

"Oh, easy. Monitoring police scanners. They've followed everything you guys have done for weeks. Any press release. Any notice of a public meeting. Any activity. They've tracked it. So when your release went out, they took it seriously and let all their units know about it over police radio, which we all listen to."

The long arm of Big Brother strikes again. The police *would* be keeping their eye on a band of pushy potheads. Luther and Julie had debated the issue with most every D.A. and police chief in the state. But we also knew what law enforcement wanted most of all: a headline reading, "Medical Marijuana Leader Arrested in BIG Pot Bust."

The press conference began. The doctors and nurses were excellent. They outlined the need for medical marijuana in order to provide relief from debilitating pain and nausea. They explained the horrors of glaucoma and the misery of AIDS, the unpredictability of MS.

*Okay,* I thought. *Maybe this won't be so bad after all.*

But then the activists took to the podium.

Here was their one chance to tell people why they should vote "Yes" on Amendment 20, and they weren't going to pass it up. To say that our spokespeople went "off message" is to suggest that Little Big Horn was a minor blemish on Custer's military record. One person told of the "tens of thousands of likely users" of medical marijuana, when for months the campaign had used the figure "5,000 at the most." Another said, "It would be easy to obtain a medical marijuana card," undermining our mantra of "strict access." Another claimed this amendment "was a stepping stone to legalization." (A good thing, as he saw it.)

For once, the reporters didn't lie. Highlights of the press conference, focusing primarily on the activists' comments, were shown on the morning news, then again at noon, followed by the five, the six, and the ten. The only solace was that neither of the two major newspapers sent reporters because they, in fact, did observe a strict embargo on hard news for their editions on election day, which was the next publishing date.

That night, I closed my eyes every time I heard the news conference being aired. But I kept repeating the numbers. Absentee and early voting meant that as much as 50 percent of the votes had already been cast. The

Denver media market reached only 70 percent of the voters in the state. The news channels reached maybe 30 percent of the voters on a given night. We knew that fewer than 10 percent of the voters were undecided or "soft" in their support. When we did the math, we saw that maybe 3 percent of the voters would be swayed by the news coverage.

But then we caught a break. *Monday Night Football*, the highest-rated program on the highest-rated channel for news, went into overtime.

The ball is on the twenty-seven. It is a short thirty-four-yard field goal for the Vikings to win this Central Division match-up. The ball is snapped; it's down. OH NO! It is wide left. We go to overtime.

Tie game: Packers 20, Vikings 20.

Brett Favre and the Packers needed only about four minutes on the clock to settle the affair in OT. But four minutes of play (plus stoppages, plus commercials) was enough to push the ten o'clock news past most viewers' bedtime.

I wonder if the members of the 2000 Green Bay Packers know just how much they contributed to sensible drug policy in the State of Colorado.

Election night arrived, and in the midst of the Bush-Gore fiasco, Colorado passed medical marijuana 53 percent to 47 percent. Every time the news reported on the victory, clips from Monday's news conference were shown in the background. But clearly, few of the unconvinced had seen coverage of the conference *before* voting.

As mortified as we were by the coverage of the press conference, its timing had been right. A post-election poll showed that the "pot" initiative was the least known and understood of the four major initiatives.

Sometimes, the winning strategy is to do nothing, stay below the radar, and hope the opposition is as incompetent as your own team.

• • •

Damn that First Amendment.

# 1:00 P.M.

It all started with a simple phone call to our Denver office in 2005. Molly Stewart, campaign manager for our client Linda Bascone, wanted to speak to

Tyler, our senior associate with responsibility for the Bascone for Congress campaign. Those who knew Molly in her youth confirm that she intimidated her kindergarten teacher with her direct personality and salty vocabulary.

Tyler put her on speakerphone and motioned to me to come into his office.

"I am in the fucking bathroom of Linda's apartment *in* the Congressional District," Molly said in a vehement stage whisper. "I came inside here because I saw a fucking Channel 7 TV truck pull up outside."

"Why don't you go out and talk to them?" Tyler asked.

"I can't. They'll want to come in the fucking apartment."

"So?" I said.

"They will see that Linda doesn't fucking live here."

"What do you mean? We told the press that she moved into the district more than two months ago," Tyler said.

"Yeah, she has the apartment but she never moved in."

"None of her stuff is here. Things you would have if you actually lived someplace . . . like, say, A FUCKING BED!"

After those last three non-whispered words, Molly resumed her hushed tone.

"All that's here are a couple of tables and folding chairs so we could use the place as a campaign headquarters or . . . or something. . . . Shhhh. . . . I have to go. They're knocking on the door."

She hung up.


## 2:30 P.M.

Lindsey, the intern covering the phones, shouted, "Molly's on the phone!" Tyler hit the conference button again. The stage whisper came out of the speaker.

"They keep calling my cellphone asking, 'When is Linda coming back home?'"

"Are they still there?" Tyler asked.

"How the fuck should I know? To repeat: I'm in the fucking bathroom. If I come into the living room to look, they will see me through the windows, which, naturally—did I mention that Linda never moved in?—don't have any fucking blinds. Then they will want to come in."

"Where's Linda?" I asked.

"She was at a senior event. Then she is headed to her home downtown."

"As long as she's not going to the apartment in the congressional district," said Tyler.

"Because if she goes to the apartment in the congressional district, she will have to let the press in." Molly added.

"Which would not be pretty," I said.

"What's not pretty is this fucking bathroom! Fix this, Ridder."

"Hang tight, Molly. Channel 7 will have to leave soon for the four o'clock news."

## 3:15 P.M.

"Molly on line one!" shouted Lindsey.

"I think they're still here," Molly said, still whispering. "Wait . . . I just heard another knock. I need to get out. I told you guys we shouldn't put out that press release before she moved."

"But she intended to move," I said. "Within a few days."

"Well, she didn't, goddammit. And now I have goddamn Channel 7 casing this goddamn apartment on a goddamn story revealing that the goddamn candidate for the goddamn Fourth CD doesn't live in the goddamn Fourth CD even though she says she does."

"Not good," I said.

"No shit, James Carville. So what are you going to do?"

"They have to leave at some point. Maybe we can think of a diversion."

"Make it quick. Get me the fuck out of here."

She hung up.

Tyler looked at me "Do you think any of the interns would volunteer to get into a three-car pileup on I-70, just west of the airport? That would divert the satellite truck."

I replied that since all of our office interns rode bikes to the office, he should volunteer his car.

He declined.

"I've got a 4 p.m. meeting," Tyler said. "I will catch up on this afterward." He left.

## 4:10 P.M.

"Molly again," said Lindsey.

I picked up.

"Where are you?" I asked.

"Still in the bathroom. Have you assholes thought of anything yet?"

"I have an idea. We'll send someone to drive by and see if the truck is still there. It will take us a bit to get somebody there in rush hour, so hold tight," I said.

"Good. Now we're making progress. Oh, by the way, Ridder, have you spoken with Linda about this?" Before I could answer Molly continued. "I have. She was on the way here to pick up some papers. I caught her, got her redirected."

"To where?"

"Your office. I told her you would figure this shit out."

Timing is everything, and before I could say, "No, not here, anywhere but here," the candidate walked in.

I told Molly I would call her back with Linda on the phone.

I brought Linda up to speed on the apartment, the truck, and the bathroom. She admitted that she should have moved, but explained that she wanted to stay with her son through the end of the school year. She now agreed to move in immediately, bringing with her some clothes and A FUCKING BED (although neither she nor I phrased it that way). But this did not solve our immediate problem.

We called Molly, and I told her that I had dispatched my trusted partner, Craig Hughes, to drive by the apartment complex. Craig, a former White House operative, was familiar with press stakeout procedures and would be able to make a quick assessment.

• • •

## 5:20 P.M.

"Hughes on line two," announced Lindsey.

I put Craig on speaker and conferenced in Molly. "The truck is still there," he said. "I didn't see anyone in the truck, but I couldn't get too close. So I slipped a fiver to a neighborhood kid. He knocked on the truck door, and someone rolled down the window."

"So they're still fucking there," said Molly from the bathroom.

"Yeah, and according to the kid, they're gonna be there awhile," Craig said.

"What do you mean?" asked Linda.

"Well, the kid asked them what they were doing and how long they would be there, and could he bring over his buddies to see the cool stuff inside the truck? And the guy in the truck told him that he was waiting until a woman got home before he could leave."

"Then he's going to be there a while," said Linda, "because I won't be there for a couple of days."

"BULLSHIT!" Molly wasn't whispering. "I am not spending the next two days in this goddamn bathroom."

"We're working on it," I said, despite having no clue as to what we were going to do.

Molly hung up.

Linda went out for dinner.

## 6:35 P.M.

"Channel 7 looking for Linda. Who wants it?" Lindsey said.

"No one wants it," I said.

Lindsey looked at me.

"But I'll take it," I said.

The first thing I did when I got on the phone was get off the record. I said, strictly off the record, that I had no idea where Linda Bascone could be at that moment, given that she'd left an hour before. Off the record, I posited that perhaps both Molly and Linda weren't answering their phones because both devices had run out of battery, and you know how phones are.

"Look," said the Channel 7 reporter, "we are running a story on the ten o'clock news saying that Linda Bascone doesn't live in the Fourth CD."

"She doesn't have to be living in the district to run for Congress representing that district. That's in the Constitution."

"True, James Madison, but I have a campaign press release saying that she now lives in the fourth congressional district. We've had people at her supposed home in the fourth congressional district for two days, and she has not shown up."

"I'm sure she was there in the evening."

"Nope, hasn't been there."

"In the wee hours—after attending late-night fundraisers."

"Nice try, but uh-uh. Our people are equipped with night-vision goggles."

I laughed. He didn't. Was he serious? I couldn't tell.

What I could tell was that my effort at damage control wasn't controlling any damage.

I kept trying.

"She does spend a couple of nights a week in downtown with her son," I said. "Maybe she spent last night downtown and will be coming back to the 'burbs tonight."

"Yeah that's why I want to talk to her—to find out when she is headed home to the district, so we can get some video to show that she really lives there."

"Great."

"If she does."

"Right. Let me see if I can track down the campaign manager or Linda. Okay?"

"No problem, but I need at least a comment by nine-fifteen."

"You got it."

"By the way, there *is* someone in the apartment. We saw a woman enter at about eight this morning. But no one's come out or even opened the door since our truck arrived."

"Ah. Interesting. Thanks for letting me know. Yeah, I wonder who that is. Okay. I'll get back to you right away."

I hung up. I dialed Molly first. "We are soooo busted," I said before detailing the conversation with the reporter.

"Okay, let me get this straight. They know I'm here, but I can't come out. Because if I come out, that will be *admitting* I'm here."

"Right."

"And I can't *admit* I'm here because then they'll want to go inside and I'll have to refuse to escort them in, and they'll want to know why, and I'll say something ridiculous, and the whole thing will be on the ten-o-fucking-clock news."

"Yeah, that sums it up."

"So I'm stuck in this goddam bathroom until they run the story. I'm hungry, Ridder."

"It's a bathroom so you do have water. I've read that you can survive on water for months and months before you die."

"Get. Me. The. Fuck. Out. Of. Here."


## 7:00 P.M.

I called Linda, and we hatched a plan. She would call Channel 7 and say to them that she's been downtown the last two days. And that she's moved into the district more slowly than she'd expected to because of her son. And that she hoped to completely move in shortly.


## 7:15 P.M.

"Linda on the phone." Lindsey's voice had gone from cheery to resigned.

"I did the best I could," said Linda.

Twenty-five years of campaign experience told me that when a bright, intelligent candidate—which Linda was—says, "I did the best I could," you are about to be a chestnut roasting on an open fire.

I patched in Molly.

"Did you guys get me the fuck out of here?" was her substitute for "Hello."

Linda and I expressed our dismay at Molly's situation, but didn't feel that, under the circumstances, she could be seen in the apartment, because Linda had told Channel 7 that no one was there.

. . .

## 7:25 P.M.

"Bob Nelson on line one for you Rick," said Lindsey. Bob, a long-time employee of our firm, was also a good friend of Molly's.

"Molly's calling everyone she knows to scream about being stuck in a bathroom," Bob said. "What the hell is going on?"

I tried to explain the conundrum when Lindsey called out, "Hughes on the line."

I hung up on Bob and picked up on Hughes.

"I just got back from getting something to eat," Hughes said. "They're doing a stand-up outside the apartment. . . . The reporter is pointing at the apartment. . . . Now he's reading something. . . . Okay, they're doing cut-away. . . . Lights off. . . . They're packing up. . . . Shit, I may have been spotted. Will call back in a bit."

## 7:50 P.M.

"Hughes again," said Lindsey.

"They've left," he said. "I had to pull away because someone saw me in my car and started to walk toward me. But now I'm back and they're gone."

"The reporter and the truck?" I asked.

"All gone. I'm headed home."

I hung up on Hughes and called Molly.

"They're gone," I said. "You can come out of hiding."

"Well, isn't that just fucking peachy. I've seen enough of this bathroom, enough of this whole goddam apartment, for a whole damn lifetime. I am going to leave and never return. Call me if anything goes on the air. I will not be watching fucking Channel 7. I will be drinking whiskey in a fucking bar. And the next time Tyler and Linda suggest sending out a press release, you tell 'em to fuck off."

I told her I would call her after the ten o'clock news.

## 10:07 P.M.

The story led off the broadcast. As I'd predicted, it wasn't pretty: "Congressional candidate doesn't live in the congressional district, as the candidate claims." The video included the press release, the apartment, Molly's car as proof *someone* was in the apartment, a transcript of Linda's comments, and a lousy headshot of her.

I waited until after the weather report to call Molly. But before I could call her, my phone rang. It was Molly.

"I just talked to Linda," she said. "She thinks now that the story is out, she can wait until next year to move."

Linda lost the election.

# RULE #6

## ALWAYS HIRE BETTER PEOPLE THAN YOU. AND YES, YOU CAN FIRE VOLUNTEERS.

You can't win them all, so if you're going to lose, you might as well try to look good. I am not talking about wearing an Armani suit (although I have one somewhere in my closet for that meeting with some foreign billionaire candidate, which means it has never been worn) or women wearing Gucci; I'm talking about maintaining some semblance of a positive reputation.

Inevitably, activists blame campaign managers and consultants for a candidate's defeat. They ran lousy commercials. They didn't target hunters and anglers—all twenty of them in London, England (yes, this was an actual complaint). They didn't use volunteers effectively. They ran on the "wrong" message.

Rarely do activists realize that the candidate was flawed or worse, the jurisdiction was simply unwinnable for a candidate of a particular party, or the campaign was outspent fifteen to one. Never have I heard an activist say the words, "You lost. But in that district, with that candidate, and being outspent two to one, you did damn well." Just doesn't happen.

So, early in my campaign career, I realized that you always have to leave them (the activists) something to maintain their faith in why they supported the candidate or cause in the first place. Generally, that means providing them with an interaction with someone on the campaign whom they like and even respect, but more important, someone who is really good at what they do.

And if someone does a good job, it reflects on you—even in a campaign where the candidate and cause should get the attention.

The key to success in hiring in the campaign world—and concomitantly making yourself look good—is:

1. Follow the advice of Satchel Paige: "Age is mind over matter; it you don't mind, it don't matter."
2. Listen carefully to those who have seen it before; and
3. Never underestimate the observations of unlikely sources.

• • •

I was living at home in Washington, D.C., in late 1971, ostensibly in the midst of "a gap year" between high school and college—except there was no defined end to the gap. During my senior year of high school, I had failed to apply to any college that I remotely wanted to attend, and now, after much parental prodding, had only recently sent in applications to start college in the fall of 1972.

But the college application exercise was over and my daily chore of picking up my younger sister at high school while pondering my ambitions in life (I decided my aspirations had something to do with women and avoiding the draft and any participation in President Richard Nixon's Vietnam war—not necessarily in that order) was becoming tedious. So, I called the McGovern for President campaign.

After being rebuffed in an attempt to secure a paid position with the campaign, I called back my contact there to say that I was ready to "do anything to help." Perhaps this generous offer to help *the* anti-war candidate had something to do with a letter I'd received from my draft board, indicating my eligibility for armed forces service.

I was sent to the mailroom at no pay.

I handled only outgoing mail but my responsibilities were far greater, because I also did the duplicating. In the days of mimeograph and stencils, I was the ink-stained wretch at McGovern for President.

After two months of arduous work at the postage meter and duplicating machine, my superiors recognized my talents. I was asked to go to New Hampshire for the primary. Actually, what they recognized was my car— more accurately, my four-wheel-drive Jeep—which was perfect for navigating the snowy roads of New Hampshire.

Goodbye, mailroom. My little Jeep and I arrived in Concord on a Friday evening in late February 1972.

. . .

Once I'd arrived in Concord, my former boss at the mailroom, Rob Gunnison, gave me my assignment. (Gunnison was already in New Hampshire, having been dispatched there shortly after I had mastered the mysteries of the postage meter and stencil machines.) "We want you to go up to New London," Rob said, "about forty minutes away. It's rural, but McCarthy did well there in sixty-eight. Don't know why. We'll send two others with you tomorrow morning. As far as I know, no one from the campaign has been there, because a lot of the roads haven't been cleared of snow."

Yes, I owe my career to my Jeep.

I received a one-page description of New London that read somewhat like this:

> A small community of 800 voters situated on the crest of a hill. The town center is comprised of a post office, a grocery, a diner, the town hall, a church, a small pizza takeout, and a hardware store. There are single-family homes near the town center that are as close together as found in the average suburb. Mostly there are old homes, about a mile apart, down rarely plowed dirt roads. Politically, New London has a history of voting Republican in general elections but for liberals in Democratic primaries.

That was it. Not much to go on. It was eight days before the balloting.

I had a crew of two in my Jeep on my first full day in New Hampshire: Julie and Billy, both college seniors taking a week off to work for McGovern in the Granite State. We took the interstate to New London and as we exited the highway, we saw signs for Colby Junior College. Julie checked the briefing paper and found no mention of this institute of higher learning.

We decided to investigate this potential bastion of newly eligible voters; it was the first year that 18-year-olds could vote. We parked and sought out the chair of the political science department. That neither Julie nor Billy was shy became clear when we learned from the chairman that Colby Junior College was, in fact, an all women's institution, that it had conducted a voter registration drive at the outset of the school year, and that it had a Young Democrats group on campus.

"I'll work the college," Billy announced immediately upon leaving the chair's office. "I've been the campus coordinator for the campaign at Williams, and I'll—"

"Hey, I've been organizing for over a year at Vassar," Julie said, "and I know how to communicate with women on *their* terms."

"Listen," said Billy, "these women have been snowed in on this mountaintop for two months and haven't seen a guy the whole time. They will gravitate to my sign-up table just to interact with someone of the opposite sex."

"They won't trust you or your motives," Julie retorted. "Besides, I bet they visit Dartmouth"—which was in Hanover, New Hampshire, 30 miles away—"every weekend."

Not eager to step directly into the crossfire of this minor skirmish in the war between the sexes, I offered a delaying tactic. "Let's find the head of the Young Dems here and see what's up."

Billy and I were prohibited from entering the bedroom area of the girls' dorm, so we waited in the building's common room while Julie went in to knock on the door of Nancy, the group's chair. The two women quickly came out to meet us.

"Thank God you've finally shown up," Nancy said. "Where have you been? I talked to the Concord McGovern HQ over a month ago and they said they would send somebody up immediately. You have big problems here with the Young Dems."

"We do? Is there a lot of Muskie presence here?" I asked, referring to the leading contender for the Democratic presidential nomination, Senator Edward Muskie.

As I responded, I noticed her eyes were fixed on Billy. She barely looked in my direction as we continued our conversation.

"Yes and no. You have big problems, but we are losing support to Pete McCloskey, not Muskie."

"McCloskey? He's a Republican."

"How can the Young Dems vote for a Republican with zero chance of winning?" Julie demanded.

"Two words," Nancy said.

"'Richard Nixon?'" Julie posited refering to the then sitting Republican President.

"Nope."

"'Mom and Dad?'" Billy asked. "Their parents are Republicans and their DNA doesn't allow them to vote for a Democrat even though they are YDs?"

"Nope."

"I give up," I said.

"The two words are 'Paul Newman.' The McCloskey campaign brought Paul Newman here to speak on the candidate's behalf. Those blue eyes. . . ." She paused to sigh, still looking at Billy—I guess he bore more of a resemblance to Paul Newman than I did. She resumed, "There are Paul Newman/Pete McCloskey posters all over campus."

"So," Julie said, "this is what happens to women stuck in the middle of fuckin' nowhere for three months in the middle of winter?"

"I told Concord a month ago," Nancy told us. "I said, 'All you have to do is get Warren Beatty to show up for George McGovern.'"

I paused to silently curse the goddamn McCloskey organizer who had brought Paul Newman to this windswept bastion of same-sex higher education.

"I will make the request," I said. "In the meantime, Billy will work with you to develop a plan to identify McGovern supporters on campus—what few there are after the visit from Cool Hand Luke. Have the plan ready by five—Julie and I will be back then to go over it."

Once Julie and I had walked out the door, she started in on me.

"You copped out. *I* should be organizing an all-girls college, not that guy from an all-boys school. What does he know about women anyway? And what are you going to do about Warren Beatty?"

We hopped into the Jeep and I started driving, looking for the nearest phone booth to call Concord . Julie continued to hammer me.

"Great. You really think it was a good idea to leave Billy in charge of the campus? Did you see how she looked at him? There will be zero, I repeat, zero work from those two. And how is he going to organize if he can't get into the dorms?"

The phone was outside a café, and putting quarters in a pay phone, with gloves on, in a New Hampshire February made the process of calling

Concord for a farfetched request seem even more like a fool's errand. I removed them.

Concord HQ answered, and I made my request to Rob. He was not amused.

"Let me get this right. You want Warren Beatty to go to an all-girls college? Is this a set-up for him or for us? Forget it. Tell them Mr. Beatty would love to come but he's fully booked until election day."

"Right. Fully booked. Got it." I hung up.

"You didn't try very hard, did you?" said Julie.

"I knew we weren't going to get Warren Beatty up to this godforsaken mountain. Besides, all I want is to get one more vote out of this town than Ed Muskie gets. And so far, I have heard nothing about Ed Muskie on that campus. At least we now have an organizer there."

"Okay, so now what are *we* going to do for the next six days?"

"We're going to talk to voters. We have 311 to contact before next Monday, when we start preparing for primary day. Let's do some door-to-door, then we'll check back on the campus organizing plan at five."

Forty-six doors and seven hours later, we returned to the campus to review the plan and pick up Billy. Nancy and Billy had developed a pyramidal structure of dorm and floor captains, identified prospective captains, and had a task list for each position—all mapped out on a detailed timeline within an accountability structure that placed Billy and Nancy in charge. Julie grudgingly admitted that the plan had merit, although she added in front of the two that "Billy could accomplish in three days what the plan called for in six." Left unsaid was the exact method Nancy and Billy would employ to recruit their captains.

I gave Nancy the bad news about Warren Beatty. "His schedule won't allow a visit here in the next week, but maybe in the general election we could make it happen."

Her response was surprisingly positive. "I guess Billy and I will just have to do without Warren Beatty, eh, Billy?"

Billy nodded in enthusiastic agreement.

Billy, Julie, and I headed back to Concord for the night. I had three cassette tapes in my Jeep—Janis Joplin; Rod Stewart; and Crosby, Stills, Nash & Young. Billy wanted Rod Stewart. Julie wanted Janis Joplin. I was sick of all of them. We settled on CSN&Y.

I met one of my friends from the Washington office at the front door of the Concord headquarters. He was in charge of "Advance" for Concord.

"Hey, Ridder. I need one of your team to help with a McGovern rally on Friday night, here in Concord. Which one?"

I then received an essential lesson of my political education: Advance always has the money and the priority over Field Operations, not to mention the glamorous job of arranging activities for the candidate. Field simply talks to voters. So, when Advance arrives at a campaign office, the field operation is appropriately nervous, because they're about to see personnel and resources vanish.

"How about her?" He pointed at Julie.

Seeing no other option, I agreed. I said my goodbye to Julie with two requests: that she first write the follow-up letters from the day's canvassing and that she return to the New London team on Saturday.

The next morning I met Billy at headquarters for our drive to New London. He had his suitcase with him.

"You taking a trip?" I asked.

"Nancy has arranged a guest room for me on campus so I can work in the evenings."

I spent the next four days going door-to-door in New London, putting my four-wheel drive to good use on the snowy roads and driveways. Many of the voters had never had a canvasser come to their door before and welcomed their guest. I drank a lot of coffee, talking with voters who turned out to be either voting Republican or not voting at all. Occasionally, I would find myself at the home of a Democrat, and even more occasionally at the home of a Democrat who was as yet undecided. Many were convinced that McGovern was no more than a stalking horse for Senator Ted Kennedy's entry into the race.

I saw Billy sparingly over those four days. He was a no-show at one meeting we'd arranged and had only "a few minutes" when I found him Thursday on campus. Our next meeting was to take place at the library on Saturday morning, to begin developing our Get Out the Vote (GOTV) lists.

Even Julie, released from the Evil Advance Empire, was initially impressed at the Saturday meeting when Billy provided a list of forty-one supporters. But, brimming with even more confidence now that she'd helped organize a rally featuring the actual candidate himself, she was quick to raise doubts. "How do I know these are real supporters? How do I know they even exist? Where's Nancy? Why isn't she here? I need to check these names with her."

Billy squirmed. "No, no. You don't want to do that. Some of these girls told me of their support in strictest confidence."

"She can at least confirm that they are *likely* supporters."

"Actually, Billy," I said, "where *is* Nancy? I asked you to tell her about the meeting."

"I dunno. Maybe she had something else going on."

"Like what?" Julie asked.

"I dunno. I dunno." Billy said.

"It doesn't make sense that she wouldn't come to the meeting if she knew about it," said Julie. "That's what we get for relying on a student at this two-bit—"

"That's not it," said Billy, looking out the window. "It's . . . um . . . because Nancy is a bit, um, unhappy with me."

"And why would that be?" Julie asked.

"Lets just say that I got a little too . . . shall we say . . . enthusiastic in my outreach efforts to the Colby student body."

"What?" Julie demanded. "Can't you fucking control yourself for *six days*? I'm going to find her. I'll be right back. Don't either of you move."

With that, she stormed out of the library and toward Nancy's dormitory.

As soon as Julie was out the door, Billy said to me, "It's not as bad as it sounds. I mean, it's not as if I've been romancing every single girl on the list. But I have been, um, very successful in scoring some, um, support. Nancy is a bit upset that I've been spending so much time broadening our base here."

I looked at him and sighed. "Just be careful and don't get yourself—and me—kicked off campus."

Ten minutes later Julie returned to the library with Nancy. There were sharp glances but no verbal blows among the three of them while we categorized each registered voter at the college as:

1. strong supporter;
2. leaning McGovern;
3. undecided; or
4. supporting another candidate.

Nancy rarely refuted any of the information Billy provided, although, after one name, she simply said, "Her, too?"

Nancy and I were the only McGovern representatives allowed in the counting area in New London on election night, and Julie was working Advance for the election night party in Manchester, so Billy was at liberty. He caught a ride with a friend from Dartmouth who, I was told, was on his way to the party.

The absentees were counted first. McGovern was leading Muskie 27-3. "Must be all the kids away at college getting to vote for the first time," said the town clerk, referring to the newly lowered voting age.

At eight, they started counting the non-absentee ballots. When I left at 8:45 to drive to the party in Manchester, over an hour away, my guy was up 76-27. I told Nancy I would call her the next day about any thank-you notes that might need to get written or ruffled egos that might need to be smoothed in New London.

The party was smoky and crowded. I didn't know anyone, couldn't find Billy, couldn't find Julie. I made an early exit, drove to Concord, watched the news, which highlighted McGovern's extraordinary second-place performance, and went to bed. The next day, Wednesday, I dropped by the Concord office early to find only a couple of volunteers there. I tried to reach Nancy with no luck, and waited briefly for Billy to show up. He didn't, and I never again saw the Don Juan of campus organizing. After leaving a note for Rob Gunnison, informing him that I would be in Washington on Monday, I departed for a few days of decompression.

I arrived back at the national office on Monday morning as promised, to resume my indispensable work as king of the mailroom. I was halfway down the hall, headed to the broom closet masquerading as an office that housed the duplicating machines and postage meter, when I heard a loud voice behind me.

"Ridder! Ridder! Where have you been?" I turned to see Rick Stearns, the national field director, staring at me.

"I went skiing, then to see my sister and a friend. I thought it was okay, because I left a note for Rob . . ."

"We've been looking for you for four days. Do you know what happened in New London?"

"Uhh, I know we were leading by more than two to one when I left to go to the party. Did something happen?"

Shit. What happened while I was on the ski slope? Was Billy arrested? Had an angry father come after him with a shotgun? Was the college dean changing visitation policies?

"You don't know what happened?"

"Uhh, no. Look, I'm sorry if—"

"The McGovern share in New London was the highest in the state—over 70 percent! And the turnout. Much bigger than in 1968. Over 100 more votes from that small town. Extraordinary. How did you do it?"

"I had good staff," I mumbled.

"Well, find that staff and take them to Wisconsin. Because you're headed there as soon as you get packed."

"Yeah, but Billy's back in college."

"Billy? Who's Billy?"

"He's, um . . ."

"Well, whoever he is, he must be one hell of an organizer."

• • •

A few days later, in early April, I was sent to Wisconsin and assigned to Madison because, according to Stearns, my success in a college town and knowledge of rural issues warranted an assignment to another college town with large agricultural areas adjacent. My supposed "agricultural expertise" was based on nine days of working in New London, New Hampshire.

Six days before the Wisconsin primary, in which McGovern would square off mainly against Senator Hubert Humphrey of Minnesota—who had entered the race a few weeks previously, with the demise of Ed Muskie—Polly Hackett, a member of the campaign Advance staff, showed up in the Madison, Wisconsin headquarters. I knew her from my days in the mailroom.

Polly spotted me in a cubicle with a phone to my ear. "Hey Rick," she asked, "What are you doing?"

"Calling students."

"Not anymore. I need some help on a project in a rural area. Stearns said you were the rural organizer."

So Advance once again raided Field Ops, but this time, I was the spoils of war. I had no idea what Polly wanted me to do, but I was enthusiastic about whatever it was once she suggested we go get breakfast.

Over eggs and cups of coffee, Polly got down to the task at hand. "Leonard Nimoy—you know, Spock on that TV show *Star Trek*—is coming in to help the campaign, and we want to send him to rural Wisconsin. We need you to arrange his speaking engagements and radio and newspapers interviews. We have names of organizers and supporters. Call them—they'll help you."

But," I said, feeling that as "the rural organizer" I had leave to actually express an opinion on this matter, "are you sure he's the right person to send to rural Wisconsin?"

"We don't have a choice. We need someone to go to these towns this weekend. Every other politician and celebrity wants to be seen with McGovern in and around Milwaukee. This guy actually *wants* to go to rural Wisconsin. I'm told he's a big deal. I need you on this because the guy I had working on it has been pulled onto another assignment: advancing Warren Beatty as he travels with McGovern."

Ah, so Advance can be raided, too—by Advance.

And so it began. I spent the next three days planning events and transportation for Leonard Nimoy's visit to Wisconsin. I talked with McGovern contacts in towns all over the western part of the state and in one town up north, Rhinelander. For Easter Sunday and part of the following Monday, I worked out interviews, travel times, motel reservations, flight schedules, leafleting sites, and advertising plans. Polly helped me a bit, but she was focused on a big rally in Madison, also planned for Easter.

Late Friday evening, I went to Polly with the final typed copy of the schedule. Given the frequency of last-minute changes there was more Whiteout than paper. "It's done," I said. "Everything is set, except one thing."

"What's that?"

"We need a volunteer to drive him around—all day Sunday and half the day Monday."

"That's you."

"Me? I don't know if my Jeep is appropriate for driving around a TV star."

"Forget about the Jeep; you'll rent a car."

"I can't rent a car, I'm not old enough. You have to be at least twenty-one. Maybe twenty-four."

"How old are you?"

"Nineteen."

"Shit. Okay. Take the Jeep."

Promptly at 9 a.m. on Easter Sunday, I met Leonard Nimoy at the Madison airport with my freshly cleaned Jeep. He looked at me in my khaki pants, white oxford shirt with tie, and jean jacket—my attempt to be Sunday respectful while remaining anti-establishment. Then he looked at the Jeep and said, "Well I guess this is the right vehicle to travel rural Wisconsin in." I agreed. Later that day, after eight hours in the cramped quarters of the Jeep, he would not be so complimentary.

Our first stop was the town of Baraboo, an hour north of Madison. I had spoken to the Baraboo coordinator, John Daniels, once—on the phone, for twenty minutes, the night before. He had been fastidious about the arrangements recruiting 15 volunteers to help with the event. In the past four days since the event had been confirmed, they had made more than 830 phone calls, which meant that they had reached every household in Baraboo. He had printed more than 500 leaflets and hit every grocery store and school in the area. He had met with the local peace group twice and the county chair on a daily basis.

As we approached Baraboo, Nimoy asked me, "So what's the drill here?"

"Small town on Easter Sunday. We're meeting John Daniels at the first sign that says 'Welcome to Baraboo.' Then we go to the high school. I suppose we'll meet in a classroom or something."

"It is Easter Sunday morning. Forty or fifty people, right?"

"Right. Daniels didn't give me an estimate, but he has worked the town. The Democratic county chair should be coming, plus a Democratic elected official or two. Do you want a brief on what to say?"

"No, I've got my spiel. Did it a lot in New Hampshire. But I am told you will take care of the rural and ag policy stuff, if someone asks."

"Uhh . . . right. Yeah. Right."

As I answered, I saw Nimoy cock his head sideways at me, Vulcan style. "Let's hope there are no questions in that area."

We pulled over at the appointed meeting place, where a station wagon with a "McGovern for President" bumper sticker was parked. A middle-aged man and his son, approximately fourteen years old, stood beside the car. Nimoy and I got out of the Jeep. I introduced myself to the dad. "Hi, John. Good to meet you in person. I'm Rick Ridder."

The man extended his hand and said, "Good to meet you, Rick. But I am *Peter* Daniels. This is John." He pointed at the young man to his left.

This kid is the local coordinator? The person I was talking to over the phone?

Nimoy rescued me from my dumbfounded astonishment. "John, good to meet you. Where are we headed?"

John stood straight up—to his full five-foot-two-inches—and said, "We're going to the high school, where you'll be talking in the gym. Everyone's real excited that you're here."

"I'm glad to be here," said Nimoy. "Can I ride with you over to the gym? Rick will follow."

"Dad," John Daniels asked Peter Daniels, "can Mr. Nimoy ride with us?"

Peter agreed, and we headed to the high school, but not before Nimoy turned to John and said, "Please, call me Leonard."

"Yes, sir, Leonard," said John, his eyes open wide as if he'd seen a spaceman.

The ride to the high school took all of five minutes, but that was long enough to see that calling the town "excited" didn't begin to describe it. Nearly every home had a homemade "Welcome to Baraboo, Leonard Nimoy" sign hanging from its white picket fence. Some of the signs featured pictures of the Starship Enterprise; some, pictures of Mr. Spock. A few had drawings of a hand giving the split finger sign with the words "Live long and prosper," the Vulcan saying that Nimoy, a Jewish actor, had appropriated from a ceremony in which members of Judaism's priestly class bless their less exalted brethren. (I'm guessing that few of Baraboo's citizens were members of Judaism's priestly class.)

A couple of signs even made reference to George McGovern, who, to my knowledge, was neither Vulcan nor Jewish.

As I drove my Jeep into the crowded high school parking lot I saw a twenty-foot banner arched over the driveway: "The Thunderbirds Welcome Leonard Nimoy." Balloons were tied to every lamppost and to the handlebars of every bicycle.

After I parked my car, I ran to catch up with John and Nimoy, who were working a receiving line. John introduced his friend Leonard to the Democratic county chair, members of the state legislature, the county commissioners, the mayor (a Republican), and the high school principal. Nimoy, a courteous man, said to the principal, "It must be great to have a good student like John here."

To which the principal responded, "We look forward to having John come to the high school next year, after he finishes at the junior high."

We headed to the gym, with a quick stop at the campaign sign-up tables, where Nimoy thanked the volunteers and autographed a few McGovern brochures. The principal led the way, followed by the child prodigy coordinator, the star of the small screen, the legislators, and the county chair (who was loving it). The mayor, balancing civic pride with party loyalty, remained at the rear of the room. The procession made its way to the front of the gym, packed mostly with people too young to vote. The principal led the Pledge of Allegiance, then turned things over to the master of ceremonies.

The youthful master of ceremonies.

John recognized the elected officials, the county chair, and the volunteers who had "worked tirelessly to make this event a success." He then asked those same volunteers to work "just as hard in the next forty-eight hours to help George McGovern bring peace to our country." He then introduced "my good friend Leonard Nimoy."

I was watching from near a side door when I heard an elderly man turn to his wife and say, "Don't know who this guy is, but this is the biggest political crowd in Baraboo since Fighting Bob La Follette came through for his son, just before he died in '25. Of course, his wife was from Baraboo."

Nimoy began simply. "I will first talk about why I am here for George McGovern, then answer questions about why I am committed to making George McGovern president of the United States. Then I'll take a few questions about pointy ears and the Starship *Enterprise*."

He kept his word. He focused on the war in Vietnam and why he was opposed to it, citing the civilian losses caused by land mines and cluster bombs as well as the fallacy of the "domino theory" positing that if one country fell to Communism then others would quickly follow. He was forceful, compassionate, and believable.

Then he took questions. One of the first ones came from a young nonvoter: "You know the episode where you telepathically communicated with the Klingon leadership, and then Captain Kirk and Scotty had a fight, and then you took Scotty's side because Kirk's argument was not logical, and the Klingons were about to destroy the *Enterprise*? My bedtime is right before the end of *Star Trek* and I never found out what happened, and I've been wondering, and I knew you would be able to tell me."

"We worked it out," said Mr. Spock. "Next question."

There were one or two questions about McGovern's stance on the war, and perhaps a dozen about the TV show: the makeup used to create Spock's ears, the address from which one could obtain "official Star Trek uniforms," Spock's full powers, and, from one middle-aged mom, "Why don't women play a larger leadership role on the show?"

Forty-five minutes into the Q&A, John ended the program by thanking Nimoy, and issuing an emphatic call to "Vote McGovern on Tuesday." He then turned the microphone over to an individual whose collar denoted him as a clergyman. I expected a closing prayer, but instead heard an announcement: "I would like to remind everyone that the Easter services for all Christian denominations have been delayed until noon today to accommodate the scheduling of this fine event. We look forward to seeing you in an hour."

Mr. Spock had bumped God!

The event was over. After Nimoy signed a few McGovern posters for John and his volunteers, we said our thanks and goodbyes. We hopped into the Jeep and headed to our next stop, a radio station an hour away. As we drove down the highway, a station wagon passed us with four kids peering out the back window and flashing their split-fingered hands. Leonard responded in kind.

We'd been driving in silence for a few minutes when Nimoy asked, "How many?"

"The gym was packed. I counted twenty rows of seats with twenty seats each. I'd say there was a minimum of 400, plus the people standing. Probably 450 to 500, total."

"Easter Sunday morning," Nimoy said, shaking his head.

We visited four towns and two radio stations that day. The crowds were impressive but nothing like the Baraboo gathering.

Eight days later, after McGovern won the Wisconsin primary, I walked into the offices of Utah Citizens for McGovern, home also to the western states office of McGovern for President, where I was assigned for the next few months.

Mary Ellen Simonson, the deputy western states director, met me with the words, "Call Washington right away. Stearns wants to talk to you."

"Stearns?"

"Yes. Stearns. The national field director."

I dialed Washington and asked to speak to Stearns.

"Ridder, where the hell have you been? You were supposed to be in Massachusetts."

"Massachusetts? I was told to go to Salt Lake. Then to Idaho for the caucuses."

"You were? By who? Oh never mind. Everybody is looking for you, including some press."

"What? I didn't do anything. The trip with Nimoy went fine, right?"

*Shit. What had I done now?*

"Apparently the trip did go well. Very well. There was a big fundraiser in San Francisco on Thursday night with all the biggest California donors—everyone. A huge dinner, 500 people. McGovern was there, Mankiewicz, Hart. We raised $250,000. It was a big event."

"Yeah. A big deal. So?"

"So we eat, and then it's time to make the money pitch, and we'd asked Leonard Nimoy to do it. He stands up and tells this story about traveling around Wisconsin in a Jeep with a nineteen-year-old volunteer named Rick Ridder. And somehow you made sure that there were 500 people on Easter Sunday, in some remote town miles from Madison."

Stearns continued. "So now everyone wants to know where you've been assigned to next, and why you're not in Massachusetts for the next primary, and where the press can find you. To the press guys, this is about commitment, youth, and God knows what else. It's become a story."

"Uhh, okay."

"But, you had to go to Utah where no one will find you."

"Sorry."

"But what I want to know is this: how did you pull off 500 people in Beaver, Wisconsin, on Easter Sunday morning?"

"It was Baraboo, and I had a very good local contact."

"Great. Well, get him moving to the next contest. Do you need him in Idaho?"

"I don't think his parents will let him go on the road before he gets out of junior high."

"What?"

"He's in eighth grade."

. . .

Sometimes, it's not just about hiring but about firing the right people. Campaigns are filled with true believers whose commitment is grandiose and whose capabilities are limited. Generally, these people are very low-paid campaign workers or volunteers, and not necessarily an asset to a campaign. I've told numerous campaign managers that when they spend 15 minutes a day undoing the mess a volunteer has created, that is nearly a full day over the course of a month. So, its okay to fire volunteers or reassign them to some area of the campaign where their capabilities are better employed, such as permanently waving signs on a corner.

Generally, firings are a necessity for financial reasons. In 2000, I became the George Clooney in *Up in the Air* of the Bradley for President campaign. (Of course, Clooney doesn't have my good looks.) I "released" more than fifty staffers in Iowa in a twenty-four-hour period, and then a week later went to New Hampshire to release thirty more.

It isn't easy making a judgment about future employment in a ten-minute interview with a person who has just spent eighteen hours a day working for a candidate who, in their minds, could save mankind from imminent destruction.

I've worked hard to be right in my assessments *most* of the time, because keeping the right people makes you look good, too.

. . .

Six weeks after the Wisconsin primary, in May of 1972, I was on my way to Oregon. At that time, the Oregon primary was considered a stepping-stone to the major California primary. I traveled there from Utah with two veterans of the Massachusetts and Ohio primary battles—Hattie Hartman, age 18, and Nina Wilds, age 17. Also along was Leonard McGee, a University of Utah student who excelled at going into Latter Day Saints communities and convincing these LDS Democrats (yes, there were some of those back then) that George McGovern was not going to foist a radical atheist agenda upon the nation and deserved their support.

Upon our arrival in Oregon, Hattie and Nina were sent to Tigard while Leonard and I were stationed at a small storefront headquarters in Hillsboro staffed by two former Ohio organizers. We were to report to those two, but within a few hours it became clear that either they were stunningly inept or something else was going on. It turned out to be both.

In ten days of working Hillsboro, the two former Ohio staffers had identified fewer than ten McGovern supporters—no surprise, considering that they had made fewer than fifty phone calls and knocked on exactly five doors. They had recruited one volunteer to the office, a Vietnam vet in his mid-twenties whose major contribution, we would find out, was the provision of alternative-lifestyle supplies.

Upon our arrival, Leonard asked, "What do you need us to do?" Bobby, our supposed boss, responded, "Whatever you want. I'm headed out for a smoke break. See you in a few."

He returned two hours later—which told Leonard and me that the smoke in the smoke break didn't come from tobacco—to find us preparing to make canvass calls. He stared at us, "Wow. You guys are really going to do it, huh?"

There was a single phone line at campaign headquarters, and another a block away at Washington County Democratic headquarters. Alternating our locations, Leonard and I dialed eleven hours a day for six days, averaging fourteen connections per hour. We identified 616 McGovern supporters. After writing more than 300 follow-up letters, we agreed that we would never do anything like that again.

All six days were not completely monotonous, however. The third featured a bit of excitement. That morning I was collecting my lists before heading to the county headquarters, when in through the storefront door walked Paul Sullivan, the statewide field director. His name was familiar from my early days in the mailroom; the lowdown at national headquarters was that he was a good but tough organizer from Hawaii. Leonard and I introduced ourselves, but he didn't want to talk to us. He was there to do an "unannounced spot check." He wanted to talk to the two guys in charge of the place—the two guys from Ohio. I pointed to the individuals in blue jeans who were giggling and staring at a poster in a far corner of the headquarters.

"What's wrong with them?" Paul asked.

Leonard looked toward the ceiling and might as well have begun whistling. It was left to me to answer. I tried to do so as carefully as possible. "Well, um, specifically now? Or, um, in general?"

"Now, yesterday, the day before, last week, next Christmas. What the fuck is going on here?"

"They're stoned," I said.

"How did they get here?"

"They were on staff in Ohio and were sent here after the primary there."

"Jesus," said Paul. "What idiot sent them on to Oregon? Fire them."

"What do you mean? *We're* reporting to *them*. They are our bosses."

"Fire them. Clearly, they are not providing oversight to anyone, including themselves. From this moment forward, you two are running this place, not them. I am going down the street to the coffee shop to make a few calls. I will be back in thirty minutes. They'd better be gone."

He walked out before I could ask, "Why us? *You're* their boss."

"Well, Leonard," I said, "I'll let you fire them. I've never fired anyone."

"No, no, you do it. It will give you experience."

"No, no. Please? You do it. You're older."

"No, no. You're the national staffer."

"No, no. You're tougher."

Our Alphonse and Gaston act went on for five minutes, until we realized that we had only twenty-five more before the Hawaiian Hammer would return, looking to nail us if we hadn't nailed the Ohioans. We agreed to do the deed together.

We approached our midwestern friends slowly, and as officially as possible, informed them that their tenure with McGovern for President was over. Further, we asked that they leave the premises immediately. Upon hearing of his dismissal, the taller of the two simply said, "Wow. We were going to go to the beach this weekend to drop acid anyway. Now we can leave early."

They were gone in ten minutes.

Paul reappeared fifteen minutes later, as promised, and went over our phone plan for the weekend. He left muttering, "So help me, I'm going to find out what idiot sent those two guys out here on the campaign's dime."

Over the course of the McGovern campaign, I learned to dread a Paul Sullivan "unannounced spot check," particularly in California. Thirty-six years later, he flew from Hawaii to volunteer at my daughter's Obama HQ in Colorado.

"This guy from Hawaii showed up who is just awesome," she reported. "My numbers went through the roof tonight. He rocks."

His only comment to me after a few days in her HQ: "Hers is a lot better than your Oregon ops."

• • •

For the Gary Hart presidential campaign, November 1983, it was the worst of times. And there were no best of times. Our polling numbers lingered in the low single digits. Funds were extremely limited. Indeed, no one had been paid for October and some hadn't gotten anything for September. Our candidate loved to meet with voters in New Hampshire, but hardly anywhere else. And he loathed making fundraising calls, so he made few of them. The field staff had been pared to a handful in New Hampshire and Iowa, along with one southern coordinator and me.

The comptroller of the campaign walked into the field office, which had once housed the five-person full-time field staff but now consisted of two very part-time volunteers and me. "You have to cut your staff," he announced.

"What staff?" I asked.

"Your staff."

"Okay, okay," I said, knowing that it really wasn't okay.

"We can't cut the Iowa staff or the New Hampshire staff because that will cause another 'Hart Campaign in Disarray' story. And—"

"You could cut yourself," he interjected.

"No, thank you. I am not doing this as a volunteer, at least not on paper."

"Well, then that leaves one person, doesn't it?"

I agreed. It was the coordinator who lived in the South somewhere.

At that point, with the Super Tuesday southern primaries four months away, I had spent zero time working on any state but Iowa and our presumable "base" in the west. New Hampshire was not really my concern because we had a very talented state director up there, Jeannie Shaheen. She later became governor and U.S. senator from that state. Not bad for a field organizer.

So, I picked up the phone, and called our southern coordinator. "James, this is Rick Ridder at the Hart campaign office. We spoke a few days ago."

The man at the end of line responded in a heavy southern drawl. "Yes, yes. I remember. How're things goin' up there?"

"Ah, well, not so good. Listen, James, I am going to release you of your contractual obligations with this campaign because we can't pay you, and—"

"Well, I figured that out a few weeks ago when I got a call from the comptroller saying he couldn't pay me for September," he said.

"Oh. I didn't know that we didn't pay you for September. I knew about October, and—"

"Don't worry. I wasn't planning on you guys making it to the south anyway. I've got a job starting next month. I am going to be Lloyd Doggett's campaign manager for his Senate race."

"Okay, great. Good luck! Send me any notes or files you might have." And I hung up with James Carville.

• • •

There is a moment in a campaign when it is time to acknowledge that all is lost. It is not necessarily when poll numbers show your candidate in single digits with three weeks to go, or when the heat has been cut off in the headquarters for lack of payment, or when paychecks have trickled to the nonexistent level, or when the staff is cooking lunch on camp stoves in the office and selling the cooked food to the other staffers to make rent money. (My wife still wants her wedding gifts back from this use of our pots and pans.)

No. It is when you observe more campaign staff resumes than campaign schedules or press releases in the printer tray.

All of these conditions existed at the Washington-based national headquarters of Gary Hart for President in early February of 1984. With the Iowa caucuses two weeks away and the New Hampshire primary in less than three weeks, it appeared to all of us, and to the national pundit community, that the Gary Hart for President campaign would cease to exist in less than a month. Although the campaign had been airing TV ads in Iowa and New

Hampshire for two weeks, the buy was anemic and there was some question as to whether there would be any money to sustain it for the next three weeks.

Late one afternoon, walking by the only printer we had, I heard Ginny Terzano, the receptionist/office manager/assistant press secretary, scream down the hallway from the front desk, "Ridder, telephone call. It's the Secret Service."

I got that dreaded sinking feeling in my stomach that this was not going to be a good call. The campaign had been assigned a Secret Service detail a month earlier, and this was certain to be another installment in the weekly ritual of the Secret Service informing the national field director (me) of the Iowa field staff's recalcitrance in accommodating the Service's protocols.

I, of course, had heard from the Iowa field staff of the unreasonable demands of the Secret Service, and was told directly by one of the field staff, "Tell them to cool it. I can't do my job with them around."

I did no such thing, but did suggest in the weekly colloquies with the Secret Service that changing the behavior and organizing techniques of our team would be an "ongoing effort, and I hoped the Service could be more flexible in letting my staff do their job."

My request was always met with a very cordial, "No. We do this to protect the candidate. That's *our* job."

I picked up the phone, and before I could say "Hello," the agent began, "Mr. Ridder. This is Agent Johnson. I need to see you and the campaign manager, Pudge Henkel, right away. I have already spoken to Doug Wilson, the campaign's liaison with the Service, about all of us meeting as soon as possible."

"Sure. Sure. When?"

"Tomorrow, 9 a.m. at your offices."

"Okay, I will tell the campaign manager, and we will expect you."

"Thank you. Goodbye." He hung up.

So, now they were coming in person to discuss the Iowa staff. No more Mr. Somewhat-Nice-Guy on the phone. This would certainly be a full-blown dressing down in front of the campaign manager.

I walked down the hall to check with Doug Wilson. "Did you get the call from the Secret Service?" I asked.

"Yes," he answered. "Did you get one? He said he was going to call you."

"Yeah. Did he tell you what this was about?"

"No. Generally when they call it's about the schedule or timetables or about the Iowa field staff. This time he wanted to make sure that you, me, and Pudge would be at the meeting."

"That's all he said to me, too. I'll go tell Pudge."

The next morning, Doug and I entered Pudge's office at eight fifty-five to prepare for our nine o'clock meeting. We were both wearing ski parkas as the office temperature hovered in the mid-fifties due to the campaign's failure to pay the office heat bill. Pudge wore a tweed jacket but benefited from a heating pad draped over the back of his desk chair. He was always leaning back in the chair.

Promptly at nine, Agent Johnson entered Pudge's office. Before any of the Hart team could say a word, Agent Johnson stared directly at Pudge Henkel and began, "This campaign is about to take off, and you're not ready for it."

Silence as three jaws dropped to street level, two floors below.

We could acknowledge the second half of the statement, but the first? Finally, I stammered, "And . . . just what makes you think that?"

Johnson looked at me. "People are coming up to Hart and want to touch him."

"What?" Wilson asked.

"Look, " Johnson said, " I was in Iowa with Senator Hart three weeks ago, in mid-January, and there was nothing going on. But I was back there for the last four days. People are coming up to him. They want to touch him." He stopped briefly to take a breath. "I have to keep people from pushing him and trying to get a piece of him. This is always the first indication that something significant is happening for your candidate."

Silence.

"Now, let me talk about your Iowa team," he said, shifting to look directly at me. "First, they are very nice kids. Very smart and working extremely hard. In fact, you are highly understaffed for what is coming. But they have got to listen and do what we tell them."

Pudge leaning forward off the heating pad. "What do you mean, specifically?"

"Okay, here's an example. On Saturday night, there was that Carole King concert in Des Moines, at a theater. Good crowd. We told the campaign staff that Hart could walk down the aisle to the stage but Hart could not, *not*, go back the same way through the crowd. After the concert, the field staff took him right back down into the crowd. Exactly what we told them not to do."

"Well I'm sure they wanted him to meet other possible supporters who he'd missed before," I said.

"Yes, and a couple of weeks ago, it was of far less concern. But not now. Here is the problem with what they did. An assassin will often not pull the trigger the first time he or she gets near a candidate; he'll have second thoughts. But when you give him another chance by going back, then you're in trouble. Just talk to Governor Wallace about this. He will tell you that if he had followed our directions and not gone back into the crowd, he would be walking today."

Johnson stood up. "I've got to go," he said, "but I think you really need to prepare for something that you have not been expecting. You need to get your staff ready now."

We stood up and said good bye and thank you. Then Pudge turned to me. "Rick, you better call the Iowa and New Hampshire staffs and tell them to be a bit more cooperative with the Secret Service. Doug, perhaps we should get some Advance staff ready—for free, of course."

Then we stood there in silence, looking at the floor, shaking our heads.

Three weeks later Gary Hart won the New Hampshire primary.

# RULE #7

# CASH UP FRONT PREFERRED IN ALL CASES.

Here is what a new client says at the start of a typical first meeting with our campaign consulting firm: "We have no money. You *do* believe in our cause. So, we were hoping you would give us your special low rate—understanding our situation."

"Uh . . . no."

Actually, try as we do to give off the impression that we are a bunch of hard-boiled, ruthless operatives selling our services to the highest bidder—and consider libelous the unfounded rumor that we can't be bought—we do from time to time work for the lowest bidder. In fact, a newspaper article on pro bono work in politics—an article we've tried to scrub from Internet search engines—quoted a fellow consultant as saying, "Right cause, no money? Call Ridder/Braden."

The article got us plenty of calls. And no money.

Some cash-poor clients have paid us in kind: bad aboriginal art, bottles of vinegar masquerading as wine, enough gift baskets to clean out Harry and David's warehouse, a bag full of coupons from Bed, Bath and Beyond, and season tickets to the local rodeo in really outback Wyoming.

But every once in awhile, something special comes along.

In April 1986, Joannie and I opened our own firm with one major congressional client, the aforementioned Ben Nighthorse Campbell, who was running against a House incumbent in western Colorado. Not only did Campbell's campaign have no money—this was before he wowed the Jewish donors in Denver—but the candidate was also averse to making fundraising calls. By June, we had not been paid for two months. Then we got a phone call from Sherrie Wolff, the campaign manager.

"I have good news and bad news," Sherrie said. "The good news is that the Cheyenne Indian Tribe wants to do a fundraiser for us."

"That's great!" I said. Campbell was a chief of the Northern Cheyenne. Tribe members would chip in tens of thousands to send him to Congress, and we would get paid. "But wait," I said. "Wasn't there bad news?"

"They want to do it on the Fourth of July."

"No problem. We'll just squeeze it in between parades in the district."

"We can't."

"Why not? We'll do some creative scheduling. He'll miss the end of one parade, the beginning of another."

"Rick."

"I've got it all worked out. He'll . . ."

"Rick."

"What?"

"The fundraiser's in Montana."

"So we cancel all the parades?"

"We cancel all the parades."

This was a problem. Anytime there was a parade in the district, Campbell attended in full Indian chief regalia, replete with feathered headdress and buckskin trousers. Newspapers and TV stations loved the pictures, which meant that every parade meant press coverage.

Together with Sherrie, Joannie and I weighed the political calculus: parades and media coverage versus no parades and money. We opted for the money—and certainly not because all of us (including Sherrie) wanted to get paid.

Off Ben went to northern Montana—by himself. We weren't going to waste money on a plane ticket for a staffer. No, we trusted the candidate to handle things on his own. (Never a good idea.)

Expecting a haul of many thousands of dollars, we eagerly awaited his report. He didn't call on the Fourth of July, nor on the fifth. But after his return to Colorado on the sixth, Sherrie called me to say that she'd spoken to him. "It was wonderful," she said. "There were quite a few people there, and they held a blanket dance for him."

"A blanket dance?"

"Yes, a blanket dance. It's a Cheyenne tradition. Ben said it was amazing."

"Fabulous. Super. Terrific. And this blanket dance—was it held before the fundraiser? Or after?"

"No, it *was* the fundraiser. It's a traditional way of raising money— instead of passing the hat, they hold out a blanket."

"Fantastic. Marvelous. Great." I was building up to the big question. "So, how much did we raise from this amazing blanket dance?"

"According to Ben, he has $478 in hand." She was blurting this out, trying to get through the pain, just as you remove a Band-aid from a hairy arm.

"$478?"

"Yes, and promises for a couple hundred more."

"Even with that additional windfall, you realize that the take doesn't cover Ben's airfare, not to mention the hotel, the rental car . . ."

"But that doesn't include the horse," Sherrie pronounced.

"The what?

"We *got* a horse. In the blanket dance."

"That was one big blanket."

"No, the horse wasn't tossed into the blanket . . . I don't think."

"So," I said, "here's my next Federal Election Commission filing: we received $478 from unknown sources and one horse of undetermined value. Sherrie, is it my job to provide amusement to government bureaucrats?"

"He said it's a good horse."

"Where is this good horse?"

"In Montana."

"Okay. So we transport—this good horse—to Colorado. Then what?"

"We can—"

"Wait! They must have glue factories in Montana. We sell it for cash, most of which we use to pay a small portion of our fees, leaving us $1.50 to add to the $478."

"Well, ahhh . . ." Sherrie was now speaking slowly and deliberately, "Ben and I . . . Ben and I thought that in lieu of your fees . . . you would like the horse."

"A horse, in lieu of my fees? No. Lets begin, I live in central Denver, where, I'm sure, there are codes against keeping a horse."

"This is the west. Anyone can have a horse who wants one."

"I don't want one. I grew up with horses. I didn't like them then, I don't like them now. I left Virginia, my family home, to get away from horses. I'm allergic to horses. I get near one and my asthma makes Wheezy in Snow White look like a marathoner. I don't like riding horses, I don't like smelling horses, I don't like hearing horses. Are you seeing a pattern here? Do you think that by offering to pay us with a horse instead of money you were whinnying up the wrong tree?"

Sherrie sighed. "I knew it was a long shot, but I had to try."

"Why don't you take it?" I posited.

"Me? I don't want it, thank you very much."

To my knowledge, the horse never left Montana, and it may still be living there, known to one and all as Ridder's Horse. I will also say, at great legal peril, that we never listed the horse on the campaign's financial disclosure reports.

Campbell's campaign was underfunded but he won because he was a superb candidate who looked great in photos and on TV. His image astride a horse was featured in numerous TV spots throughout his political career, which included five electoral victories.

As far as I know, he rode his own horse, not Ridder's Horse.

• • •

Sometimes, money isn't everything for a candidate—although it helps a lot. Many candidates point to their experience in the private sector when running for office. "Government should be run like a successful business," these successful business types say. "And I've run a successful business."

"I've met a payroll," some CEO will declare. "I've created jobs. I've balanced budgets. I've flown to golf weekends on a corporate jet!"

Actually, most—but not all—avoid bragging about that last bit—at least in public.

Unfortunately for these candidates, most of them quickly find out that not everyone wants government to be run like a business.

But candidates with money are rare in Democratic politics, so when a call comes from a potential client with deep pockets, despite the probable negatives, we answer the call.

In 2003, one such potential client, Blair Hull, asked me, "How much will it cost to run for U.S. Senate if I don't take any contributions?"

"The primary in Illinois might cost twenty-five to thirty million dollars," I told him. "No one knows you and you'll have stiff opposition in State Treasurer Dan Hynes. The general election will cost you another ten to fifteen million."

Blair thought for all of two seconds, then said, "Okay, forty million. Won't hurt my lifestyle or my children's lifestyle one bit."

Clearly, this time I was not going to be looking at a gift horse.

Hull spent twenty-eight million in a hard fought primary. He lost to an obscure state senator with an unelectable name: Barack Hussein Obama. Whatever happened to him?

• • •

In 1987, Bill Farley of Farley Industries decided he wanted to explore a run for the presidency.

An entrepreneur best known at the time for appearing in TV ads for Fruit of the Loom in his underwear—he owned the company—Farley was one of those it's-time-to-run-the-country-like-a-business candidates.

Unlike most of those candidates, however, he wanted to run as a Democrat, which was unfortunate because extensive polling in Iowa showed him with zero chance in that state's caucuses as a Democrat, but a real chance as a Republican. But . . . damn the polling, full speed ahead.

I got a call from Jack Albertine, Farley's political guy, when my wife and I were in Zurich visiting friends after attending an international campaign conference. "We need you in Washington tomorrow afternoon at 2 p.m. for a meeting to make the go/no-go decision," Jack told me.

I put my glass of red wine down next to my half-eaten stash of chocolate and looked at my watch: it was 6:30 p.m. "Jack," I shouted—because even though you can be heard perfectly well over international telephone lines, the geographic distance, not to mention the absurdity of the request, called for amplification—"I'm in Zurich. Headed to London tomorrow, where I have a meeting at 2 p.m. the next day. I can't be in Washington tomorrow."

"What do you mean you 'can't'?" Albertine, a political pro whose speed talking was legendary, was starting to rev up. "Hop on an early-morning flight to Paris. Concorde over to New York. Grab the shuttle. You'll be in DC by 1 p.m. at the latest. Concorde back to London in the evening. Land at 7 a.m. London time. You make our meeting here, you make your meeting there, everyone's happy."

I paused for a few moments because I was unfamiliar with the verb infinitive "to Concorde."

"Okay . . . I guess."

"Good. I'll tell Bill you'll be here."

"Sure, I just . . ."

"See you tomorrow, Rick."

Five years earlier, I had been nearly fired by my boss, Ralph Nader, for submitting an expense bill in the outrageous amount of $394 for six weeks on the road, but now I found myself at the Air France counter in Paris signing a credit card slip for five grand so I could "Concorde."

I still wasn't home free—I was on standby, because the flight was sold out. However, it was worth the five thou just to wait in the Concorde lounge. Air France clearly wanted no complaints from their master-of-the-universe passengers that the food and drink in the waiting room was *comme ci, comme ça. Non, monsieur.* Plenty of first-rate *vin, pain, fromage,* whatever the French is for roast lamb on a carving table. Plus champagne. Plus a chocolate fountain. It was as though we were the Bourbons and the Bastille had never been stormed. I could swear that I heard a woman with really big hair say, "Let them eat pretzels!"

I tried to look as if I belonged there. I tucked in my shirt and mumbled some imprecations about "creeping socialism."

One of the swells failed to appear in time for the flight, so I got my seat in the plane's only class: "Concorde Class." Three hours more of food and wine, and more food and more wine, and we were circling the Statue of Liberty.

As we landed, I realized that Concorde-ing came with an added benefit. Before I'd gotten off the phone with Albertine, his last instruction was, "Keep track of your time. We'll pay you on an hourly basis—even for the travel." So now I started figuring: Let's see. I left Paris at 1 p.m. but landed at 8:30 a.m. in New York. That meant that I could bill twice for the time between eight-thirty and one.

I made it to Washington for the two o'clock meeting. After a few minutes, Farley looked at me and asked, "How much will it cost to get me to the New York primary in April?"

Having prepared an initial campaign budget a few weeks prior, I knew the answer: fifteen-to-twenty million.

"So, fifteen million. Not a penny more, am I right? I hate it when a project comes in over budget."

I never had thought of a presidential campaign as "a project" but I assured him that I would watch his pennies.

The meeting adjourned with a decision to move forward slowly on Mr. Farley's project. I headed back to London that night but "Mon Dieu!" the Concorde did not fly to London or Paris in the evening, and Washington-to-London business class was sold out. Steerage on the DC-10 was neither fast nor comfortable, and I think the cheese came from Pennsylvania. I arrived in London in time for the meeting with two representatives from the UK's Liberal Democrats. We didn't quite use orange crates for chairs, but it was pretty close.

The Liberal Democratic Party was our client for twenty-four years. After much fanfare, Bill Farley decided not to run for president after all—and the "the project" came in below budget.

• • •

In the midwinter of 1999, Joannie and I received an email from a colleague in Argentina. He spoke halting English and my Spanish is limited to *cerveza, por favor*, but I did understand this much: Come quick. Important client. Has money. That last bit, especially, had a lovely ring to it.

I arrived with Benjamin Kupersmit, my associate/translator in Buenos Aires, where we met our Argentine partner and local pollster, Hugo Haime. Over coffee at a plaza café, the well-respected and dapper Hugo began the discussion. "The candidate is running for governor of the province of Jujuy," he said without a smile, in heavily accented English, and perhaps not cognizant of the irony that three Jews were about to head to work in Jujuy. "The president wants him elected. We must find a way to elect him. To keep the president happy."

All well and good, I thought, but there was this one pesky problem—people had to vote for him. "What if we find the voters prefer someone else?" I said.

"That would not be good," Hugo answered, still in English. In Spanish, he provided further detail to Benji, who nodded his head occasionally as he listened, then translated for me. In the morning we would head to Jujuy, where we would talk to the candidate about conducting a poll and developing a campaign plan.

"Jujuy is holding a special election because the previous governor died in office," Benji explained. "The president wants to win the election as a show of support for his policies."

This seemed perfectly reasonable. Leaders often seek solace in the results of special elections. The only problem is that special elections are precisely the best vehicle for voters to display their dissatisfaction—if not outward anger—at the people in power. In the UK, political observers have always looked to by-elections as indicators of the level of voter disdain for the sitting government.

As we were finishing our coffee, I asked Hugo, "Say, how did this guy make his money? Mining or something like that?"

Hugo smiled and simply said, "Business. *Agricultura*."

"Oh, in the States we call that 'farming and ranching.'"

"*Sí*, business. *Agricultura*."

The next day we flew to Jujuy. The candidate's entourage—four well-groomed men in dark suits and sunglasses—met us at the airport in two black Suburbans. They were men of few words. "Come with us," the tallest among the tall commanded.

We obeyed. They drove us to a hotel and told us to wait there until the candidate was ready. As I looked out the window at the streets of Jujuy, it became clear that this was the kind of place where Butch Cassidy and the Sundance Kid met their fate and where escaped Nazis get together to talk about the good ol' days. It was northwest Argentina on the Bolivian border. Dusty. Hot. Dusty. Dry. Everything was a shade of brown, making scrub brush the local equivalent of flowers.

We waited in a bedroom of the hotel until we were told that we should get lunch because our client would not be ready until early afternoon. Over empanadas and coffee at the hotel bar, Hugo, who had been twitching nervously since our arrival in Jujuy, turned to me and whispered, "I need to tell you something." He then looked toward Benji and said, "I will speak in Spanish because it easier."

He spoke in lowered tones to Benji, who offered simultaneous translation. "Some of Hugo's sources here say . . . that the candidate may have a bad reputation . . . in this community . . . because he may have . . ." Benji stopped the simultaneous translation, turned to me, and said in unlowered tones, "Killed an eighteen-year-old girl! Holy shit!"

"No, no," said Hugo, waving his hands and shaking his head. "*Solo posible, no se seguro. Solo posible, no se seguro.*"

"It's only possible," Benji translated, "not certain."

And that's when the men in black suits returned and told us that the candidate was ready to meet with us. Hugo clammed up.

We piled into the two Suburbans, headed out of town, and began climbing up the nearby mountain. After five minutes, we saw green trees and verdant grasses. As we climbed higher, there were forests of native woods and what looked to be orchards. Maybe our candidate's "*agricultura*" was the growing of apples or peaches. The campaign story was beginning to form in my head. Did they have apple pie here in Argentina? Peach empanadas? Someone who grows apples couldn't have really killed a girl, could he?

Thirty minutes outside of town, we arrived at what I first thought was a gated community. Well, there was a gate—along with a ten-foot-high barbed-wire fence—but not much of a community.

It was an *estancia* with security. Lots of security. Indeed, the place was a demi-Twelve Days of Christmas of security operations: six men in black suits, holstered pistols at their hips, earpieces in their ears, barely moving a muscle as they talked into their sleeves; five German shepherds roaming freely, always searching for their next meal—which could be you; four guard towers with posted sentries, all smoking large, black cigars; three video cameras in every room, swiveling to and fro; two bodyguards who never left the candidate's side, their faces as steely as their Uzis; and a man on horseback, holding a shotgun, looking sideways at the three mild-mannered city types who had come to visit.

As we stepped out of the car, I had a moment to lean over to Benji and whisper this confidence builder: "Don't fuck up the translation because if you do, we could be puppy chow by morning."

The candidate greeted us. He was a silver-haired fox with a trimmed mustache, fit, tan, and sporting a diamond ring that rated high on the bling index. We shook hands and went to sit down in an open-air living room overlooking a small orchard.

We watched the dogs. The dogs watched us.

We began with some cordial chitchat. Benji and I indicated our great pleasure in being in Jujuy with him. He thanked us for coming all the way from Denver.

We started to talk about his campaign. "What issues are important to you and the people of Jujuy?" I asked.

He replied with a solid answer: he wanted to make Jujuy more competitive by diversifying its economy.

We then spent an hour talking about all the issues facing Jujuy—transportation, water, education, and jobs. This guy actually knew what he was talking about. Maybe he was a natural. Or maybe I was talking to a future president of Argentina, a future folk hero, the next Simon Bolivar. I might just want to work with this guy.

In my halting Spanish, I asked him the basic question: "Why do you want to be governor of Jujuy?"

His response was deeply heartfelt: "Because my business background will be helpful in government and because the president wants me to."

Hugo immediately jumped in to suggest that perhaps the candidate could draw on his business experience to make the state operate more efficiently and effectively.

Benji translated the candidate's response: "He says that, 'Yes, he could use his experience in *agricultura*. But mostly, he is running because the president wants him to run.'"

We then moved very quickly into the campaign plan and timeline for the polling. But you can't leave a planning meeting with a new client and not ask, "Do you have anything in your past which might become an issue?"

I wasn't asking about the dead girl. I wasn't. It was a standard question.

Benji glared at me as he translated the question for the gubernatorial wannabe. Señor Agricultura said, "No, I don't think so."

Few politicians will readily air their dirty laundry during their initial meeting with me—so I probed a bit more. "Is there anything on the public record that any reporter or opponent might find? Driving while intoxicated, for example?"

"No, I have a driver."

*Hmm, a driver. Good answer,* I thought.

Hugo was shuffling his papers loudly and placing them in his briefcase, trying to signal to me that the interview was over and maybe I should shut up before I sent us both to untimely, painful deaths. But I didn't think we could do a proper campaign plan or poll without a couple more pieces of information.

Look, I have a responsibility to anyone I take on as a client. And before I took this nice gentleman's money, I was going to meet that responsibility.

"You seem to have a fair amount of security here. I was wondering—for the bio profile in the poll, we test positives *and* negatives about a person's background. What line of work are you in?"

Benji shortened the question; the candidate supplied the answer, "*Agricultura*. Agriculture processing and import/export. Mostly export."

I was about to ask, "What kind of *agricultura*? Apples? Sheep? Cows? Arugula?" but our host talked some more.

Benji's back straightened and his face turned gray. He turned to me and said, "He says, 'There might be a problem because some people think he killed a young girl.'"

Oh, right, I thought. An accusation of murder might increase a candidate's "unfavorables."

Trying to keep cool, I drew on the other half of my facility with the Spanish language: "*Por que?*" Hugo's papers were now entirely in his briefcase. As he was fastening the latches, his eyes were darting about, looking for the driver who'd brought us here.

The candidate began speaking to Benji in Spanish. They conversed for at least a minute as I wracked my brain to see if I could come up with any other murderers I'd worked for. Nope, this guy would be the first.

Benji and the candidate finally stopped talking. Benji sipped some water, then motioned to me to come closer. I leaned in.

"Uh, apparently there was an eighteen-year-old girl who happened to get pregnant and was found dead. Some people in the community thought he had been sleeping with her and wanted her killed so she wouldn't have his child."

*Well, it's just "some people." That changes everything.*

I thought carefully, then looked at Benji and said, "Tell him, um, we will test it in the poll to determine if this rumor is widespread. Perhaps we could use a simple open-ended question such as 'What do you know about the candidate?'"

As Benji relayed my words, I noticed that one of the Uzis happened to have its muzzle directed at my left shoulder. No, actually a few inches below my left shoulder. Let's see . . . yep, that's where my heart would be.

The candidate seemed anything but offended by all this talk of his past.

He smiled, gestured with both hands in an open and friendly manner, and said a few words to Benji that sounded as warm and reassuring as a bowl of cherry cobbler with vanilla ice cream on top.

Benji translated. "He said . . . he said . . . let me be very careful here . . . that even if he did kill the girl, he wants us to help him win the election."

"Okay," I said, standing up. "I think we have all the information we need, and, gosh, look at the time—we have a plane to catch."

We shook hands, thanked the candidate, and hustled over to the two black Suburbans. As the German shepherds looked at us loading ourselves into the vehicles, we could see the disappointment in their eyes.

Hugo, Benji, and I said nothing during the ride and nothing on the plane back to Buenos Aires. Finally, at the hotel bar, after drinks were poured, I announced that my firm would decline the opportunity to work for this candidate. This left Hugo with sole responsibility for discussing the campaign with the president and the government leadership, and, ultimately, conducting a poll.

About three weeks later, Hugo called me with the results of the poll. Apparently, more than "some people" thought the guy had killed the eighteen-year-old. On the open-ended question about "What do you know about the candidate?" nearly everyone of those surveyed in Jujuy used the words "murderer" or "killer."

He lost.

• • •

Sometimes in politics, the compensation doesn't come from a client, a contributor, or conspirator. For some campaigns, you simply have to take a chance and play the odds.

I was in London in the late summer of 1990 for a meeting with my pro bono client, the Liberal Democrats of Britain. The pro-bono aspect was not by choice, but due to the stark reality that this was a political party with very limited resources. American consulting help was an immediate candidate for a line-item veto by the party's treasurer. Nevertheless I was there, and we discussed the strategy for the upcoming by-election in the constituency of Eastbourne.

At the time, the country was in the throes of a debate regarding Prime

Minister Thatcher's poll tax. Unlike the U.S. variety of poll tax, this was not a tax on those seeking to vote but a flat tax on the number of people living in a home. It hit the elderly and homeowners particularly hard.

Despite Thatcher's unpopular poll tax, to say that the Lib Dem prospects in Eastborne looked dim is a gross understatement. The previous Conservative MP had died in an IRA bomb attack, setting off a surge of nationalistic Conservative fervor. The Tories had held the seat since some time around the signing of the Magna Carta, and Labor was not even contesting it, so there would be no three-way split that could benefit the Lib Dems, which was an indication that realistic politicos were fully aware of the hopelessness of defeating the Tories in Eastbourne. Indeed, the British betting establishment Ladbroke's recognized this futile position with 100-1 odds against the Lib Dems winning.

That's when I suggested we do a poll—survey research. This was a novel notion for the Lib Dems at the time. They had done one poll. It was one I had written for them during a by-election in northern Yorkshire. We had finished 100 interviews before they terminated the survey to use the phones for "knocking up." That's British for getting out the vote. I told them that the margin of error for a survey of this size was over 10 percent, but *if* these results were from a poll with a much larger sample—perhaps 500 with a lower margin of error, the Tory candidate William Hague would get about 40 percent of the vote. That would be just enough to win, as the Lib Dems would split their vote with other left-of-center parties. Well, Hague got around 37 percent and the Lib Dems came in third. The Lib Dem leadership thought I was a polling mastermind for predicting the result. Statistical margin of error was not part of their calculus.

For Eastbourne, the leadership took an hour to debate the merits of a poll. At first, they were convinced they shouldn't do a poll just to show they would lose. But others wanted to know what issues were of concern to the voters; it couldn't be the poll tax in this Tory stronghold, they reasoned. They finally agreed that survey research was in order as long as it cost nothing, and the sample size would be no more than a paltry 250 respondents because the Party leadership didn't want staff to waste time on this endeavor. After five nights of volunteers and staff calling from the parliamentary offices in Westminster, we had our 250 respondents. (Note: This methodology would not remotely pass standard methodological sniff tests.)

I met with the leadership the following morning to inform them that, surprisingly, the poll tax proposed by the Prime Minister was very unpopular in Eastbourne. Moreover, our poll showed that less than 30 percent of the voters thought their next MP should be another Tory—not good news for the Tories. And, over 50 percent of the voters were over age 60—those most affected by Thatcher's poll tax. The Lib Dems were 20 points down, but all the data suggested that the PM and the Tories were in a heap of trouble and the Lib Dems might possibly pull an upset.

At the end of my brief presentation, I uttered words that have made some people briefly wealthy: "You know, we can win this."

The immediate and rapid departure from the room of the party staff made me think they wanted nothing to do with this polling nutcase from the Land of the Revolt. Then I learned their destination.

They all went directly to Ladbroke's to place 100-pound bets at 100-1 odds.

As in many campaigns, the winner ran the least worst campaign. The Tories, assured of victory, selected someone as their MP candidate who lived at least 100 miles from the constituency. They followed this by failing to address the poll tax's impact on the overwhelmingly elderly Eastbourne electorate. But ultimately, they hoisted themselves on their own petard when they held a press conference citing all their great works in Eastbourne, including a new hospital. Unfortunately for the Tories, the address they provided for this institution was a rubble-strewn vacant lot. Within hours, the Lib Dems were distributing a leaflet with a photo of the vacant lot and the headline, "The Tories Call This a Hospital."

The Lib Dems won by 10 percent.

The day after the election, there was a line of Lib Dem campaign staff at Ladbroke's cashing in their bets, while the London tabloids called it "the biggest upset in over eighty years in British politics." Shortly thereafter, Margaret Thatcher resigned as Prime Minister and I had a fine quote from the Lib Dems extolling my political and polling acumen.

Today, I visit homes of former Lib Dem staff members who point with pride to their purchases made in late October of 1990. Indeed, only last summer, one former staff member poured me a Scotch and announced, "Let's have a seat outside on the Eastbourne by-election patio furniture and drink to Margaret Thatcher's poll tax."

# RULE #8

# KNOW THE RULES OF ENGAGEMENT.

Often, success in a campaign is a matter of simply understanding the political system or rules better than the opposition does. When it comes to their mastery of the legislative process, ballot language for initiatives and referenda, *Robert's Rules of Order*, and even convention procedure, some folks are wizards. These people are to be cherished because they often make sure that mistakes are minimized and ultimately help you win.

When you don't have these political Merlins on your side, your campaign can head down a path toward an unseemly fate. It is said that the Clinton 2008 campaign leadership was unaware of critical elements of the rules of delegate selection for that year's Democratic nomination. Some senior staff apparently thought there were still "winner-take-all primaries," when this practice had been eliminated decades before. The results showed.

Some of the best political operatives are stunningly ignorant of the importance of the system and rules in other countries. Top American political media consultants often approach me about my work over twenty-five years in the UK. They begin with the pronouncement that they could produce some great stuff in the UK. They tell me they have watched BBC shows since they were twelve and that, apart from the U.S. Sunday news shows, *Question Time in Parliament* is their favorite viewing. They explain how they would use *Question Time* material in their thirty-second spots, and how, if they were just given a chance, they would revolutionize political ad-making in the UK.

I ask these consultants, "How good are you at billboards and door to door?" Their answers range from "Why?" to "What do you mean?" to "I don't do billboards or go door to door. I produce TV spots." At which point I explain to them that party television advertising is limited to at most three five-minute spots in the entire UK during the election period. (It's banned entirely in many other countries.) These data points reduce their interest considerably.

The U.S. political system is quite straightforward compared to those in the rest of the world. In the U.S., generally it is just the two major parties opposing each other, thus side-stepping the multi-candidate and multi-party situations found in places such as Sweden or the Netherlands. America also has a pretty simple balloting process: you mark your favorite. Compare that to Australia, where in some cases, voters have to mark eighty different party preferences.

The major exception to the standard of electoral simplicity in the U.S. is our political party presidential caucuses. By understanding the rules and the peculiarities of the caucuses, savvy political organizers have made themselves into legends. The opposite is also true. Caucuses, with their myriad rules, traditions, and multi-candidate fields, are where the reputations of fine operatives go to die.

• • •

April 1972, Idaho. "Okay. Delegate selection caucus. Here's the deal," declared Angie Johnson, the McGovern state director, as we sat at her Pocatello home so I could receive my marching orders. "You need to find McGovern supporters, encourage them to show up at their county caucuses at 7 p.m. on Monday night the eighteenth, and be willing to run as delegates to the state convention in May. The more people we get at the county caucuses, the more people we'll have at the state convention. The more people we have at the state convention, the more delegates we'll have at the national convention. Got it?"

I nodded, even though all I understood was that this was unlike a primary and that I would be trying to get people to commit to do something. What I'd be trying to commit them to do was less clear.

Angie then dispatched me to the town of Preston. "It is in southeast Idaho, about an hour and half from here." she explained. "Farming. Ranching. Very small communities. Washington said you were the rural issues guy."

As I took my leave, my pocket held a list of the names of six residents of Franklin County and a few from neighboring Caribou County. Four of the

Franklinites were members of the county's Democratic Central Committee—in fact, they were the only members of the county's Democratic Central Committee. One came from a list of supporters of a peace group. The sixth had sent ten dollars to the McGovern campaign.

From an acorn a mighty oak may grow. It was time to grow an oak amidst the sagebrush in Franklin County, Idaho.

Before I left Pocatello, I called the Franklin County Democratic Chair to arrange a meeting to go through the list. We met in Preston, the county seat, at a café where everything was covered in Formica except for those items covered in Naugahyde.

The chair was an older woman with silver hair coiffed into an inverted snow cone. Also present was the vice chair, who confided at some point after her third cup of coffee in 30 minutes that, "Just between us girls, Jackie Kennedy was a bit too much for me, but Bess Truman . . . now she was my kind of gal."

The three of us talked about food prices—I was, after all, the rural/farming issues maven—including the cost of round steak and bread. We also discussed George McGovern.

"He's too liberal for this part of Idaho," said the chair. "As for me? I'm with Scoop Jackson."

The vice chair nodded in agreement, "You're wasting your time in this county," she said. "The entire central committee is supporting Jackson."

I took their word for it: 50 percent of the county central committee was sitting across from me; I assumed they spoke for the remaining 50 percent.

I had not encountered support in Wisconsin or New Hampshire for Henry "Scoop" Jackson, the hawkish Democratic senator from Washington State. In fact, the only person I knew to be supporting him was a D.C. lobbyist who represented the aircraft industry, a big employer in the Northwest. Here in Preston, however, Jackson seemed to be a towering figure, the darling of perhaps the only four people likely to show up at the caucus. It seemed quite evident that when the big event took place, McGovern would come up empty.

After finishing my discussion with the Jacksonians, I headed off to find the peace group supporter. I drove to the address listed but found that the activist had moved out of the county and State of Idaho over six months prior. This left me with one name: Williams Christiansen, the guy who'd contributed ten bucks. I didn't have a telephone number for Williams, only an address, so I asked around and got lost three or four times before I found his home and small farm down a dirt road about ten miles from town.

When I knocked on the door, a young woman in her early twenties answered. She was wearing a long dress with an apron and a high collared blouse—think Granny in *The Beverly Hillbillies* but about 50 years younger. My thought was, *Wow, this is so cool that someone in the actual west would be dressed so western retro; I must have stumbled onto some hippie/commune thing.*

"Hello," I began affably, "my name is Rick Ridder and I am with McGovern for President. Is Mr. Williams Christiansen available?"

The woman peered at my attire—a black sport coat, blue pinstriped shirt, black tie, and khaki pants—and asked, "You mean, you're not with the Church?"

"No, no. I'm with McGovern for President."

"Oh, I thought you were from the temple looking for help before you go on your mission."

"My miss—uh, no. I'm from McGovern for President. Mr. Christiansen is a contributor to the campaign, and I came by to thank him and see if—"

"Why don't I get Williams for you? Stay right here."

I stood on the doorstep for a few minutes until a thirtyish bearded male came to the doorway. "I am Williams Christiansen. How can I help you?"

"It is good to meet you, sir," I said. I thanked him for his contribution and said I'd like to talk to him about helping McGovern in Preston.

"Oh. Him. Well, all right. Why don't you step inside?" He opened the door and I entered, passing through a mudroom into the foyer of an immaculately clean home with numerous children running about. Williams led me into the living room and pointed to a chair. As I sat down, he said, in a stern but not elevated voice, "Children, leave the room."

They did. Immediately.

I tried small talk. "Do you run a day care here?"

"No. All mine."

"How many kids do you have?"

"Six right now. Two more on the way."

"Oh. Twins. Great." I said.

"What can I do for you?" he asked.

"We're contacting all McGovern supporters in the area to encourage them to come out next Monday night for the county caucuses. The caucuses are the first step in choosing the delegates from Idaho to the Democratic National Convention, which will be held in Miami Beach in July."

"What do I have to do?"

Trying to conceal my amazement that he was showing an inkling of interest, I said, "Show up at 7 p.m. at the Franklin County caucus, which is being held at the high school in Preston. I imagine there won't be more than five or six people there, so it's possible that if we can find a couple more people to come for McGovern, we could elect McGovern supporters as the county's delegates to the state convention in Boise."

"So I could go to Boise as a delegate to the state convention, eh? Excellent. I'm a Vietnam vet. It would be cool to have a vet there for McGovern. Whatcha think?"

"That would be great for the campaign, you bet. There might be other veterans in the area who would support you. You should contact them."

"Nah, I know them all and none are Democrats. But can I bring my wives?"

"Absolutely, yes. You can bring your wife. As long as she's a Democrat and registered to vote in this county."

"No, my wives. I have five wives."

"What? Oh. Five wives. Well, um, yeah. Well. Well, yes, technically, I, um, don't see a problem with that, as long as they are registered to vote in the county and they are eighteen."

"Good."

"Uhh . . . do you want to bring them all?"

As we spoke I was flipping through my three-ring binder containing party rules to see if there were any rules relating to the number of wives allowable at any given caucus. Nope, no rules.

"How about Judith? She's seventeen," Williams asked.

"Um . . . when does she turn eighteen?"

"December, I think." He stroked his beard. "I have trouble keeping track of their ages and birthdays." He got up and walked toward the kitchen. "Judith," he called, "your birthday is in December, right? And you'll be eighteen, right?"

A young woman appeared in the doorway. Like the woman who'd

greeted me, she was wearing a dress down to her ankles and an apron. "Yes. December sixteenth."

"She wouldn't be eligible," I said. "She has to turn eighteen before election day to vote in a caucus."

"Okay," said Williams. "That means I could guarantee five votes: four wives, plus myself." As he spoke he paced in front of a wood stove. "Will I have to make a speech or something?"

"Well, it might be a good idea to tell the other folks why you're supporting McGovern."

"That's easy, the war. When I was in Vietnam I realized that we shouldn't be there. And I came back pretty messed up. Thank the Lord I found the teaching of the Lord Jesus Christ and Joseph Smith. Say, would you like something to drink? How about some tea? We don't have coffee or alcohol here."

"Sure."

He directed a request toward the kitchen, but not to anyone in particular. Shortly thereafter, another young woman, whose name turned out to be Louisa, appeared with tea. She was clearly pregnant.

"Okay, we get to this meeting. What happens?" Williams asked.

I explained how it worked. "There'll be two county delegates to the state convention. They'll probably want a male and a female. Best to have gender balance."

"Gender balance?"

"Yes, the party is trying to get more women to participate at all levels."

"So one of my wives could be elected as a delegate, too?"

"Yes, if she gets enough votes."

"And if we go to the Boise convention, we could run for national convention delegate, right?"

"Yes, you could," I said, thinking that the campaign might never recover from a *New York Daily News* headline, "McGov Dels Make Love Not War: Polygamist and One of Five Wives Are for George."

I needed to get out of there. Looking conspicuously at my watch, I rose and started toward the door. "I'm due in Soda Springs to meet the Caribou County Chair," I said. "Why don't I call you in a couple of days?"

"We don't have a phone. We like to stay under the radar."

"But . . . won't you be above the radar if you show up at a caucus with four wives?"

"Don't worry about that. This part of Idaho is full of believers in the words of Joseph Smith. Everyone here knows. It's outsiders we have to worry about. I would appreciate it if you didn't say anything about our family."

I agreed to be silent and to return in a couple of days, after he'd had a chance to speak with his wives about a potential conflict he told me about: the caucus was on Monday, which was traditionally the Mormon Family Home Night.

In Soda Springs, the members of the party leadership were friendly, but each one supported one of the other candidates: Jackson, Humphrey, or George Wallace. My next stop was the Caribou County Courthouse, where I looked up the names of people who had voted in the last Democratic primary. I cross-referenced those I found—fewer than 100—with the local phone book. I found the phone booth off the atrium, changed dollars for a pocketful of dimes at the County Finance Office, got back in the phone booth, and started calling. The politeness shown by the local party leadership was not matched by the voting public—the receptivity to my calls was muted at best, hostile at worst. And those in the "best" category were few and far between.

I reported back to Angie that southeast Idaho was not a hotbed of McGovern support. When she asked how many supporters I had identified, I told her "one, but he has a lot of family in the area that might attend the caucus as a favor to him."

She was not happy, and sent me farther east for the next couple of days, into areas even more rural. In some places along the Wyoming border, I thought I had stepped back in time. The coffee shop of choice in Twin Falls was Sambo's, which featured on its exterior a giant, plastic, caricatured black man carrying pancakes, and, on the interior, a ten-cent cup of coffee. Driving north along the far eastern edge of Idaho, I found the town of Freedom, Wyoming/Idaho. The road delineated the border between the two states; on either side of it were homes identical to one another. In a previous period (it was unclear to me just when), Mormon families would cross from one state to another to avoid prosecution for polygamy. And why not have two identical houses per family, to make it easy to find the bathroom in the middle of the night, no matter which side of the street you happened to be sleeping on?

As I talked with prospective supporters, nearly every conversation began with questions about where I'd gone for my mission, where I'd served in the military, and whether I'd be entering Brigham Young University—not *the* Brigham Young University in Utah, but the Idaho version in the town of Rexburg. I generally acknowledged that I had not gone on a mission, that I'd received a high draft number and thus had not joined the armed forces—I thought it wise to omit the fact that I'd applied for a 4-F deferment as "unfit to serve" on the grounds that I did not meet the U.S. Army's minimum weight/height standards (I was 6' 2", 132 pounds)—and that I was likely to go to school "back East."

No surprise, looking back, that after those answers, almost no one wanted to talk presidential politics with me. One rancher, pressing me on the matter of my religion and discovering that my background was Catholic and Jewish, annouced that "cross-breeding of religions, just ain't right." Then he backed away from me as if I were a green goblin. Strangely, he did not support George McGovern.

Late Thursday afternoon, four days before the county caucus, I checked in again with Williams Christiansen. Louisa greeted me at the door. "We are very glad to see you again. We didn't know if you would come back. We have lots of questions."

She called for Williams as I stepped inside, and soon, five women surrounded me, all wearing the standard long dresses and aprons.

"How many men and how many women get to go to Boise?" Louisa asked.

"In this county, two delegates are selected and the Democratic National Committee rules would like the choice to be reflective of gender balance."

"So you're not saying that it *has* to be a man and a woman, right? It could be two women."

"Correct. There is no mandate that it be fifty-fifty."

"So, two of us could go, right?"

"Yes, that's true," I said.

"Given that this valley is 70 percent female, it would be more representative if we sent two women."

While I speculated about the opportunities for romance in a valley in which 70 percent of the population is female, Williams stepped into the room, glaring at Louisa. "Two of you are not going out of this valley together to Boise."

"Honey," Louisa shot back, "if all of us support one another, and my sister and her husband show up with all of *his* wives, we can elect anyone we want."

Williams sighed and turned to me. "You see what you've stirred up here? They all want to be delegates. For two days I've been telling them that it needs to be one man and one woman. Like in the Bible."

"Well," I said, "there is supposed to be an effort to bring more women into the system. I'm not sure of the, um, biblical connection."

Lindsey, the other pregnant wife, handed me a glass of water. Then Williams came close and whispered in my ear, "I need to talk to you without the women." He motioned to the door.

Outside on the stoop, he placed his hand on my back. "Listen, I've got problems. I can't let two of my wives out of this valley alone for two or three days in Boise. It just ain't right. You understand?"

I didn't. But I nodded. I needed his full cooperation to get *any* delegates out of southeast Idaho.

"And there's another problem," he continued. "I was reading *Time* magazine and I learned that George McGovern is a women's libber. I'm not sure how that fits with Church doctrine. You understand?"

Even at this young age, I knew that when attacked politically, you should do one of three things: respond, ignore, or change the subject. In this case, I chose option number three. Relying on language provided to me by the McGovern Senate staff, I asked, "What are you running out here? A cow-calf operation?"

Williams looked a bit stunned, but quickly answered, "A few head. Nothin' serious. Mostly run a mechanical repair operation in the back. Got a knack for mechanics. In Vietnam they had me repairing every dang motor, machine, and new toy the Army had. The Vietnamese can repair a scooter all right, but anything more than a souped-up lawn mower engine and they're worthless. Kept me busy and out of the danger zones. Now I make a living out of it. I'll show you."

We walked behind the house, where four children played on a swing set, and entered a large barn. It held tractors, trucks, and a variety of mechanical devices that I could not remotely identify. He was describing the problems that accompanied each piece of hardware in what might as well have been Serbo-Croatian. I switched the subject again.

"About that *Time* article, I wouldn't worry about it. You know how the press can distort things. Just remember why you sent the money to the campaign in the first place. Keep focused on getting out of Vietnam."

Williams sighed. "You're right. But I need you to go in there and tell my wives that they have to choose between 'em—which one is going to Boise with me. Because two of 'em can't leave the valley, then sign in somewhere with the same last name, then lie that they are in-laws. That ain't right."

I nodded. "Right. You should never lie in politics."

He led me back into the living room where he announced, "Look here. Rick is going to tell you all to choose among yourselves who will be the other delegate with me. Right, Rick?"

I stood up, cleared my throat, and said, "Yes, it's best before you get there to choose who would be the other candidate, so you don't split your votes."

"You mean we have to vote for Williams and someone else?" said Melissa, the oldest wife, the one with the yellow apron who had initially met me at the door.

"I think it would be best to have a gender-balanced delegation," I said. "Yes."

"Well," said Melissa, "I'm Williams's first wife, so I should go."

Before I could halt the outbreak of spousal rivalry, Anna, who had never before said anything in my presence, took aim at two of the other wives. "Louisa and Lindsey can't go because they are with child, and it would be unseemly for Williams to be lying down with them. So only Melissa and I could go."

"But I'm the one who actually knows something about the caucus and I know more than anyone about George McGovern," Louisa said.

For some reason I can't now identify, I stood up and got involved in the dispute. "Generally, it is a good idea to have a delegate who is committed to the candidate and the cause."

Melissa was having none of it. "Louisa can't go because she is with child."

"And," added Anna, "I will *learn* everything there is to know about George McGovern."

"So," I offered, again for no reason I can now discern, "maybe you should both run, and the one who gets the most votes, goes."

Melissa scowled. "She has more family members in this valley than Abraham had wives."

I waited for a smile from her, but . . . no.

"Well," I said, inching toward the door, "I think it is only fair that you both stand up at the caucus and tell people why you are for McGovern and let everyone choose. That would be best, right, Williams?"

"Good idea," Williams said. "We will all choose in a secret ballot at the caucus. And let the best wife win." He draped his arm over my shoulder and gently accelerated my transit to the door.

Once outside, I extended my hand to him. "You're down to two. Hope that helped. I will be in touch."

"Yeah, really helpful," he said, opening the door of my Jeep. "I now have four, soon to be five, angry wives."

"Wait . . . five? How can Judith be angry?"

"She has to watch the kids alone while the rest go to town."

"You have another problem, you know," I said.

"What's that?"

"It is not a secret ballot. Caucus delegate selection is done openly."

"I've got a problem," Williams said.

I left.

Late Sunday evening, I left for Salt Lake. There wasn't much to do on Monday, the day of the caucus, except re-call everyone we'd called during the past two days. Besides, I was meeting friends for three days of skiing in Alta, Utah, where I had once worked as a dishwasher. Late Monday night, the phone rang in the room I was sharing. It was Mary Ellen Simonson from the western states office in Salt Lake.

"Sorry to bother you, but I just got a call from Angie. She said you might know something about this because the Idaho caucuses were held tonight."

"Uhh . . . yeah?"

"She got a call from the Franklin County Chair, in Preston, Idaho. Apparently, this chair is a bit upset. There were more than twenty people at her caucus, none of whom she had seen before. They elected two delegates to the state convention, both named Christiansen. A man, Williams

Christiansen, and a woman named Anna. Living at the same address. She is too old to be his daughter. So, husband and wife, right?"

"That's right. She's his wife." The truth, if not the whole truth.

"Here's what we don't understand. Apparently, the county chair was so angry that she was not elected delegate herself that she suggested she go as an alternate. I guess she figured the Christiansens wouldn't actually show up in Boise and so she would get to be a delegate after all."

"Okay," I said, expecting disaster.

"However, the chair is still angry because, well, they had an election for alternate and she lost the spot to a Melissa Christiansen. She has the same address as Williams Christiansen and Anna Christiansen, but she is also too old to be their daughter. Angie wants to know if she's his sister or something."

"Or something," I replied and hung up. I went to find a beer.

• • •

Every four years, in the run up to a presidential election, there is an event that attracts more concentrated news coverage than any other news event of the year except perhaps the Summer Olympics and the final two weeks of the presidential campaign: the Iowa caucuses. Along with the caucuses themselves comes a yearlong examination of the voters of one state and its quirky electoral process—a deluge of punditry on the implications of the presidential preferences of slightly more than 300,000 likely Iowa caucus attendees.

Much is made of the likely results of the caucuses, and indeed the actual results, but little is written on the peculiar characteristics of what has become an American democratic institution—an institution that may not be that democratic at all.

Considering they are the first in the nation to select presidential delegates, the Iowa caucuses present quite the contrast to the United States as a whole. As any political consultant or election junkie can tell you, Iowa is not remotely demographically representative of our nation.

It is significantly more white, rural, and Christian than the national average. Only 12.4 percent of Iowans are minorities, while nationally, minorities comprise 28 percent of the population. Thirty-six percent of

Iowans live in rural areas or small towns, whereas in the United States overall, 19.3 percent do. About 44 percent of Iowans identify as religious, whereas 49 percent of Americans do. This disparity in the level of religious involvement is not exactly shocking, but the percentage of those religious people who identify themselves as Christian stands out. Of the 54 percent of religious Iowans, only 0.5 percent of them identify as Muslim, Jewish, or any Eastern religion. This is markedly lower than the 4.7 percent of Americans nationally who identify themselves as religious but practice a religion other than Christianity.

On a racial basis, the Iowa caucuses skew significantly from the national average. The attendees are really white. Indeed, at the Republican caucuses of 2012, a full 99 percent of attendees were white, while nationally about 89 percent of the Republican Party is white. There was virtually zero representation at the Republican caucuses from the near 12 percent of Republicans in the U.S. overall who are from minorities.

The makeup of the Democratic caucuses is somewhat more representative of America, but not much. In 2008, the last time there were contested caucuses in Iowa before the 2016 election, 93 percent of Democratic caucus-goers were white, 4 percent were African-American, and 3 percent were "other." Nationally, in 2008, the Democratic Party was 66 percent white, 16 percent African-American, and 12 percent Hispanic.

The lack of participation among minority voters has something to do with the caucus process itself. On the face of it, the process seems simple. On a designated winter night at 7 p.m., political party members—or independents wishing to associate with the party—venture out into the upper midwest cold to a home, school, church, or other designated location within a precinct, and participate in the selection of delegates to go to a county convention. At that convention, delegates are selected to a state convention, where delegates are again chosen for the national conventions.

Very quaint. Very small-r republican. Very small-d democratic. But not really.

The structure of the caucuses limits access to the process for working men and women, families with children, business people who travel, the sick and infirm, and anyone else who has less than junkie veins for politics.

To show how this is so, let's go through a few scenarios. First, the 7 p.m. deadline is real. The caucus chair can close the door and bar entry at seven,

even if you're in line to enter the venue. Snow, ice, traffic, job, and kids are not an excuse. In the past, there have been no proxies or absentee voting. But what happens if you show up at 7 p.m. and your caucus host hasn't returned home? This happens frequently; hosts are late, too. Well, you hang around in the cold until he or she shows up.

Once the caucus has convened, you have to listen to your fellow precinct neighbors make impassioned speeches about their favorite candidates. And there could be other political party business as well. Don't think you can show up, indicate your preference, and leave. You can if you are a Republican, but if you're a Democrat, you must wait to the end of the meeting before expressing your candidate preference. And if your Democratic candidate does not reach a 15 percent threshold, you must join another candidate group or a group of undeclared voters.

In 2004, I was working for Howard Dean's presidential campaign in Iowa. In Muscatine, I was trying to ensure that a group of young Latino voters attended their caucus for the first time. They arrived at the caucus site at 6:45 p.m. and waited for the doors to open. At 7:15, no one else had shown up so they left. At 7:20 p.m., the caucus chair arrived home and proceeded to phone the usual gang who had come to previous caucuses—all white— to tell them she was home. When she was questioned afterward about her tardiness and what followed, she simply remarked, "I called all those who had come before. I didn't know any others were interested. Besides, I don't know any of them."

The Iowa caucuses are unrepresentative, exclusionary, inconvenient, dysfunctional, and undemocratic. But they could be worse. A few years ago, I was explaining these problems to a group of international students. At the end, one student commented, "Yes, it is not good. But it is much better than the military leaders picking the candidates."

How true.

# RULE #9

# BEWARE OF SPOUSES.

Some consultants claim that a "good spouse" can add as much as two percentage points to a candidate's vote. They describe spouses who, without complaint, trek for hours to remote outposts where no candidate has been seen since William Jennings Bryan stepped off a train to give his Cross of Gold speech for the 755th time.

They sing of spouses who, with good cheer, travel to those burgs in a volunteer's vehicle that features a leaky exhaust system, fast-food wrappers as upholstery, and the shock absorption of a pogo stick.

They rave about spouses who, once they have arrived in East BeJesus, show nothing but enthusiasm as they work a reception attended only by six octogenarians, all eager to share in great detail their lifetime supply of stories describing their eternal loyalty to the party.

They wax nostalgic about spouses who, after delivering the compulsory you-are-the-core-of-what-makes-our-party-strong speech, head home and are ready, at six the next morning, to do it all again.

I am told these spouses exist.

I have never met one.

One of my friends in the campaign consulting business proudly announced one day, "I no longer do candidates. I only do ballot initiatives and referendums now."

"Why's that?" I asked.

"Because they have no spouses," he answered.

But since someone still has to "do candidates," here are a few guidelines for working with candidates' spouses.

## 1. FEAR THE SPOUSE CAPTIVE IN A GROCERY STORE.

What is it about a political spouse behind a shopping cart that draws an onrush of campaign advice? It's as if the public-address system has announced, "Attention, shoppers. Today only: a candidate's spouse is in the store. Criticize the campaign for free. Repeat: for free." Strangers materialize in the Frozen Food aisle to kvetch to the spouse about the music in the latest radio spot. Television junkies line up in Dairy to dish with the spouse on the candidate's makeup during the last debate. Self-styled political scientists plant themselves in Produce to run down for the spouse the four issues killing the campaign and what can be done to fix them. Moralists and Peeping Toms alike gather at the checkout line to insist on learning from the spouse whether the candidate is really having that affair headlined in the *Weekly World News*.

My favorite shopper comment took place in the San Francisco Bay area. With a straight face, a shopper told a candidate's wife that her husband's biggest problem was that he didn't "look gay enough." Upon hearing of this charge, the candidate immediately sought the counsel of his "best gay friend" on how he could remedy the problem. Fortunately, his best gay friend responded, "Don't even try. You will never pass the gaydar authenticity test."

When the candidate told his wife about his friend's comments, she immediately responded, "Well, what does he know?"

## 2. NEVER LET A POLICY PAPER GO HOME.

Count on it: if a candidate takes a policy paper home, his or her spouse will read it and disapprove. The spouse will not wait until the next day to deliver the verdict; inevitably, the candidate will call you at 10 p.m., beginning the conversation with, "My husband/wife thinks . . ." and continuing with, "This policy will kill us with business"—or "women" or "Latinos" or "cross-eyed plumbers."

The spouse will then come on the line. Before the horse's mouth can neigh, you, the consultant, speaking slowly, will explain that:

1.   There is no chance your wife will win the business vote in a Democratic Party primary because
2.   There isn't any, and

3.  Even if there were, she's running to the left of Leon Trotsky in order to pander to the Democratic base that will decide the matter, or

4.  Your husband will get exactly one woman's vote, yours, because his three opponents in the primary all possess two X chromosomes, and thus his only chance to win is to play the alpha male, or

5.  The only person in the district who speaks a word of Spanish is the owner of the just-opened O'Leary's South of the Border Hacienda and Irish Bar ("Serving Corona and Guinness!")

As for cross-eyed plumbers, however, you will sadly note that, yes, that vital constituency must be sacrificed for the greater good of the country, politics be damned.

## 3. CUT OFF THE HOME INTERNET.

Some of the best candidates I know are married to brilliant and creative individuals—but as election day approaches, their spouses' IQ sinks to room temperature. Soon, the spouse turns to the Internet for guidance, where every blogger in footie pajamas is the next James Carville/Karl Rove, declaring the right path for the campaign. Upon reading up on this late-night Internet wisdom, the spouse immediately emails the campaign and consultant team a link to a blog post from *Huffington Post*, Daily Kos, or Bob the Blogger: a daily journal of politics, baseball, and stamp collecting. The blogger is undoubtedly bemoaning the quality of the TV ads, the content of the TV ads, the failure of the campaign to be sufficiently positive, the failure of the campaign to be sufficiently negative, or the candidate is not focusing on his/her opponent's position on abortion or gay marriage or marijuana legalization or the spread of a rare food gene that will wipe out every known grain on the earth. And because the campaign manager is not obeying without hesitation every single word of instruction from this blogger, said campaign manager is, ipso facto, screwing up.

The campaign team then holds a 1 a.m. conference call with the spouse to point out that:

1. The blogger doesn't have their research, which shows he knows not of what he speaks;

2. The campaign strategy is to avoid hot-button issues such as abortion, gay marriage, and marijuana legalization because the swing voters ain't where their candidate is on these matters; and

3. The CEO of the company that manufacturers the rare food gene is chair of the candidate's finance committee.

After an hour of heated conversation, the issues are settled. It is then time to begin preparations for combatting the next blogger threatening to derail the campaign.

# 4. NEVER, EVER LET THE ROUGH CUT OF A TV SPOT FALL INTO THE HANDS OF A SPOUSE.

At our consulting firm, we call this one the Chauncey Rule.

Why?

Years ago, during the last week of a very tight race, the candidate's spouse asked to see the campaign's final spot before it aired. Against our better judgment, we agreed. Off went the videocassette containing the spot to her home. We wanted to run it immediately, so we asked the spouse to report back with her comments within three hours.

She took thirty-six. "I don't like it," she said over the telephone. "It's too negative. It's not inspirational."

"Um," I said. (The reader will note that "um" is among the most often used words in a consultant's lexicon, along with "w-e-l-l" and "hmmm.") "We are *suggesting* that our opponent's business broke every environmental law and regulation enacted since the days of Gifford Pinchot and, in doing so, spilled toxins into the city's water supply. We *suggest* that our opponent either knew about it or should have known about it, and did nothing. That, you see, is, um, against the law. Therefore, the spot is *intended* to be negative. It is *not* intended to be inspirational."

"Well, it's *too* negative. Our gardener doesn't like it, either."

The gardener, of course—that changes everything.

"How old is this gardener?"

"Pablo is twenty-eight years old."

"Young Hispanic males are not our target audience with this spot. We're trying to reach middle-aged Caucasian women who worry about toxic substances in their children's drinking water."

"Well, Pablo says he didn't understand it."

"Does Pablo speak English?"

"Not very well. But he watches a lot of television."

"Univision, probably—where we won't be placing the ad because the network is not a favorite of, um, middle-aged Caucasian women. Besides," I added, "I'm sure Pablo will vote with us anyway."

"Oh, Pablo can't vote. He's not a citizen."

"Green card?"

"Don't know."

"Okay, let me be sure I got this. You focus-grouped this spot with one person, in the wrong demographic, who doesn't speak the language, can't vote, and may be deported at any moment?"

"I still don't think we should run it."

"I tell you what. Why don't I get back to you on this?"

She agreed but added, "I still don't like the spot."

The candidate and the spouse eventually approved the ad. Before we sent it out, the producer named it *Chauncey,* after the gardener in the movie *Being There.*

## 5. ANTICIPATE THE UNPREDICTABLE.

Art Linkletter made a fortune from a TV segment titled, "Kids Say the Darndest Things." Kids have nothing on political spouses.

Near the end of one heated campaign, a reporter asked the candidate's wife if she was looking forward to the end of the race.

"You bet I am," she said. "I'm looking forward to having sex again. And so is my husband."

Fortunately, the reporter didn't probe for details.

A spouse gave perhaps my all-time favorite campaign speech. The husband of the county coroner in Gilpin County, Colorado, appeared as a surrogate for his wife at a local gathering of party faithful. When the time came, he rose to press the case for his wife's re-election.

"Well," he began, "Judith is running for re-election. You all know her. She's been coroner for over twenty years. I could tell you why she's done a good job or will continue to do a good job. But, let me just say, by the time you need her, you won't much care."

He sat down.

• • •

Spring in the western United States dovetails with the beginning of the campaign season. Full-tilt political ambition surfaces, as the inhibitions of the winter are unbuttoned and discarded.

Other things may also be unbuttoned.

One beautiful afternoon—sunny, warm, with more than a hint of summer in the air—the campaign's director of fundraising and I, the campaign strategist, were leaving the local brewpub where we'd discussed the finance plan for the campaign. We had determined that a) we had no money and b) none was expected. But we were only fifteen points behind the incumbent with five months to go. We left the pub feeling optimistic and relaxed. Then we got back to headquarters.

The campaign manager met us at the door. A savvy political operator who had run campaigns across the country, Paul dealt ably with staff and candidates. He was experienced and generally unflappable in the heat of battle.

"Where have you been?" he asked.

"At a liquid fundraising meeting," I said. "Why?"

"We've got a life-threatening situation here. I am going kill his wife," Paul said.

We knew immediately which wife: the candidate's.

"Did she miss her flight from *est* training, or whatever it was?" I asked. *est*—that's not a typo; it's written in all lower-case letters—was a personal development program popular during the 1970s. Its chief claim to fame was not permitting attendees to use the bathroom during four-hour sessions in which they were repeatedly told, "You are not all assholes" in order to develop their self-esteem and help them create meaning in their lives.

"Did she tell a staff and volunteer meeting, 'You are not all assholes'?"

"No and no. The plane landed, she met the driver—Charlie, the eighteen-year-old volunteer. Everything was fine. He was driving her south on I-5, to her meeting with the Young Dems in Fresno and then . . ."

"And then?"

"Ummm . . . you need to talk to him."

Paul got Charlie on the phone and handed me the receiver. "What happened?" I asked.

"I picked her up at the Modesto airport. Her flight was a bit delayed from San Francisco, but we had plenty of time." Charlie's voice was quivering even more than might be expected of a high school kid describing a snafu to a campaign hack thirty years his senior. "She said something about it being a beautiful day. She asked me to pull over so I could put down the top—I've got an old Saab convertible."

"I guess she wasn't worried about the appearance of her hair at the Young Dems. The windswept look, eh?"

"Uh, no."

"No?"

"No. After I put the top down and we got going again, she started chatting about est—how free she felt, how liberating the whole experience was."

"Okay, okay. This is not good, but nothing out of the ordinary for someone who just went to est."

"So we get on I-5 . . ." Charlie was speaking in starts and stops. ". . . drive for about twenty miles . . . twenty miles . . . and she starts talking about how beautiful the day is . . . the day is. . . . And that it's time . . . time to . . . time to . . . time to 'let the girls out.'"

"Let the girls out?"

"Y-y-yes. 'Let the girls out . . . to breathe.' Then she took her shirt off."

"Aha, *those* girls. She had something on underneath, right?"

"No. There was nothing. Nothing for over forty miles."

"Did you politely say something to her, like 'I'd feel more comfortable if you had your clothes on,' or simply, 'What the fuck are you doing?'"

"After a few miles I said, 'We're approaching a town. It might be best if you put your shirt back on. But she told me that she was expressing her freedom and that I needed to focus on my own . . . space. That's what she said: 'space.'"

"Holy shit. I am all for expressing freedom, but there are nude beaches for that. You put the car top back up, right?"

"Uh, no. She wouldn't let me stop. In fact, she put her seat way back so she could, I think she said, 'fully expose the girls.'"

"Where is she now?"

"Talking to the Young Dems."

"BARECHESTED?!?!?!"

"No, she did put her shirt on just before we got to Fresno."

My heart returned to its normal rhythm.

"Thank God for small favors."

"Do I have to drive her back, Mr. Ridder? The sun hasn't gone down."

"Stay where you are, Charlie. I'll call you back."

Before I could hang up, Charlie asked, "Mr. Ridder, Mr. Ridder, is this going to hurt me when I apply to college?"

"Charlie, I guarantee you there is no college application that asks, 'Have you ever driven a candidate's wife bare-breasted down an interstate highway?'"

I hung up and turned to Paul. "We're lucky no cop cruised by and busted her for indecent exposure," I said. "Imagine the headlines. 'Pol's Wife's Naked Knockers.'"

"Bare Bazungas," Paul responded.

"Spousal Exposure."

"Uhh . . . back to work."

We paused a moment to recover our wits.

"We still have the candidate's wife cruising in a convertible," said Paul, "topless, down one of America's biggest highways, with a shell-shocked volunteer behind the wheel."

"Letting the girls out to breathe."

"You have to call her," he said firmly.

"Me? Oh, no. That's the campaign manager's job. I'm just a strategist."

"Nah. This is where you have to step up, big guy."

I responded as bravely as I knew how. "Let's call the candidate, and have *him* call her."

"Okay. You do that," said Paul, poking his finger into my solar plexus.

I picked up the phone and dialed. The candidate was an easygoing guy who made people smile with his sunny disposition. Volunteers loved working for him because he was friendly to them and held views far to the left of center. He answered his mobile right away.

"What's up?"

"Well. I . . . um . . . well. You see . . . it's about your wife."

"Everything okay? She's in Fresno, right?"

"Yeah, yeah, Fresno. She's fine. But I need you to make a phone call."

"To whom?"

"John, would you please call your wife and tell her to keep her clothes on when she's riding down an interstate highway in a convertible?"

"What are you talking about?"

I told him.

"I was afraid this was going to happen when she went to est," he said.

"What? You were afraid she might go cruising down a highway topless, and you didn't tell us?"

"No. No. I just had a feeling she might take it too far. Any reporters see this?"

"No—at least, not to our knowledge. No cops, either."

"So, Rick, just call her up and tell her to keep her clothes on next time."

"You're her husband. Wouldn't you like to make that call?"

"Not me. Nooo. I can't. I'm the one who told her it was fine to go to est to find herself. I can't undercut that now. You have to call."

"You encouraged her to go to est?"

"Thought it would be good for the campaign to get her off the trail. Listen, gotta go raise money. See ya."

He hung up. It was first time in three months he had mentioned raising money.

I reported the conversation to Paul, who thought for a moment, then rendered his decision.

"Goddammit, I'm calling her."

He headed to his office and slammed the door. Through the window I could see him dialing, then speaking into the phone, then slamming down the receiver.

He emerged shaking his head, grabbed me, and said, "We are going to that brewpub. And I am not talking until I have a pint in my hand."

Over the fifty yards to the pub, Paul muttered to himself. The second we found a table, he grabbed a waiter and ordered a pale ale, then sat staring at the table. Upon receiving his beverage, he looked up and said, "She told me I was not listening to her needs; that she had to express herself in her own way; that the campaign was trying to control all elements of her life; and that if I didn't stop harassing her, she would have her husband fire me."

"Oh."

"But she did say she would keep her clothes on for the return trip."

• • •

Candidates' spouses not only *say* the darndest things. They also *do* the darndest things.

Sometimes consultants' spouses do, too.

A Republican political consultant friend of mine (I have a Republican friend, perhaps two), Tom Edmonds, returned to his Washington, D.C. home, after five days on the road in Montana with his party's candidate for that state's governorship. It was a tough race; their only advantage was that they had a bit more money than their Democratic opponent. As he approached his destination, he noticed campaign yard signs directing people to an event in his neighborhood. Then he realized the event was at his home.

"I kept thinking," he said to me, "I've seen these yard signs before somewhere. I couldn't immediately place it. When I walked into my own home, I was greeted by a volunteer, for my Montana client's opponent. My Democratic wife was hosting a fundraiser for her. We lost our financial edge that night, but we did win the election."

His wife's response to his return in the middle of the fundraiser: "I thought you were coming home tomorrow."

# RULE #10

# NO COALITION IS TOO BIG. UNLESS IT IS.

In theory, when you're working to build a solid campaign—whether for a candidate, political party, issue, or referendum—no coalition is too big. You should bring in all the groups, whether there is complete agreement on the mission or not. This is known as expanding the base. You want to include those who may have some semblance of interest in the campaign's purpose, and garner their support.

It's a lot like putting together a good dinner party: invite guests of varied interests who might have a mutal interest. Labor union and chamber of commerce leadership, working together for road and transit funding initiatives, will join you at the table, or doctors and trial lawyers who both support health-care reform programs.

Sometimes, though, the dinner party becomes too big and the demands of each guest are in serious conflict; it's a case of too many political vegans and paleos at the same dinner for a truly harmonious experience.

How these coalitions are formed is often a source of wonder. In 2012, in Colorado and Washington, two recreational marijuana legalization campaigns took separate directions in building the coalitions for their successful initiatives.

In Colorado, the initiative was a highly grassroots-driven campaign with extensive support from the medical marijuana community; labor unions; minority groups such as the NAACP and La Raza; libertarians; and a leading anti-immigration voice, former Congressman Tom Tancredo. Key to this coalition's success was its connections with a broad swath of the community. Perhaps most essential, the organizers never allowed disparate members of the coalition to be in the same room at the same time.

The major opponents were nearly every elected official, every former governor, a slew of law enforcement officers, and members of the business community. In some part, the opposition lost because they were under the misconception that voters respected the opinion of elected officials. When the opposition aired a radio spot featuring two former governors, a Democrat and a Republican, telling voters to vote "No," the polling numbers for the "Yes" vote went up. There is nothing voters dislike more than being told by a politician how to vote.

The opposition also forgot that there is more to building a coalition than the political, law enforcement, and business establishment.

Strangely, in Washington state, the pro-marijuana legalization advocates took a top-down approach to building their coalition. Heading the campaign was a highly regarded lawyer from the ACLU who corralled law enforcement officers and ex-federal prosecutors into being its spokespeople. Leading citizens such as Rick Steves of travel fame stepped forward in support. There was significant business, labor, editorial, political, and marijuana-business support as well. In essence, the proponents had managed to co-opt the potential opposition and bring them into the coalition.

The formal opposition in Washington state consisted largely of marijuana activists who argued that the initiative lacked a provision to allow individuals to grow marijuana at home. They also decried the limits of possession to one ounce or less. These criticisms were not a *causa belli* for most Washingtonians; therefore the opposition coalition did not expand and the opponents lost.

• • •

We were north of Siena, Italy, in the spring of 2000, in a conference room in an industrial building. Copies of the full drawings and writings of Leonardo Da Vinci in heavy leather-bound volumes sat neatly on cherrywood bookshelves, along with hundreds of other Italian tomes including a sixteenth-century copy of Dante's *Divine Comedy*.

Long-time campaign consultant Joseph Napolitan looked up from the stapled pages of translated polling data and announced to our client, Marco Malzoni, and me, "Our candidate has the worst numbers I've seen in forty years of campaigns. He has only a 13 percent favorable rating and a 75 percent unfavorable rating. They know him and they really *don't like him*. These numbers are worse than Richard Nixon's the day he resigned as President."

*Inferno*, here we come.

Marco, the owner of the library, stared at Napolitan and me, then pronounced, "But we can win, no? We must win!"

In his laconic style, Napolitan responded, "Marco, I gotta tell you. Give this one up. Right now, our client is the incumbent mayor of the town and he is getting 8 percent of the vote. He is behind his closest rival by 25 points. With his negatives, we would be lucky to get him to 15 percent."

"No. We *must* win," Marco told us. "If we don't win. I don't get the contract."

"What contract?" Napolitan asked.

"The graveyard! What do you think this is all about?" Marco shouted, pointing out a glass window to a room of twenty people in cubicles. "We electrify graveyards."

"Oh, I see." I said, not seeing at all.

"In Italy, it is a tradition to light a candle every night over the graves of your family members," Marco said. "Your wife, your mother, your grandfather. All get a candle over their graves. People go to the graveyard every night to light the candles."

"Very nice, but somewhat inconvenient," I remarked.

"That is right. Very inconvenient." Marco beamed. "But our company solves that problem. You see, the graveyards are owned by each of Italy's 8,000 municipalities. And we get contracts with the municipalities to electrify the graveyards, and . . ."

Marco stopped for emphasis, then continued.

". . . we put a light over the graves that goes on at night, so people don't have to travel to the graveyard to light a candle."

"Oh. Do people like this change in tradition?" Napolitan asked.

"Oh, yes! It is very good for our customers. They pay us about ten dollars a month and we pay for the electricity and change the light bulbs as necessary. It costs, maybe, five dollars a month and I get ten dollars."

"Yeah, but don't you have trouble collecting?" I asked. "I mean, if I was low on cash one month, I might skip Grandma's light."

"No. No. Ninety-nine-point-nine percent collection rate. People would rather go without food than dishonor their family members."

"So why this graveyard, in this town?" Napolitan asked, returning to the issue of the viability of the campaign.

"I need this contract to keep it from the competition, but most importantly so the citizens don't have to light candles every night," Marco said, expressing his deep-seated concern for both his pocketbook and his fellow citizens. "So . . . how do we win this election?"

After we consultants shared a series of "dead" jokes ("This campaign is dead on arrival. We are at a political dead end," etc.) Napolitan, asked, "Marco, just who will benefit from this person being re-elected mayor?"

"Well, me," Marco replied. "But also, all of the contractors who work on the graveyard electrification process—and their families."

"That's a start. A coalition of contractors and gravediggers," Napolitan said. "Ridder, how many of those do you think there are in a town of 20,000?"

Marco quickly arranged for a staff member to provide me with a list of all the occupations generally associated with graveyard electrification, and we identified all of the town residents associated with those trades. There were 191 electricians, contractors, dirt removal teams, large machine operators, and light bulb vendors. I printed the list and asked, "Now what?"

"Have the client call each of them," Napolitan instructed Marco, "and tell them that if he is re-elected as mayor, there will be more jobs and construction opportunities. That's it. Nothing more."

"But that's only 191 voters. We need 8,400 to win." I said.

"Family, Rick. Family. Each of these individuals has brothers, sisters, cousins, in-laws. There are very big families in this town. Very traditional Italian families. Once they learn that a family member could get work, they will know how to vote." Napolitan said.

"So, it is a coalition of family members? Hmm. But even if we got all 191—unlikely, but if we did—each one would need at least 40 family members to vote with us to come close to our goal of 8,400. I'm not sure—"

"It's our best chance," Napolitan said. "Probably our only chance."

"Yes, this is good," Marco said, beaming. "This is very good, Joe and Rick. Thank you."

Over drinks and dinner, Marco assured us that the mayor understood the plan. He would start to talk to all 191 individuals and we would receive a progress report from him at the end of the week.

After composing a five-page masterpiece memo on how the construction coalition plan could bring victory to our client, Napolitan and I left Italy. At the end of the week, we received the progress report during a conference call.

"I need your help," Marco began. "I am not sure what to do. Our client, the mayor, made many of the calls."

"Good, so how did it go?" Napolitan asked.

"Not so good. I don't the think he understood my directions. He promised each of them the business."

"Oh. So each of them get some of the business, right?" I asked.

"No. All of the business," Marco said.

"ALL of the business?" Napolitan and I responded in unison.

"Yes. And of course, I can't hire all of them to do all of the work."

"Right, yeah."

"But then, many of the contractors have family members who are married to other contractors, and soon everyone realizes that he has promised their relatives the same 100 percent of the work."

"I think there was a movie about this," Napolitan remarked.

"Well," I said, "the good news is, he broadened his coalition. The bad news is that they really don't like him now."

We hung up.

The mayor received 9 percent of the vote. He lost. Marco did not get the contract. Neither did his competitors. Somewhere in Italy a graveyard still flickers under candlelight.

• • •

After three fine days of skiing in April of 1972, I was back at the McGovern headquarters in Salt Lake City, Utah, organizing for the precinct and county caucuses. The Utah McGovern operation was run from the second floor of a Victorian mansion on one of the city's main streets. On the walls were precinct maps of every major city in the state, with the requisite pins indicating where identified caucus precinct leaders resided, and beside the maps were taped organizational charts for every legislative district in the state. For every eight precincts there was a precinct captain and for every legislative district there was a legislative coordinator. Arrayed along the wainscoting was our database—shoeboxes filled with 3 x 5 cards, one for each identified

McGovern supporter, sorted by precinct. On each card were handwritten notes regarding the individual's commitment level and volunteer capabilities.

Our information technology was sophisticated—for the early nineteenth century.

The Church of Latter Day Saints-style penchant for organization was the only attribute of the campaign that remotely met local cultural and political norms. Chuck Nabors, the McGovern state chair, was an African-American in a state where full acceptance of his race into the Mormon Church—which made up 70 percent of the population—was still six years away. A professor of physiology at the University of Utah and a friend of McGovern's, Nabors knew where to find just about every left-of-center Utahan. He had corralled two brilliant student organizers from the U of U, John Lear and Leonard McGee (who went with me to Oregon), each of whom had sufficient LDS credentials to be sent to county conventions where neither Chuck, of an inconvenient race, nor I—a Catholic-Jewish-Easterner who hadn't gone on a mission, served in the army, or enrolled in BYU (Idaho or Utah)—was welcome. John and Leonard traveled far and wide across the state, representing the campaign and rooting out McGovern support. They organized supporters and turned them out, often winning county conventions in areas where McGovern would receive less than 10 percent of the vote in the general election six months later.

Utah, on the whole, was not McGovern country. (Then again, as we would learn in November, the United States wasn't McGovern country, either.) Not only had nearly every major political figure in the state—the Democratic governor, the Democratic U.S. senator, almost every Democratic state legislator—endorsed Edmund Muskie or Hubert Humphrey, but all of them were actively hostile to McGovern. The lone exception was the president of the Utah AFL-CIO, Frank Lay, who incurred the enmity of national AFL-CIO president George Meany, national AFL-CIO treasurer Lane Kirkland, and just about every other important labor official in the country by being the lone state AFL-CIO president to endorse McGovern.

In many ways, the McGovern operation in Utah resembled a solid Democratic coalition: African-Americans, the Left, and Labor. The problem was that these groups together made up only about 5 percent of the voters in the state. We needed to expand our base. The best way: find other political outcasts.

On a Saturday in early May, we organized a door-to-door effort on the west side of Salt Lake City to try to find any support we could. This was hard work because there were no voter lists, so we had to knock on every door. We were not looking for massive support. One supporter in each precinct would give us a presence in a precinct caucus. After four hours of going door-to-door, we returned to the headquarters to share our successes.

"I found one person who indicated he might support McGovern," I began, "but he won't go to a caucus. I got a lot of, 'Who's George McGovern?'"

Hattie Hartman, who was canvassing with Nina Wilds, experienced much the same. "This is a lot harder than Massachusetts," she said, "or even Ohio. Is all of Utah like this?"

"No," I said, "Salt Lake City is the liberal center of the state. This is our hotbed of support."

"The good news, then," Hattie said, "is that I didn't find anyone for Humphrey, Muskie, or George Wallace either. So I guess the two supporters we found look pretty good."

"You found two supporters?" I asked, practically astonished.

"Yes. Two of them in one household."

"That's great! Will they go to the caucus?"

"Probably," Nina chimed in.

"We have to convince them to go," I said. "We need everyone."

"They seemed a little nervous about getting involved," Nina said.

"Nonsense. It will just be a couple of hours on a Tuesday night, and then perhaps a couple of hours at a county convention. We can get them to do that."

"That's not the point," Hattie said.

"What do you mean?"

"Rick," said Nina, "they are . . . um . . . gay."

"And, this being Salt Lake not San Francisco is the problem they have with attending," Hattie added.

Sheesh, I thought, it was always something. "Five wives, not such a big problem. Gay, a big problem. Let me talk to my bosses, Jean Westwood and Chuck Nabors, about how we should proceed. In the meantime, put their names in the supporter files."

The next day, in an update meeting, I mentioned our new supporters and their sexual orientation to Westwood and Nabors. Westwood smiled and said, "Not a big deal. Steve Holbrook, who was a homosexual, ran for county commissioner of Salt Lake City last year. He got something like 20 percent of the vote."

That seemed like a weak endorsement considering that 80 percent had voted against him.

Chuck pointed out that even the 20 percent was misleading. "Half of the people voting for him didn't know he was homosexual. If they had . . ." He shook his head soberly. Finally, he agreed that we should encourage the two new supporters to go to their caucus. "But," he added, "keep this quiet."

After two weeks of working in Oregon, I called up Johnny and Stevie, our two gay supporters. Johnny answered the phone. I introduced myself, told him I'd received his name from Hattie and Nina, and encouraged him to go to his caucus. Johnny asked to meet with me at the headquarters.

At around five the next afternoon, Johnny and Stevie arrived together. Their orientation was apparent even to someone such as my nineteen-year-old self, with minimally developed gaydar.

After I described the caucus process, Stevie announced, "We have thought about this a lot and have decided that it is important to us. We are going to do it."

"Great," I said. "Now you have to organize your precinct for McGovern. We went door-to-door in your area and didn't find any other supporters, but you may know of some."

"Can we check your card file of supporters?" said Stevie. "We may know some people."

I led him to the shoeboxes against the wall. A few minutes later, I saw Stevie and Johnny whispering in a corner. After a few minutes they walked over to me with a 3 x 5 card.

"Can we talk to you alone?" Stevie asked. The three of us found a spot in the office where there were no volunteers or staff.

"We found this," Johnny said. He handed me the 3 x 5 card he was holding. It was the card for Johnny, with his name, address, and phone number, a "1" designating him as a McGovern supporter, and the comment in Hattie's scrawl, "Gay Citizens for McGovern."

I turned pink.

"Look," Johnny said. "We know you know. We could ignore it, but actually, we think we can be helpful.

"You can?" I asked.

"You don't know how many gay men there are in this city. Hundreds, probably thousands. Attorneys. Businessmen. Even a couple of judges. We can get them to go to their caucus for McGovern."

"Really?" I was at a loss—this was all quite new to me. (Please remember that this exchange took place some four decades ago, when Don't Ask, Don't Tell referred more to hair coloring than sexual orientation.)

Stevie reached into the hip pocket of his jeans and pulled out a mimeographed piece of paper. "I got this in California last week," he said. He handed me the sheet—it was a flier titled "McGovern on Gay and Lesbian Rights." Put out by the San Francisco office of McGovern for President, the page detailed the candidate's relevant positions. I had never seen it before. Even in the mailroom. I didn't know McGovern *had* any positions on gay rights.

"Can you reprint 500 of these?" said Stevie. "We'll distribute them in bars and bathhouses."

I hesitated. The movement for gay rights had just begun; the old attitudes still prevailed. "Ah, yeah. Bars and, um, um, bathhouses. Yeah. Let's see. Hmm. I will have to get approval from Nabors and Westwood to spend this kind of money. We don't have a Xerox machine here, not even a mimeograph or something to cut a stencil. I would have to go to a copy shop, and this could cost fifty dollars or so. I don't have authority for that kind of expenditure."

"You're going to get it done. Right, Rick?"

"Well, I have to talk to—"

"You're not going to be like all the others—asking for our help, then leaving us out there alone—are you?" Stevie asked, peering into my eyes.

"Well, no, no. I just, um, don't have the authority."

"So, when will you speak to Nabors or Westwood?" Johnny asked.

"Later today. Why don't I call you with the answer and we'll go from there."

Stevie and Johnny looked at each other. Stevie shrugged, "All right, but I want that flier back regardless of your decision."

Thirty minutes later, Jean Westwood arrived, joining Chuck and Mary Ellen Simonson in her office.

"I, ah, met with Stevie and Johnny this afternoon," I told her. "The two gay guys who are McGovern supporters."

"What?" Mary Ellen said, turning in her seat.

"Ridder has identified two gay men who are McGovern supporters," Westwood told them. "So how did your meeting go?"

"Not too badly. They want to organize their precinct. And they want me to reprint 500 of these fliers to distribute in bars and bathhouses." I held the sheet out toward Westwood. Nabors wheeled his chair next to hers and Simonson leaned in.

"Holy shit, Ridder," Nabors said. "You want to print 500 of these with a 'Paid for by Utahans for McGovern' disclaimer? And distribute them in bars?! And, what, in bathhouses?!"

"That's . . . that's the idea. But if you don't authorize the expenditure, well . . . that's that."

I was trying to show my reasonableness, as well as my hard-bitten appreciation of cold political realities by my statement of the obvious. Of course, if they didn't authorize the expenditure it wouldn't be expended.

Chuck was still boiling. "For Pete's sake, Ridder. Can you see what will happen if some TV reporter gets this and asks me for a comment? Chairman of Utahans for McGovern, who, by the way, is *black*, defends homosexual flier. Wonderful."

"How much to reprint?" asked Simonson.

"Fifty bucks."

"The Church will go nuts." Nabors added.

"Well, Chuck," said Simonson, "it's not as if the LDS has a lot respect for black men like you."

Westwood, an avowed "Jack" Mormon—not an *ex*-Mormon but not a particularly observant one, either—sat up straight, handed the flier back to me and said, "Let's not bring the Church into this. They are fond of few Democratic candidates. I approve an expenditure of fifty dollars."

"It's okay that I get these reprinted?" I asked. I just wanted to make sure.

"That's not what I said. I approved an expenditure of fifty dollars. If you think the printing of 500 fliers of this sort is a good expenditure, then go ahead. If there's something else you feel the money should be spent on, spend it on that."

"I'll take twenty-five dollars, reprint 250. They can distribute those, then tell me if they need more. Then we'll see about the remaining twenty-five bucks."

"W-e-l-l-l-l-l, shit," said Chuck, "just keep my name off of it as chairman of Utahans for McGovern."

"This is national money," I said. "I'll just keep the same disclaimer that's on there now—it's from San Francisco. That will give it more credibility with the target audience, anyway."

As I left the room, Simonson followed me, then grabbed my arm. "Just be careful. This is Utah. Polygamy is okay—quietly. Homosexuality is not okay—at any volume."

I visited a late-night copy shop and made the copies. The next day I called Stevie. "I got your reprints. Two-hundred fifty were all I could get."

"Two hundred and fifty?! Wow! That's great! I didn't think you'd make any. I'll come right over."

Twenty minutes later, Stevie showed up at headquarters sporting a sleeveless T-shirt, "hot pants," and perfectly coiffed golden-blond hair. I met him at the doorway but he pushed right past me, announcing to all in the room, "We're going to run for national delegate. We hear Miami Beach is wonderful!"

"That's great, but first you need to get through the precinct caucus, then the county caucus. Then, at the state convention, you can be considered for the delegation to the national convention in Miami Beach."

"Listen, we've already identified enough friends in my precinct to get me to the county, and I know that with these fliers there will be enough gay men at the county to get me and maybe Johnny to the state. Today, *I* hereby begin *my* campaign for national delegate."

And with that, he took the fliers and strode out the door.

John Lear, who resembled Wally Cleaver, glanced up from his desk. "And what bars and bathhouses have you been visiting, Rick?" he asked.

At the precinct caucuses a few days later, much to our surprise, McGovern dominated. It was quite possible we could command the state convention and thus claim as much as two-thirds of the delegation to the national convention in Miami Beach. Our amalgam of small constituencies and left-wing ideologues accounted for no more than 5 percent of the population across the state of Utah, but when organized, made up over 50 percent at a Democratic caucus.

It was nearly two weeks before I heard from Stevie again. He talked rapidly into the phone. "I had enough delegate strength to make it out of the county. No problem. Over 70 percent of the county delegates were for McGovern, so just about anyone who wanted to go to state is going. Now I need to know how to be elected at state to go to national."

My response had been well rehearsed. "Congratulations. As a member of the national staff, I cannot assist anyone in becoming a national delegate. I can only inform you of the rules and try to make sure that our delegation is a reflection of all the supporters of George McGovern and the Democratic Party."

"What do you mean you can't help me? You—you got me into this."

"I can't help beyond what I can do for anyone who supports McGovern."

He hung up.

About an hour later, I received a call from Frances Farley, at whose home I'd stayed when I first arrived in Utah. A leading pro-choice activist and later a state senator, Farley always provided me with solid inside political information and wisdom, and she kept in touch with the state's "wacktivists."

"You should be aware of a situation," she said. "Steve Holbrook is going to run for national delegate. As a former commissioner candidate and gay activist, he has a strong base of support. Expect him to win."

I hung up.

I called Stevie.

"You've got competition," I told him. "Steve Holbrook is running for national delegate."

"I know. I heard it at a bar last night. I thought you would help me win, but you can't. So I will lose. He can get the lefties and the gays in Salt Lake. I can only get the gays."

I told him that we needed his vote at the state convention to make sure we sent as many McGovern delegates to the national convention as possible. "Don't worry, I'll be there," he told me. "It's your fault, you know. If you hadn't printed up those leaflets then I wouldn't have distributed them. I'm told he got the idea of running when he saw the leaflet."

Stevie and Johnny, along with over 800 other McGovern supporters, arrived at the Salt Lake Convention Center for the state conclave in mid-June 1972. Our banners and posters covered every wall. There was little if any Humphrey presence but the Muskie contingent, led by Utahan

Randy Horiuchi, was making inroads with the uncommitted delegates, who made up about 20 percent of those in attendance. "That's odd," I thought, knowing that the Maine senator himself had suspended his campaign months previously. It seemed that here in Utah, his supporters—mostly the governor, a senator, and a young activist, Horiuchi—had kept hope for his candidacy alive. (In later years, Horiuchi defeated incumbent Salt Lake County Commissioner Tom Shimizu with the memorable slogan, "Better a new Horiuchi than an old Shimizu.")

I didn't understand why the Utah Muskie supporters were still organizing until I spoke with Randy outside the convention hall while we shared a smoke break (tobacco). "Look, among the eighteen delegates representing Utah at the National Convention, there will be Steve Holbrook, a homosexual; at least two strong advocates of women's and abortion rights, Frances Farley and Karen Shepherd; and every major peace advocate in the state. Leading them will be a black man who is originally from Cleveland."

"Yes," I said, "that sums up the current makeup of the delegation."

"The Democratic Party will truly be the party of gays, abortionists, and peaceniks. Nobody will vote for a Democratic candidate for any office anywhere in the state—and that includes every single legislative seat. All we want is for Governor Rampton and Senator Moss to be on the delegation."

"I don't know if we can pull that off. Our delegates want a 100 percent McGovern delegation. I need to talk to Nabors."

I headed to our Boiler Room, just off the convention floor, to find Nabors pacing and flinging his arms about. "They're nuts!" he was screaming. "Absolutely fucking nuts!"

"Who?" I asked.

"Our supporters. Our delegates."

"What happened now?"

"I've got to figure some way of getting Rampton and Moss on the delegation because we'll need them in the fall. All these folks care about is electing a homosexual."

"So you've talked to Horiuchi?"

"Didn't have to. I've talked to over a dozen of our key supporters and it's gay rights: yes, governor and senator: no."

"They do have a point. The delegate count nationally is very close and we need every person there to be 100 percent pledged to George McGovern. Rampton and Moss are both with Muskie."

"They'll vote McGovern if we push hard enough."

"What if we make them alternates? That way they'll be in the delegation but won't vote on the nomination."

"Not going to work. They've got to be delegates or nothing."

Nabors sat down and pulled out a piece of paper that detailed our ideal slate of candidates for the delegate slots. We went through them one by one to determine what geographic, demographic, and ethnic quota each of them would fill. We realized that the vote on the last delegate would likely come down to Holbrook versus Rampton or Moss. But we needed *both* Rampton and Moss.

"I will have to appeal to the entire McGovern delegation to vote for both Rampton and Moss and not Holbrook and someone else," Chuck said, just as Jean Westwood walked in.

As national co-chair of McGovern for President, Jean had been on a trip to the south for the national campaign; Nabors quickly briefed her.

She smiled and said, "This will be a good show. U.S. senator versus homosexual activist. Governor versus homosexual activist. Both probably against some other peace advocate. Just tell me when to tune in so that I can watch the end of my political career. After today, no one in Utah will want to be associated with the McGovern national co-chair."

Nabors headed out the door on his way to a meeting of the McGovern delegate caucus, but first stopped to talk with some of his legislative district coordinators about how to whip the members of said caucus. He left me to deal with the visit of our special guest speaker for McGovern, Congressman Don Edwards of California.

Edwards arrived at the convention hall about ten minutes later. I introduced him to the major political figures—the major ones, that is, aside from the governor and senator, who already knew him. He gave a fine speech that was well received by the overwhelmingly partisan crowd. He worked the convention aisles. Then he left.

As soon as I saw him into a taxi, I went straight to the McGovern caucus, which had just started. Chuck was standing in front of the crowd of 800, pleading with them to elect Rampton and Moss. He failed intially.

On the initial vote, the delegates elected as delegates Chuck and

Holbrook, but not Moss and Rampton. Once those results were announced, Chuck, looking dejected, stepped to the microphone to announce, "I will give up my seat on the floor of the national convention to the governor of the state of Utah, if you will elect him delegate." After thirty minutes of parliamentary wrangling—one part *Robert's Rules of Order*, one part Saul Alinsky's *Rules for Radicals*—Rampton was elected national delegate.

Within a few moments, a woman who had already been elected a national delegate stepped up to the microphone and offered to go as a half-delegate, giving the other half to Senator Moss. This, too, passed after much wrangling, but with the amendment that Nabors was to be the non-voting chairman of the Utah delegation.

In making the motion for the amendment, the delegate stated at the microphone, "Nabors can't be a priest in this goddamn state, so let's make him our delegation chair and he will make the vote announcement on national TV."

This, of course, pleased the assembled McGovern delegates, and the meeting was adjourned.

As I left the Utah Democratic Convention in 1972, I saw Stevie. He was buoyant. "This is just the beginning! We can take over the state. This is a new movement. Who would have thought that we could send a gay man from Utah to the Democratic Convention; at least three women's libbers; a guy, Fred Dietrich, who wants to pull *all* our troops out of Europe as well as Vietnam—that's gutsy; left-wing students; and a black man as our leader? And only a couple of mainstream LDS people. Isn't it great?"

I agreed that it was, and hoped that the revolution had come to Utah. It hadn't. McGovern received 32 percent of the state's vote in November. However, in subsequent years, one member of the McGovern delegation, Karen Shepherd, was elected to Congress, and others became leaders in the state legislature.

So I guess Stevie was right. It was kinda great.

# RULE #11

# PROCESS KILLS. POLICY KILLS.
# BOTH MATTER. WATCH YOUR LANGUAGE.

There is nothing more stultifying than a politician explaining the nuances of the legislative process. Talking process is a guaranteed way to lose all but your most policy-nerdy supporters.

Besides losing the audience, discussion of process inevitably leads to admission of failure—why the elected office was unable to do what the elected official promised to do. Never a good thing.

Despite the extraordinary efforts of the politician to explain in a rational and understandable manner the Herculean efforts put forth in the attempt to pass some legislative fix to the world's problems, the headline the next day will always read, "Fix Failed."

Did the message come through? Nope. Did the politician communicate a record of accomplishment? Nope. Did the politician admit failure? Yes.

Admitting failure inevitably leads to making an excuse. The excuse begins something like this: "Yes, my food safety bill is still in committee. It was originally referred to the Committee on Agriculture where it was taken up by the subcommittee on Grains and Wheat, where it was amended. Of course, once it got before the whole committee, the majority added some other amendments that were not consonant with the objectives we were trying to achieve, so we tabled it. However, we may seek a jurisdictional change and move it to the Commerce Committee under a food safety provision. We hope it will be sent to one of the more consumer-oriented subcommittees to be considered there. Of course, I don't belong to the Commerce Committee, so I will have to find someone on the committee to be a lead co-sponsor, so that we can move it through that committee."

One of my friends in the consulting industry, Steve Murphy, upon hearing a congressman describe the failure of one his bills in a similar manner, looked at the congressman and said, "So what you thought was a good idea, others thought sucked. You lost. Don't talk about it again."

Perhaps as a result of campaign Darwinism, where only those in the most secure seats survive forever, state legislators and members of Congress in those safe seats seem incapable of refraining from uttering such process gibberish. It takes a candidate who has been in engaged in a competitive campaign of some magnitude among voters who don't regularly read the op ed pages of a newspaper—i.e., those voters who don't vote in primaries—to realize that no one understands or comprehends the process; it is about results.

Naturally, a deep dive into process leads most politicians into the Mariana Trench of detail and minutiae. But this propensity is amplified when they are given the opportunity to go into what really matters to them: policy.

The *Encyclopedia Britannica* is a blog post compared to a politician who wants to demonstrate the mastery of the nuances of a particular policy. This demonstration generally occurs at town meetings, on Internet blogs, at legislative hearings, and even at rallies.

Most normal human beings run from these colloquies. If people wanted to listen to this stuff, why are C-SPAN's rating so low?

Not surprising, then, is the political success of "straight-talk" candidates who can simplify complex policy and avoid process-speak. They are understandable to all but those who want or need the detail. The "straight-talk" politician comes across as a genuine person with whom most voters can relate.

In Europe, unfortunately, all politicians and parties are determined to present their full and complete knowledge of every issue known to their constituents (and some not known to their constituents) in full-page newspaper advertisements. These ads do not come with photographs or slogans. No. Agate type is required so that no one over the age of forty can read them without 200+ reading glasses. Columns upon columns are lifted from the party's platform, manifesto, or the mad rants of a supposed policy expert. When one campaign manager in Spain placed an advertising order for ten days of these newspaper policy declarations, I tried to stop him but was told, "We must do it. Everyone wants to know our policies."

"Everyone? Hell the city's football team is on a roll. That is what everyone is reading. We don't need this stuff. We are running a forty-year-old against an octogenarian. The other party has been in power for twenty years, and the local economy is headed straight downhill. This is very simple. Young and vigorous versus old and staid. Change versus stay the same. And, yes, we will do something about the economy."

I lost the argument. The newspaper articles ran. Somewhere, somewhere in that city, somebody other than our opposition read all ten ads. I am sure there is such a person.

• • •

When I first arrived in Madison, Wisconsin, to work for McGovern, I was told to find Jean Westwood, who was running the Madison office and the western part of the state. She was sitting between two other staffers in a crowded office. In a husky, cowgirl voice she asked, "Where have you been?

I was about to say that I'd waited to leave Washington because I needed to train a new person in the science of postage, copying, and printing, but somehow suspected Jean wouldn't be impressed

"Washington tells me you're a damn good rural organizer. I presume you know something about ag policy. Particularly dairy issues."

"Ag policy? Dairy? I'm from Washington, D.C., and—"

"You don't know anything about ag policy? Stearns told me they were sending me their best rural organizer from New Hampshire, goddammit."

"Sorry, I . . ."

"You sure you don't know dairy policy?"

"No. I mean, yeah. I mean, yeah, I'm sure I don't know."

The air from Jean's sigh could have propelled three heifers from here to the next county. (I may not have known rural issues, but I was trying to get into the spirit of things.) "All right, then. Go sit down with that Humlicek kid over there who is from Nebraska and is here specifically to work on ag issues. See if you can learn something."

Jim Humlicek and I sat down in the first of what would be countless meetings over thirty years. He tried to explain the nature of "parity" to me and its importance in the ag pricing world. Then he explained the cheese wars between Vermont and Wisconsin over dairy supports. After my face failed to register that I understood any bit of it, he said, "Look, just memorize this brochure about McGovern's ag policy. You don't have to understand it. If you can repeat it, that will be good enough."

In Madison, my accommodations were the floor of a high school friend's apartment. I shut myself in one of the bedrooms to memorize and practice regurgitating the lines from the brochure. The next day, Palm Sunday, I walked into headquarters and asked Jim to test me. I passed the memory test but, surprise! failed the Q&A. He seemed to think that was good enough. For the next three days, I called farmers during the morning and afternoon and students during the evening. The work seemed worthwhile, although most of the farmers could discern a policy rookie and most of the students were away on spring break.

I thought I caught a break when assigned to take Leonard Nimoy around rural Wisconsin; I presumed that I would not have to discuss farm policy any more. I was wrong.

In the middle of the Q&A at the Baraboo High School event, a gentleman in a Sunday suit rose to ask, "Okay. I know where this fellow McGovern stands on the war. But what is he going to do about parity prices and dairy subsidies?"

Nimoy looked the man straight in the eye and said, "I don't know much about ag issues. But Rick here, from the McGovern staff, knows all about McGovern's ag positions. Right, Rick?"

I froze, then managed a weak nod.

"Can you help him, Rick?"

I nodded again, and then again, before realizing that nodding was an insufficient response. Nimoy, staring at me with Vulcanesque concentration, wanted something verbal. It was showtime. I swallowed hard, stepped to the microphone, and began reciting the brochure. I may have missed a paragraph or two, but, as far as I could tell, no one knew I was winging it except the questioner, who stared at me as if I had forgotten the words to the Lord's Prayer.

After I finished, Nimoy had the good sense to quickly ask for the next question, which came from a young nonvoter asking about *Star Trek*-related arcana.

When we got back into the Jeep later that day, Nimoy turned to me and said, "Hey, about the ag question. You looked as if you were reading the answer from a teleprompter. Maybe you want to put a little more passion into your response next time. Just a thought."

"Right. Gotcha. Passion. Good idea, " I answered and kept driving.

• • •

Sometimes, policy does make a difference and often, so does process. More often, the language we use to describe the policy or process makes a very large difference. The language that is best used is not the words and phrases offered by academics, legislators, and the grand poobahs of think tanks. Rather, this language is simple, understandable, and direct.

• • •

At one point during the Utah Democratic Convention of June 1972, I went back to the McGovern staff room to call Washington with the final delegate tally. I found Jean Westwood, busy sorting papers. After a few minutes, she looked at me, then turned her head away and, staring at the cement walls, said quietly, "I was with George Wallace yesterday. He is not so well."

A month before, Wallace had been shot in Laurel, Maryland. The assassination attempt had failed, but it put its target in a wheelchair for the rest of his life.

"He asked me to tell McGovern something," Jean continued. "Wallace said, 'McGovern's got it all wrong. People don't want tax *reform*. They want tax *relief*.' He said, 'People are scared of reform. They think it's for someone else. Not them. They want relief.'" She stopped speaking for a second, then asked me, "Are we too far down the road on all of this?"

I didn't answer.

"Rick, are we too far down the road?"

"I don't know, I think we could change after the convention."

She turned to me. "Well, what do you hear when you go door to door? All I get is from politicians, campaign management, media guys, and pollsters. You talk to real people."

I was stuck. I had to answer, "You can't change positions on the war; you would lose everyone. But on an issue like tax reform, maybe. The problem would be getting all of our people to use tax 'relief.' We have been using tax 'reform' for a long time and they think in terms of reforming stuff. You know, the McGovern *reforms* for the party and things like that."

"Is that what you hear going door to door?" Westwood persisted.

"When I come across a Republican, they don't talk to me. If I come across a Democrat, they want to talk about Nixon and the war. And if I come across someone who is undecided or independent, they want to talk about the economy and their taxes. I can't talk to them about tax reform or the war—they don't understand tax reform and they are disgusted by the war and tired of talking about it."

"So . . . we can change?" she asked yet again, as she returned to stuffing her briefcase with papers.

I shrugged. "Maybe, but we have to do it fast. Wallace is right. To win, we have to be seen as fighting for the independents, not for the reformers."

"Thanks. That was helpful."

Within a month, McGovern would name Jean Westwood the first female chair of the Democratic National Committee. But *reform* never changed to *relief*. Still hasn't.

# RULE #12

# CELEBRITIES ARE A WASTE OF TIME, UNTIL THEY ARE NOT.

There is nothing better than having a Hollywood star or political celebrity come to your campaign's aid, right?

Maybe.

In front of the right audience at the right time, the Robert Redfords of the world can be extremely effective in raising money or increasing a campaign's visibility. Leonard Nimoy in Wisconsin is a wonderful example of how a celebrity can help your campaign: a well-known star goes to a rural area to speak on behalf of a still-not-very-well-known candidate.

It is not as if voters acknowledge to themselves, "If Leonard Nimoy is for George McGovern, then I will be, too." They don't. But, if given an opportunity to meet or see Leonard Nimoy in the flesh, they show up, even if he is promoting some candidate of whom they have only recently become aware. They turn out in droves and become more aware of the candidate or cause in the process.

That's a good transaction. The campaign gets exposure. The audience meets and hears a star. The celebrity makes the mundane seem special and may perhaps provide political wisdom or a perspective that would never come forth from a candidate or political operative.

The problem is that so many campaigns are consumed with the notion that if they could just get Susan Saradon or some other Hollywood star to come do an event, and endorse their candidate, then victory would be in their grasp.

This desire is inversely related to a campaign's status in the polls. With a candidate or cause down by fifteen points with two weeks to go until election day, the campaign staff meetings become "can we get" meetings. The forlorn campaign fundraiser starts asking, "Do you think we can get Bruce Springsteen to endorse us and do a fundraiser?"

"No."

After a few more instances of, "What about x or y?" someone asks, "Rick, do you know any celebrities?"

"No."

At the end, a field operative inevitably suggests, "Well, my best friend played Willy Loman in *Death of a Salesman* at the Suburban Playhouse Theatre. He will do it. Can I call him?"

"No, you can't!" I inevitably answer.

If the campaign is up by fifteen points with two weeks to go, the celebrity may wish to be associated with a winning candidate or cause. In those staff meetings the conversation inevitably begins, "Do we really need this person?" or "What the hell will we do with him?"

And there is always the chance that the celebrity, once procured, will *not* say or do precisely what the candidate or campaign wants. Witness Clint Eastwood addressing an empty chair and effectively hijacking the 2012 Republican Convention from nominee Mitt Romney. This is particularly true when the celebrity is another politician with, perhaps, a different view on issues or the opposition than the hosting candidate.

Not long ago, a congressional campaign asked me to bring Howard Dean to a rally. No problem. He came.

As might be expected, Howard wound up attracting a large crowd. More than 700 people attended the rally, which is a stunning number for any congressional campaign. (Most congressional campaigns are happy if they can attract 150 humans.) But the candidate called me the day after the rally to complain that Dean's comments were too strident an attack on Republicans.

My reply was brief and to-the-point. "What the hell did you expect when your campaign asked for the former Chair of the Democratic National Committee? The Mother Teresa of Democratic politics?"

The candidate lost.

• • •

One of the best pieces of political advice I ever received came during the brief period I was in the entertainment business—the real entertainment business, not politics.

In the fall of 1978, I was producing a series of radio programs for ABC Radio entitled *Country Greats in Concert*, featuring artists such as Tanya Tucker and Ronnie Milsap recorded live in concert. I was trying to "make it" as a radio and television producer. This series with an established, "big-time" radio network was a breakthrough in my budding but, in the end, short-lived career in the entertainment business.

One afternoon, in a recording studio in Nashville, while preparing a program with a featured artist for airing later that month, I received a phone call from the vice president of programming for ABC Radio, Robert Fulman, our network sponsor. Over the phone line he wanted to share with me the jingle that would open each of the broadcasts of *Country Greats In Concert*. Clearly very excited, he put the telephone up to his tape deck speaker and pressed "play."

I was not diplomatic in my response. "That's awful. It's sounds like the intro for a bad sitcom. We have to change it."

Fulman then told me that he just spent $10,000 on the jingle and there was no way he was going to change it.

"Why don't we ask Waylon Jennings, who is standing here with me, to listen to it," I suggested, "and see what he thinks?"

Fulman agreed that the leading country artist at the time might be an appropriate judge. I put him on hold and turned to Jennings. "It is the VP of programming at ABC. He wants you to listen to their new jingle."

"ABC? Damn. You know, for twenty years those big boys wouldn't touch me with a ten-foot poll. Now they can't get enough of us 'outlaws,'" Jennings said. Willie Nelson, Jennings, and a number of other country artists had been dissed and maligned by the Nashville and New York entertainment establishment during the 60s and early 70s. Their bitterness toward the establishment media had not subsided. "Alright. Let me hear it," he relented.

I handed him the phone and he listened to the jingle. He was a bit more polite than I. "You could do a lot better," he told Fulman, and handed the phone back to me, at which point Fulman thanked me for our joint input, reiterated to me that he was not going to change the jingle, said goodbye, and hung up.

I put down the phone and told Jennings, "They aren't going to change it." The singer looked at me and shook his head. "ABC's in New York, huh?" I answered affirmatively.

"Well, Rick, it just goes to show that if you get in bed with the devil, you better be prepared to fuck or be fucked."

Not bad advice to consider in all things personal, occupational, and political.

• • •

In July 1972, I was the security guard for the McGovern campaign on the sixteenth floor of the Fontainebleau Hotel during the Democratic National Convention in Miami. My assignment:

1.   Stop unauthorized individuals from going up the stairs to the seventeenth floor, where McGovern and the McGovern leadership were headquartered; and

2.   Secure the political "Boiler Room" on the sixteenth floor, where the strategy and tactics that had been developed on the seventeenth floor were conveyed to the campaign's floor leaders in the convention hall.

Simply put, I had to check credentials of anyone seeking access to the Boiler Room and check with the Secret Service on the seventeenth floor before allowing anyone up there.

I was standing behind the desk on the sixteenth floor, blocking entry to both the Boiler Room and the stairs to seventeen, when a woman approached. Short, blonde, and petite, she wore a long dress that was neither hippyish nor antiquarian; more like a sophisticated Russian peasant dress. I did not recognize her from campaign headquarters or any of the staff briefings at the convention.

But, so what? Her beauty was mesmerizing, her cultured British accent was seductive, her blue eyes . . . ahh, her blue eyes. "Hello," she said, "I have a meeting with Senator George McGovern."

This woman could have been carrying a machine gun and I would have allowed her to pass. But, despite my weak knees, my practiced response kicked in.

"Yes, and your name please?"

She smiled at me, tilted her head down, then looked at me almost sheepishly. "Julie Christie."

My jaw dropped. My heart raced. I stammered, but only a bit. "Yes, yes, one moment please, Ms. Christie. I need to check upstairs with the Secret Service."

Flashes of *Dr. Zhivago* filled my head—Lara wearing her fur hat and coat in a Russian snowstorm, the music of her theme—*Da-da-da-daaa, da-da-da-daaaa-da-daaa*—as I glided up the stairs to inform the Secret Service that Julie Christie was awaiting her meeting with Senator McGovern. The agent on duty approved her without batting an eyelash.

Had he ever been to the movies? Didn't he have a pulse?

Before descending the stairway I straightened my tie. I tucked in my shirt. Trying to stand upright, I wondered why I had engaged in neither outdoor nor indoor exercise for the past three months. I regretted failing to shave at least once during the past three days. I tried to reconfigure my facial demeanor to appear at least twenty-one, although twelve years later, at age thirty-one, I would still be described in a newspaper article as "boyish."

The vision of loveliness was at the staircase landing when I announced, in my best deep, grown-up voice, "Ms. Christie, you can go upstairs to meet the senator now."

She stood on her toes and said, "You are such a dear!"—and kissed me.

I could tell you that it was on the mouth, long and sensuous, but you wouldn't believe me. So I'll admit that it was on the cheek.

But still. Julie Christie.

I waited for her to come back down the stairs. For two hours. *Long meeting*, I thought.

Finally, when I went back upstairs to check with the Secret Service regarding another visitor, I was told that she had met with the senator and staff for fifteen minutes, then taken the elevator down.

Not the stairs.

Aside from Julie Christie, what I most remember from the convention (which conferred on George McGovern the Democratic nomination for the presidency) was a tall, squarish fellow who one day I allowed to enter the Boiler Room. He was in charge of the Texas McGovern delegation. The guy's name was . . . let me see . . . oh, yeah, Clinton. (He did okay for himself later in life. Indeed, I have a picture of me at the White House with him and his lovely wife, as well as a letter from this Clinton fellow informing me that I was his official representative in Colorado for the 1996 presidential campaign.)

## RULE #13

# FIND A CAMPAIGN HEADQUARTERS THAT IS BUILT FOR COMFORT AND FOR SPEED.

"Why is it Democrats seem to feel that orange crates make the best campaign furniture?" asked leading political consultant Matt Reese back in 1982, when he observed the Lamm for Governor Campaign's office furnishings. There is a deep-rooted belief among Democrats that the more dilapidated, scummy, and ill-heated a campaign headquarters is, the greater the righteousness of the campaign. No true campaign could have both the people's and the campaign staff's interests at heart.

As a result, the décor of campaign headquarters takes on a mythic quality in Democratic campaigns. Never has a winning campaign had a headquarters that was clean, comfortable, and furnished with more than pre-World War II overstock. Indeed, some partisans have claimed that the reason a campaign lost was that it wasted its money on nice headquarters. But even in these "posh" circumstances, the environment would probably have been shut down by OSHA and would only *maybe* have had functional desks and chairs.

With this in mind, after forty years of field organizing, what follows are the worst campaign headquarters I have encountered.

## RICHARD LAMM FOR GOVERNOR HEADQUARTERS, DENVER, COLORADO—1982

From the outside, it looked perfectly reasonable. There were windows, a square lawn, and plenty of parking. Inside were cardboard desks and chairs bought from a closeout sale of a nonprofit organization terminated by Reaganomics.

Then it rained. Every afternoon the staff prepared for the inevitable thunderstorms. Typewriters and computers were covered, files were put away, and a bucket brigade was formed to place wastepaper baskets at strategic locations. Some days, we didn't manage to catch all the water and the office was blessed with the squish of saturated carpeting and the aroma of rotting flooring.

Naturally, this building was considered to be such prime real estate for campaign headquarters that it was used not only by a Democratic U.S. campaign in 1984 but again by a gubernatorial campaign in 1986.

## HEADQUARTERS OF THE LIBERAL DEMOCRATS, YORKSHIRE, ENGLAND—1989

Foreign political parties are not necessarily any better than the domestic variety. The first time I encountered a foreign HQ was in Northumberland, Yorkshire, England. Its main features involved space and heat, in that it had neither. More campaign staff was crammed into that small place than into an Apollo spacecraft. The single action of an individual moving his or her chair created a chain reaction of bodily contortions by other workers.

The lack of working space was compounded by the overcoats, which were required inside as well as outside. It was February, and northern England was more than cold. If there was central heating, no one could find the mechanism to work it. In the places where there were space heaters, there were so many workers huddled around them that finding your way to a desk was impossible. The entire experience taught me why Brits serve warm beer—which we enjoyed frequently because the headquarters was situated over a pub that had heat.

## EUGENE MCCARTHY FOR PRESIDENT HEADQUARTERS, CHICAGO, IL—1968

During the Democratic National Convention, the McCarthy campaign's duplicating and stuffing operation was located in a coat closet off the Grand Ballroom on the mezzanine level of the Conrad Hilton Hotel. During the course of the convention, the battle between the anti-establishment Yippies and the Chicago Police Department raged not more than 100 yards from the hotel's entrance.

As part of its arsenal, the police used a healthy dose of tear gas, which became subject to Chicago's fickle winds. The tear gas would slowly waft up to the mezzanine, where it promptly settled. The duplicating room staff, donning ski goggles, wet bandanas, and whatever else they could find to minimize the effects, looked like something from a bad science-fiction movie.

## GEORGE MCGOVERN FOR PRESIDENT HEADQUARTERS, BILLINGS, MONTANA—1972

Sometimes, in a campaign, all you really want is a good bed. And fortunately, the McGovern headquarters in Billings had one.

I had driven overnight from Salt Lake City for a meeting that turned out to have been cancelled before my arrival. So I headed to the McGovern headquarters—otherwise known as Joe's Waterbeds.

Joe, whose hair reached his shoulders, was there with his girlfriend, Abby, a poster child for a Woodstock refugee. As I walked in, Joe didn't hesitate before expressing an opinion: "You look like shit."

I told him I had driven 500 miles overnight for a cancelled meeting, after which he announced with compassion, "That's the west, man. Why don't you get some sleep?"

"Good idea. Where?" I answered.

Joe scanned the floor models in his showroom, ruminated for a bit, and said, "I don't want you on the 'Float for a King' model. It's my best seller. If someone comes in, I need to be able to demo it." He paused and looked around again. "I tell you what. If you don't mind, just take the one in the display window. It could attract some traffic to have a live, uh . . . model. Yeah, a live model. Far out! Don't worry, you'll like the 'Floatacilla.'"

I did. The midday sun and the downtown foot traffic made sleeping somewhat difficult, but the squishy, comfortable Floatacilla amounted to the best bedding I'd had in months.

## GARY HART FOR PRESIDENT HEADQUARTERS, WASHINGTON, DC—1984

It was a second-floor walk-up with one window and that was in the entranceway. Innumerable shelves housed only a few empty movie reels, and there were three rows of seven theater seats bolted to the center of the volunteer area. After the campaign moved in, the research department took less than a week to focus on the history of the building. Its previous incarnation was as a kiddie-porn shop. But it wasn't only the building's heritage that accounted for the ambiance.

By January, the campaign had run out of money to pay the heating bill. Unless a heating oil supplier could be conned into providing heat without an up-front payment, the office would remain chilly until 3 p.m. daily. At that time, the movie theater below the office switched on its heat for the afternoon show. The good news was that within the hour, heat had risen. The bad news was that the electrical system in the building was so bad that when the movie theater's heat turned on, it created an electrical surge that froze the computer equipment.

The volatility of the computers was only a part of the office equipment problem. Rarely did the campaign have the same copier for more than a week. What became known as the "copier du jour" syndrome was the result of the campaign's inability to pay for a copier, so the campaign "demonstrated" various brands for a week at a time before the distributor caught on that there was never an intention of renting or leasing the device. After a few weeks, all distributors in the Baltimore/Washington area had learned to avoid calls from the Hart for President campaign, and we were forced to walk ten blocks to the U.S. Senate office to copy anything that might be remotely considered "Official U.S. Senate" business.

## HOWARD DEAN FOR PRESIDENT HEADQUARTERS, BURLINGTON, VERMONT—2003

The heat worked, which is a good thing in Burlington in January, but it may just have been the staff's body heat we were feeling, the quarters were so cramped. At 2000 square feet and accommodating a staff and volunteers of more than 30, the headquarters was stunningly undersized. Even the infamously penurious candidate demanded to his campaign manager (me), "Get us out of this rabbit warren!"

But the real problem was the location. For a campaign trying to transcend Vermont's image as a haven for New Agers, the placement of the headquarters over a brewpub and a few doors down from a hemp clothing store only provided national journalists' greater license to depict the campaign as a concoction of the sometimes loony left.

I begged one major journalist not to describe the Dean operation as the "burgeoning bud and brew" campaign.

## HILLARY CLINTON HEADQUARTERS, PHOENIX, ARIZONA—JANUARY, 2008

In fairness, the status of the Democratic campaign headquarters has improved remarkably over the past thirty years. Nowadays, campaigns are rarely inclined to lease vacant storefronts or remote warehouses. In part, this improvement is a result of the length of campaigns; major campaigns now last eighteen months when once they lasted six. That being the case, landlords for more upscale offerings are willing to lease their property for the duration, rather then sending prospective tenants to soon-to-be-"redeveloped" property.

The step up in accommodations is also a result of the need to have high-speed communications and Internet capabilities. But when there are none of these modern conveniences, you have to adapt.

I arrived in Phoenix for the Clinton campaign in early January of 2008 in preparation for the February primary. The campaign team didn't have to worry about heat in the Phoenix office, so they had plenty of time to be preoccupied with the lack of phones, Internet, cable TV, and computers. Although the HQ was situated in central Phoenix, it was strategically placed in a mobile phone dead zone. The cable company for television and Internet initially announced that it would take three weeks to get service, and we were told the computers would be shipped to us after the Iowa caucuses, in "a week to ten days."

We conducted many of our phone calls on street corners where there was cell service. My computer became popular because I could poach a Wi-Fi signal from the Hilton Hotel across the street where my Hilton Honors card allowed Wi-Fi access even when, strangely, I was not a guest. The real beneficiary of this lack of technological capability was the Starbucks two blocks away, where most of the staff drank lattes while they enjoyed the marvel of telecommunications.

After two days of street-corner calling and Starbucks conferences, I sent the following to Jessica O'Connell, the senior staff member in the National Headquarters in charge of campaign toys, tools, and personnel. (Apologies to Janis Joplin. Sing to the tune of "Mercedes Benz")

> Oh, Jess won't you send me a satellite TV?
> The campaign has no cable, I must make amends.
> Worked hard for the Clintons, only a little help from my friends
> Oh, Jess won't you send me a satellite TV?
>
> Oh, Jess won't you buy me a telephone dialer?
> Dialing for supporters is beginning to tire me
> I wait for delivery every day until three
> Oh, Jess won't you send me a telephone dialer?
>
> Oh, Jess won't you buy me a laptop computer?
> I am counting on you Jess to make me into a blogger
> Prove that you love me and buy me the Dell
> Oh, Jess won't you buy me a laptop computer?
>
> Again, Oh Jess won't you send me a satellite TV?
> The campaign has no cable, I must make amends.
> Worked hard for the Clintons, only a little help from my friends
> Oh, Jess won't you send me a satellite TV?

The plea worked in part. We got the Internet and phone service within a couple of days, but the computers arrived as promised, ten days later.

## RULE #14

# WHERE THERE IS THE LEAST TO GAIN, THERE IS THE GREATEST INFIGHTING.

"Academic politics is the most vicious and bitter form of politics, because the stakes are so low," said Professor Wallace Stanley Sayre, a political scientist and professor at Columbia University. Well, academics have nothing on intra-political party wrangling. The viciousness of intra-party battles makes the Hatfields and McCoys look like tribe members on *Survivor*. I know of political operatives that will not work with each other because they were on opposite sides of a congressional primary twenty years ago. On a presidential level, there are Jimmy Carter supporters from 1980 that still do not speak to Kennedy operatives. I have heard of similar rifts in Republican ranks. With Republicans, however, the dichotomy is less candidate-based than class- and religion-based: Country Clubbers vs. the Christian Right.

Often, battles of immense insignificance revolve around titles. A campaign operative I know always says "titles are free," and dispenses lofty titles to anyone who asks. "You want to be a vice chair. No worries. A member of the steering committee? Done. Director of operations for legislative district fourteen? You got it!"

But the conflict over titles can cause hours of wasted campaign time.

• • •

After the Democratic Convention in 1972, I waited for my final assignment in southern California by performing "gofer" duties at the McGovern state headquarters in Los Angeles. It wasn't particularly challenging, but once again I met key staff and funders.

148

It was late August when I was assigned to take Rick Stearns, the McGovern national field director, to the airport. As he hopped into the Jeep, he looked at me and said, "I thought you were our rural guy. What are you doing in central Los Angeles?"

"I dunno. This is where I was told to come. Besides, I know nothing about almonds or artichokes, and my Spanish isn't good enough for Bakersfield," I replied, and then asked, "Where are you flying? Back to DC?"

"No. I wish. I have to go to Arizona to fix a problem."

"Arizona? Why Arizona? We have no chance of winning Arizona."

"I know. I know. But there's a dispute about who should be the state chair of the campaign."

"What's the dispute? Which person is going to be responsible for losing Arizona?"

"No, not quite. Some people actually want the job. But the McGovern campaign folks don't want a Humphrey person to be state chair. Some of the Democratic establishment do." He shook his head, then smiled. "You know . . . where there is the least to gain, there is always the greatest infighting."

# RULE #15

# IF YOU CAN'T COUNT IT, IT DIDN'T HAPPEN.
# BE ACCURATE IN YOUR COUNTING.

I wasn't the first person to say, "If you can't count it, it didn't happen." I am sure there was some ancient military leader who, when told that a subordinate had "captured a whole lot of enemy soldiers," responded, "How many precisely? Ten? Twenty? Two hundred? How many is 'a lot'?"

I actually learned the dictum from one of my first campaign bosses, Joel Bradshaw, who plagued me every day for detailed canvas results in a 1980 campaign. The words "some," "a lot," "quite a few," or "a fair number," never seemed to be a sufficient response to his morning canvas tally of my headquarters' efforts. He wanted real numbers.

I've seen the phrase repeated by other organizers of note, but for some reason my name is attached to it in four different languages and six countries. I'm not sure why it has become a maxim associated with me; probably not only because there are times when I followed it to success but times when I failed to do so—or watched others fail to do so.

• • •

Four days before the Iowa caucuses in 1984, as national field director of the Gary Hart campaign, I was dispatched to Des Moines to reassign the Iowa staff for the next round of caucuses and primaries. There would be no time to send anyone to New Hampshire from Iowa because it was only eight days later. Most of the Iowa staff would be assigned to states where primaries or caucuses were scheduled twelve days after Iowa.

Some people thought that my overnight trip to Iowa was a waste of campaign dollars and time; there would be no campaign after a less than stellar result in Iowa and a certain New Hampshire primary loss. So why reassign staff? Why not just tell them to go home? Besides, the staff had not been paid their salaries or expenses for weeks, so a $300 airfare for the lowly national field director was considered an extravagance.

But members of the senior campaign team had been the recipients of leaked, recent polling conducted by our opposition. It indicated that our campaign had some all-precious momentum heading into the Iowa caucuses. We could possibly come in second to former Vice President Walter Mondale and ahead of Senator John Glenn, the establishment's alternative to Mondale, and Senator Alan Cranston—the left-wing favorite. So, somebody had to begin preparing for the next round.

Late that Thursday night, I met with four members of the campaign staff at a local bar that had been selected specifically because no one, particularly the national press, went there. Also, it was cheap. There was some excitement in the voices of the staff as reports of bigger crowds and an uptick in Hart support in voter identification calls filtered down to the campaign offices. But not one of the staff believed there was enough of a surge to warrant anything but post-caucus unemployment.

Over beers, I presented to the four their next assignment. To suggest that my assignments were met with derision would be limiting the characterization of the colloquy.

"What the hell do you mean, you want me to go to Maine after the caucuses?" Laura Quinn, the First Congressional District coordinator for the Iowa Hart campaign, screamed across her beer. This was quite the outburst from the normally cool-headed, soft-spoken Quinn.

"Well, I need someone to do organizing in Maine and, given that you have caucus experience and Maine is a caucus—"

"Maine? I'm going to Florida. That is *my* plan. The Florida primary is in mid-March."

"I understand that Florida might be more appealing in the middle of February, but I need you in Maine."

"Ridder, do I need to remind you that you, or rather the campaign, hasn't paid us for two months? You owe me $1,921.21 for two months, after taxes. And now you're telling me that I have to go to Maine? Screw you. Lorelei

Lorch and I are going to Florida." At that, she waved a hand toward one of the other staff members present, who was tentatively assigned to Arkansas.

"That's not quite true, Laura," I replied. "You were paid one third of your December pay in early January."

"Yes, so the remainder owed in salary is $1,921.21. And how about the expenses? That's another $212.14. And who's going to pay for my travel to Maine? I am going to Florida. I have been freezing my butt off in this goddamned state for four months, and you want to send me to someplace colder? Besides, this campaign will be over in ten days anyway, so I don't know why we are having this ludicrous conversation."

Sipping my beer, I turned to John Whitehurst, the Waterloo, Iowa, area director. "John, I've assigned you to Pennsylvania. I've got to get someone there in case we get past Super Tuesday. Somebody has to be on the ground soon."

"Cool, man. I'll go to Pennsylvania, no problem, if I can get my expenses paid. I can't even fill up my car. I had to find some gas money just to get down here," said Whitehurst, a twenty-two-year-old recent college grad who was gaining a reputation as a talented organizer.

"What do you mean *find* some money?" asked Quinn, who doubled as the Iowa campaign's purser.

"Well, I'm flat broke and there is no money in the campaign account. So I found a way to get some money," Whitehurst said.

"You working a second job, like O'Malley?" Quinn asked, referring to one of our Iowa field organizers, Martin O'Malley, who was surviving by singing Irish folk songs in local bars.

"Ah, no. Let's say I just went where the money is."

"You robbed a bank?" I asked, thinking of Willie Sutton.

"Not quite."

"Spit it out. Where did you get the cash? Your parents?" Quinn asked.

"No, couldn't do that again. We would just get it into an argument about getting a real job." Whitehurst dropped his head toward the table, and in hushed tones that could be heard throughout the empty bar said, "I, ah, sold voter IDs to the Glenn campaign."

"You did what? Sold voters identifications of caucus attendees to the opposition?" I shouted.

"Yeah, they're flush with money and they're going nowhere, and their organization is a fuckin' mess. So I sold them the names of the twenty-seven Glenn supporters we found in Waterloo."

"How much did you get?" Quinn asked. She was clearly beginning to think this wasn't a bad personal fundraising project and she could maybe raise enough to get to Florida.

"I got two dollars for each of the twenty-three solid Glenn supporters and a dollar for the four leaners, for a total of fifty dollars. So, seventeen dollars and eighty-three cents for gas, four dollars and twenty-one cents for a burger and fries, and I've got four dollars for the beer here, because I know Ridder isn't paying. That leaves me twenty-three dollars and ninety-six cents for the next four days, until caucus night. I'll figure out later what I need to get home."

"I don't know whether to fire you for consorting with the enemy or praise you for your pecuniary creativity," I said. "Just don't do it again."

Whitehurst justified his actions further by referencing an arcane element of the caucus process: the distribution of a candidate's supporters if the candidate fails to garner at least 15 percent support among the caucus attendees.

"You know, Ridder," Whitehurst added, "the other part of the deal is that the Glenn supporters would come over to Hart when Glenn doesn't make threshold at the caucuses. They have no more than one or two supporters per precinct so they won't make threshold, but we might. I'm projecting an additional fourteen county delegates with this little transaction."

"Hmm. But they may have come over anyway because they hate Mondale. Just don't do this kind of transaction again."

"Got it. But then you have to pay my expenses before I go to Pennsylvania."

"Yeah, yeah, okay. And I'll try to convince the campaign office to pay Quinn and everyone else. Even if she thinks she is going to Florida."

I returned to DC the next day. Two days later, I got a call from Keith Glaser, the Iowa state director. There were rarely any good calls from Glaser so I prepared for the worst—and this one was one of the worst of the worst, for a Sunday before a caucus.

"Ridder, there is about to be a news story that two of our volunteers checked into a Holiday Inn in Waterloo on Friday. They paid for the rooms but used the phones. They ran up a $122 phone bill. As they left, they told the clerk that they were with the Cranston campaign and gave the Cranston campaign address as the billing address. They'd used the phone in the hotel room to make local and some long distance phone calls, then split."

"Jesus. Who was it?" I asked.

"Marc Dann and a few other volunteers from Michigan."

"Mark Blumenthal? Pete Giangreco?"

"I don't know about Pete, but Blumenthal wanted no part of this endeavor. He apparently knew what the cost of the phones would be. He has been in Des Moines all weekend."

"It's Whitehurst's territory," I pointed out. "And he is on staff. So, for press purposes, we will have to fire Whitehurst and ask Dann and the others to lie low for a couple of days. How did they find out it was our people who did it?"

"Not sure."

"Well, fire Whitehurst and tell the press that the individuals responsible are no longer with the campaign," I said, "and that we will take care of the bill immediately."

"That's fine, but we don't have any money to pay the bill and I don't have any way to reach Whitehurst. The reason the Michigan gang was using the hotel room, I presume, is that the phone in the Waterloo office was cut off a few days earlier for the campaign's failure to pay the bill."

"Oh. Okay. If he shows up tomorrow at the victory party, tell him he's fired." I hung up.

It was around 9 p.m. on the night of the caucuses that it became clear that Hart had scored a "victory" by coming in second in Iowa with 17 percent of the vote. Walter Mondale had received 49 percent. We were trounced. But who cared? We were second when nobody had expected us to come in better than third or fourth.

I called the Des Moines office to congratulate the staff and found them in quite the celebratory mood. I congratulated Keith Glaser and asked him to pass around the phone to other staff members. Clearly without thinking, he handed the phone to John Whitehurst.

"Whitehurst! What are you doing there? I thought we fired you?"

"Well, yeah, you did. Keith told me a few minutes ago. But I thought I would stay and enjoy our success."

"I guess that's okay. Hey, by the way, how did they know it was the Hart campaign who split on the bill?" I asked.

"Um. They left two of my remaining 15 Hart brochures in the room by mistake."

"You are still fired," I said. "Until tomorrow. Then get your ass to Pennsylvania. You are rehired as of 8 a.m. tomorrow morning."

Eight days later, after Hart won the New Hampshire primary, Whitehurst arrived in Pennsylvania and called me to report on the state of the campaign.

"Let me just give you the basics. I am sitting in a law office here, which has the only listed telephone for Hart for President. And in front of me are 451 'While You Were Out' messages from the past week and a typed list of 29 elected and party officials who have contacted the state party chair asking to get involved."

"Thanks for the count and update. Given our current fundraising levels, I don't think the phone will be cut off, and I can get you your expenses and maybe even your back pay."

And, yes, Laura Quinn went to Maine.

John Whitehurst is now a leading Democratic campaign consultant in California. Laura Quinn directs a major Democratic voter file and database firm. Pete Giangreco is a Democratic direct-mail vendor and was a key consultant to Barack Obama's campaigns. Mark Blumenthal is the former senior polling editor for the *Huffington Post* and is now with SurveyMonkey. Martin O'Malley served two terms as governor of Maryland and ran for president in 2016. Marc Dann is the former attorney general of the State of Ohio. I am told they are all getting paid for their work and paying their hotel bills.

• • •

During the primary season of the 1972 presidential campaign, the national staff competed to name the worst possible assignments for the fall campaign and place bets on who would land those plum postings. People would suggest some redneck location, such as Macon, Georgia, or Spartanburg, South Carolina. But these towns were never considered serious entries in the discussion because there was no way the McGovern campaign was going to target Georgia or South Carolina as states they could carry. Flint,

Michigan, on the other hand, was considered an ultra-undesirable location in a must-win state. The town, later made famous by filmmaker Michael Moore in *Roger and Me* and more recently the scene of an environmental tragedy affecting the lives of its youngest citizens, had been the site of strife between white blue-collar workers and African-Americans over new open-housing laws—and no McGovern organizer wanted to be caught in the midst of that battle. But Flint had to share first place on the undesirability list with a town in the battleground state of California: Whittier, boyhood home of the incumbent Republican candidate for president of the United States, Richard Milhous Nixon.

And guess who wound up winning this prize assignment?

After 25,000 miles and eight months on the McGovern campaign, I was sent to Whittier—well, the territory that included Whittier. I was Regional Field Director, McGovern for President, Southeast Los Angeles County. My jurisdiction ran from Compton in the north to Orange County in the south.

The territory was composed of blue-collar communities settled by Okies and Arkies in the mid-thirties; burgeoning Hispanic locales in Bellflower and Montebello; vast suburbia in Norwalk; oil fields in Pico Rivera; the North American Rockwell plant in Downey, where the B-1 bomber (opposed by McGovern) was to be produced; South Gate and Huntington Park, homes to union workers at a Firestone tire factory; and Whittier.

My boss was a tall, fresh-faced operative by the name of John Bowermaster. Married with two children, John loved politics and campaigns. His wife didn't. He would frequently apologize to me before he hopped into his sporty Datsun 240Z to go home, leaving me "in charge" while he did a meet-and-greet with his family before returning later in the evening. It was an early introduction for me to the conflict between family and campaigns, a conflict of which I became acutely aware later in life. One day in 1984, when I was working for Gary Hart, I was on the phone with my Oregon coordinator while my wife was in labor. With the phone scrunched between my shoulder and ear, I timed her contractions while writing down delegate projections. We won Oregon. Nathaniel was born.

As the campaign drew to an end, John fretted about his future and family. A week before election day, he finally acknowledged, "I don't know what I'm going to do. I want to stay in campaigns. But in two weeks, I'll be working for my father-in-law as an insurance broker."

I tracked him down a few years ago and found he was a history teacher in northern California. I guess property and casualty didn't hold his interest. Or maybe it was the father-in-law.

The southern California field director was Paul Sullivan, the same one from Oregon, but this time his beautiful Hawaiian wife Karen was aiding him. Paul and Karen had one demand: accurate canvass data from the night before, from all ten of my campaign offices, by 11 a.m. So, every morning, starting at nine, I would call all ten headquarters and speak to the canvass coordinators to obtain their results. I cheered if any of them recorded over 33 percent McGovern support on a given night, or if there was an anecdote of note, such as when one of the volunteers complained, "This guy, Donald Segretti, who signed up in the primary, never answers his phone when we call him to volunteer." I explained that Segretti was under investigation for "dirty tricks" by the Nixon campaign and was probably speaking to no one but his attorney.

Paul called one Thursday morning in early October, just as I was beginning to collect data from the previous evening. Despite the dismal national polls, I was encouraged by our volunteer efforts. We generally had all our phones staffed in the evenings and were headed for our regional goal of identifying more than 100,000 McGovern supporters among the upwards of a million voters in the region.

Paul told me to meet him at the Huntington Park HQ in an hour for an unannounced inspection tour.

*Uh-oh.* The Hawaiian Hammer was coming, and I was his next nail.

He could have picked any one of my nine other headquarters and there would have been some semblance of activity at ten on a Thursday morning, but Huntington Park rarely opened its doors before ten-thirty and consistently was the last headquarters to report its previous night's canvassing results. We heard from them every morning at ten fifty-five.

I roused the Huntington Park office manager, Gloria, who rounded up two headquarters volunteers, so that by the time I arrived, thirty minutes later, there appeared to be a baseline campaign operation in motion. She even arranged to have two people drop in to the office to ask for literature once Paul arrived. It was a nice touch, given that no one had walked into that headquarters for literature in about a month.

I never understood why the campaign had opened an office in Huntington

Park, anyway. It was a transitional neighborhood, moving from industrial Okie to illegal immigrant, featuring a McDonald's, a used furniture store, a Rexall drug store, and a series of taco stands. There was no free parking. Inside headquarters were three tables and ten chairs, lent to the campaign by the UAW local representing workers at the Firestone plant nearby. A few posters of George McGovern adorned one wall and precinct maps another. There were no pins in the maps to denote precinct leaders or captains—because there were no precinct leaders or captains. The volunteer card file held only five cards, three of which were marked "moved." A "Welcome Volunteers" banner hung over the area where there was coffee, soda, and a canvass sign-up sheet that listed three recruits for the next three weeks.

Paul walked through the door and immediately pulled me aside. "I came down here to see this operation. Their numbers have been extraordinary in their day-to-day increases. Very impressive. I wanted to see how a small headquarters like this does it."

I nodded, having no idea what he was talking about.

Paul shook Gloria's hand. "Your nightly totals have been terrific."

Gloria beamed for a second, then said, "They have?"

"Why, yes," Paul said as we all sat down at one of the tables. "Some of the best in southern California. I'd expect these kind of numbers from Westwood, Venice, Santa Monica . . . but here? No."

"Wow," said Gloria. "Then we must be getting killed overall. I would have thought their numbers would be a lot better than ours."

"Yeah, but they're not. Take Tuesday night. You ID'd 316 McGovern supporters while Santa Monica got only 291."

"We did what?" said Gloria, looking at me with one of those "What did *you* tell him?" looks.

"It's true, Gloria. 316 in one night. " Paul continued. "How did last night go?"

"Hey, Jack, how did we do last night?" Gloria shouted to one of the two volunteers, an older man sitting at one of the other tables. "I haven't had a chance to look."

"Let's see," said Jack, scanning some papers. "We didn't have a good night. We had seven ones, fifteen threes, and eighteen no's, for a total of forty contacts."

"That's a terrible night," Paul said.

"That brings us up to 323 supporters," Jack continued.

"What did he say?" Paul asked.

"I didn't quite hear him exactly," I replied, having heard him loud and clear.

"Ridder, pay attention. Did this volunteer just say that there are 323 *total* supporters?"

"Uhh . . . I guess so."

"So do you also guess that this office has been reporting *cumulative* totals, not *individual night* totals?"

"Well, yeah," said Gloria. "No one told me to do it the other way."

"You mean, over the last 30 days you have identified a total of 316 McGovern supporters? Not the more than 5,000 I have for this HQ?"

"That's the way we did it in the primary."

Paul turned to look straight at me. "

"Christ, Ridder, you should have caught this weeks ago! Are your other headquarters reporting cumulative totals, too?"

"I don't think so."

"You don't *think* so?"

"Uhh . . . no. But I will find out."

"Yes, you'd goddamn better. Let's get out of here."

We all rose from the table. Paul thanked Gloria politely for the hospitality, and he and I left.

He was not so polite once we were on the sidewalk. "I came all the way down here, fighting LA traffic, to honor the hard work of this headquarters and their 5,000 IDs, only to find out that they have identified a total of 323 McGovern supporters over the course of one month. Ten a goddamn day! That's pathetic. Ridder, I could walk the goddamn streets here and in fifteen minutes find ten supporters. Find out if your other HQs are doing the same thing. Call me later to discuss this. Got it?"

"Uhh . . . yeah."

"And if this isn't fixed by the end of the day, you will be rediscovering your rural organizing skills somewhere outside of Fresno. Stearns said I should have assigned you to the nut-growing areas in the first place."

I drove back to my office, thinking that I should tell Bowermaster what had just happened. I wanted to let him know before he heard about it from his higher-ups. I gave him the report and said I'd try to fix the problem.

"I saw those numbers, but I thought they were counting the guys down at the union hall and from the tire plant. Guess not, eh? . . . Look, you can fix it—but you can't fix the real problem," Bowermaster said.

"What's that?"

"There's no one in Huntington Park who likes George McGovern."

"Good point."

• • •

A quick way to learn to be accurate in your counting is to get a 7:15 Sunday-morning phone call from an unhappy U.S. presidential candidate.

The morning after the 1984 presidential caucuses in Kentucky, Senator Gary Hart called me from his hotel room in New York to inform me that, "You know, we only got two delegates in Kentucky. Two delegates! You told me we were likely to get eight so I cut that in half and told the press we were going to get four. If we had gotten eight, as you said, we'd beat expectations. But no, we got two. Fix it." He hung up.

I didn't even get the chance to tell him that I had cut the estimate from the Hart Kentucky state director from sixteen to eight before I talked to him.

• • •

In late July of 2012, we delivered the campaign plan to the student leadership of the University of Oregon. It was a well-developed plan—given that we had no polling data—outlining precisely how to win a $135 million bond campaign to renovate the student union, with students paying $117 per term in new fees to support the project.

We provided a timeline, a fully developed budget, talking points, and message recommendations. We advised our client to refer to the opposition as "narrow-minded," "stuck in the past," and "stubborn," while promoting the positive elements of the project such as "leaving a legacy," "pride," and the "benefits" of a renovated student union.

The president of student senate told us he wanted to share our campaign plan with the other forty student senators. Niki Hawthorne, our firm's associate working with the students, said, "I don't think you want to do that. It will get leaked to the opposition."

"Oh no, that won't happen, " said the president. "They all support the bond campaign."

"All?" Niki said. "Not one of the forty is opposed? It's lost twice previously. Are you sure?"

"Absolutely, and I feel that I have to share the plan in order to get their help in the campaign."

"That's a lot of people to share it with," Niki pointed out.

"Absolutely. I am sending it now." He hung up.

In thirty seconds, our campaign plan landed in our email. He had courteously cc'd us.

Within twenty-four hours, we had resigned our duties as consultants in passing a bond for the University of Oregon's student union renovation. Why? The hometown newspaper, the *Eugene Register Guard*, and the University of Oregon newspaper, *The Daily Emerald*, disclosed the entire contents of the campaign plan. Moreover, there were attacks from the opposition stating that the proponents had hired an out-of-state, high-end, campaign consulting firm to advise on a student referendum. This was viewed as highly unseemly by the university administration, the student newspaper, and some members of the student senate. Rather than become an issue in a campaign for a new student union, we resigned.

When I called to deliver the news, I said to the student-senate president, "I thought you said there were zero members of the senate opposed to this bond."

"I guess there were some after all," he said.

"How many, do you guess?"

"Three, four, five, I dunno. Maybe ten."

"And how many of those three, four or five leaked the campaign plan to the newspapers?"

"Dunno. Possibly two or three. Maybe more."

"Accurate counting is important in this business," I said.

"What? Gotta go." He hung up.

Oddly enough, four months later, we got a call from the director of the student union informing us that the bond had passed. "We just followed your plan and message recommendations and it worked," she told us. "The opponents may have known what we were going to do, but they couldn't stop us."

# RULE #16

## BEWARE OF YOUR OWN DIRTY TRICKS.

Much has been written about opposition research in campaigns and how a campaign sleuth might find a revealing video from fifteen years earlier that could undermine a candidate or campaign. But that is the exception rather than the rule.

The rule itself is very simple. Almost all of a campaign's major mistakes or demonstrations of candidate deficiencies occur during the campaign at hand, and are either very public or readily available to the public. Undoing a candidacy doesn't require a staffer to dumpster-dive or harass a town clerk to find some damning document or statement from twenty years earlier.

No. It is almost always what a candidate says or does during the course of the race, or something the campaign authorizes, that takes him or her down. Indeed, candidates often hoist their own political petard. And if it can happen to the opposition, it can happen to your campaign or you as well.

• • •

By the night before the 1972 presidential election, reality had set in. But there was consolation to come.

At about 11 p.m., my friend Curtis paid me a surprise visit. A college student who believed that the right prank, properly directed, could foster the right political end, Curtis was holding a roll of duct tape.

"Your job is done," he announced. "What more can you do to save George McGovern from one of the worst political defeats in history? It is time to hit the streets, my man. Hit the streets."

"Can't. Gotta prepare for the Get Out the Vote effort tomorrow."

"Is your boss here?"

"No, John left a couple of hours ago. But someone should be here."

But Curtis knew me and my parentage too well.

"Ridder, if there's anyone with more guilt than the Catholics, it's the Jews—and you're both. Forget the guilt. Look at the clock. In one hour, it will be your last day of work for this sinkhole of a campaign. No one works hard on their last day of work."

"But tomorrow is election day. This is what we have been working toward for months."

"You've been working for months to get slaughtered all over the country?"

"No comment."

"Whatever. Just give me a couple hours to liberate your soul and ease your transition back to civilian life."

"We're not going drinking, are we? I'm not old enough to drink in this state legally."

"A minor inconvenience, my law-abiding friend—we are not doing something as unimaginative as merely going drinking. No, what we're doing is much more exciting and creative. Behold what is in my hand." He held up the duct tape.

"I behold. What are we doing?"

"You'll see."

"Okay, what the hell. But I have to be back by 1 a.m., because I have to be up by six to be here for any poll-watcher calls. They're supposed to check the voting booths around six-thirty to make sure they're all operating properly and set to zero."

"Which is where the McGovern totals will stay, my friend. But never mind, you'll be back. Let's take your Jeep—we may need the four-wheel drive."

I retrieved the remaining three-foot-by-four-foot posters we had used at rallies. They were simple: a photo of a smiling George McGovern and the words "McGovern for President" in large block print. We rolled up the three posters, locked the doors, and left.

As we got into the Jeep, Curtis informed me of our destination: "Whittier."

"Where in Whittier? The college? Central Whittier?"

"No. We need to circumnavigate Whittier," he announced.

We took the route toward the center of town, through the thriving oil fields of Santa Fe Springs and Pico Rivera. It was one of those car-wash-waiting-to-happen drives. Smoke, grime, and dust spewed forth. As we were about to enter Whittier, as evidenced by the emergence of lawns and large homes, Curtis shouted, "Stop! Pull over! First target in sight."

Still having no idea what was going on, I pulled onto the gravel shoulder on the right side of the road.

"There it is. Proceed slowly to target Number One." Curtis was pointing directly at the "Welcome to Whittier" sign. He directed me to stop when we reached it, jumped out of the Jeep and surveyed a landscape that was made up of the gravel, the two-lane highway, the ten-foot welcome sign, and not much else that we could see in the darkness or by the headlights of passing cars.

"Let me see if I can reach it," he said, as he sprang onto the hood of the Jeep, then stepped carefully onto the roll bars, which were covered by the canvas top. He used most of his six-foot-four-inch frame and immense wingspan to touch the top of the sign.

"Excellent. Poster and tape, please," he shouted as cars whizzed by.

I got out of the car. I handed him a poster and, at his direction, cut four strips of duct tape. Once he had the strips, he reached up and placed the McGovern for President poster right below the words "Welcome to Whittier," totally obscuring the line beneath it: "Hometown of President Richard M. Nixon."

He hopped down and jumped into the car. "Let's get outta here. Looks great, doesn't it? 'Whittier: McGovern for President.'"

We were back on the road in seconds. Mission accomplished. Or so I thought.

"On to target Number Two," said Curtis.

Target Number Two—the next Welcome to Whittier sign—was planted in a patch of gravel on the side of a four-lane road. By the time I stopped the Jeep Curtis had already cut the strips of duct tape, so this time the operation took no more than two minutes from beginning to end.

"That was good," I said. I was smiling now.

Curtis nodded. "One more, and the citizens of Whittier will be fully apprised of their town's rewritten history—if only for as long as it takes the public works department to strip the posters down."

A short drive and target Number Three was in sight. It was to the right of a narrow two-lane drive through the Whittier hills. At almost midnight, the road was deserted. We heard nothing but crickets. We pulled over. Strips of tape attached to his forearm, Curtis grabbed the last poster and jumped up on the hood, then onto the roll bars. Moments later he was in the passenger seat and the residents of Whittier had one more reminder of their town's overwhelming support for the liberal senator from South Dakota. I pulled the car onto the road and we were off, seeking a convenient place to turn around and head back to the office.

That's when we heard the siren and saw the blue lights in the rearview mirror.

Curtis spoke first. "Shit. This is why we took the Jeep. Make a right up here. Head for the hills. We'll find a dirt road that requires four-wheel drive."

That plan lasted thirty seconds; about a quarter-mile down, the right turn dead-ended into a barbed-wire fence.

I stopped driving and awaited my fate: Caught! Nabbed! Apprehended! Collared!

I hoped they'd let me off easy—three-to-five years in the State Pen at most. Less if I could figure out how to unionize the inmates.

As the policeman approached the Jeep, I reached into the glove compartment for the car's registration. The cop knocked on the window and I rolled it down.

"I'm Officer Palmer. License and registration, please. Both of you—licenses or identification."

He pointed his flashlight into the Jeep. I handed over the documents.

"I'm not sure what I saw there," said the lawman, "but I think I saw some destruction of public property and then, by your actions as you departed the scene, resistance to arrest. Not to mention going fifty in a twenty-five-mile-per-hour residential zone. Let me check you fellows out. I *will* be back."

"Holy crap," I said. "We're screwed. Please, tell me you don't have any pot on you! Do you?"

"For once, no. I went clean for this op."

"Well, that's something. Maybe we'll get off with ten years on a chain gang. Now what?"

"I was going to tell the officer that we were trying to take the posters *down* when he saw us—but his flashlight caught the duct tape."

"Yeah," I said, "and our heading for the hills wasn't such a good idea, either. I was going to tell him we were looking for a convenient place to turn around, but we were going too fast and too far to make that plausible."

We sat quietly for a few minutes, then Curtis said, "At least we didn't use spray paint."

Officer Palmer returned with our identification and the registration. "Just what is your association with the McGovern campaign?" he asked, moving the flashlight from my face to Curtis's.

Curtis immediately answered. "I have none, Officer."

"I am a member of the national staff of McGovern for President," I announced.

"Well, I don't care whose national staff you are a member of, because there have been two other reports of defaced city property within the last hour and I have a feeling you boys had something to do with it."

Curtis and I looked at each other. We had the right to remain silent—and we were using it.

"Listen, boys. I am willing to forget about this whole incident if, within the next two hours, *every one* of those posters comes down and the signs are restored to their previous condition. You got that?"

"Yes, Officer, we certainly do," I said, as Curtis nodded vigorously.

"And, boys, I have your names and addresses. So no running off. You got it? If I ever again find you boys in this town screwing with our property or speeding or trying to race up to the hills, you will be talking to a judge. And we have some disagreeable judges in these parts. You got that?"

"Yes, Officer," we said in unison.

"You got two hours."

We needed half that. We were back at the headquarters at about 1:30 a.m. We hadn't said much on the return tour of Whittier, other than what was necessary to recall precisely where targets One and Two were located.

As Curtis started his car's engine for the return trip to college, he rolled down the window and said, "We were stymied in achieving our full objective, but for ninety minutes we changed the dynamics of this election here in the Land of Milhous. Onward!"

And he drove off.

I went into headquarters, grabbed a beer, drank it, and lay down on the couch for a few hours of sleep. I awoke at 6 a.m. and went across the street to McDonald's for a cup of coffee. I generally eschewed this establishment because Ray Kroc, the company's owner, had given a million bucks to Nixon's Committee to Re-Elect the President. (It was known as CREEP— yes, that was the name. And the Nixonites were actually proud of it.) But it was election morning, and coffee was imperative.

As I walked back into the HQ, the phone rang. It was a volunteer from the Whittier office. "This is Tommy Johnson. I'm the poll watcher at Whittier 103. There's a problem."

"What's up?"

"You know how you told us to check the counters on the machines before the voting starts, to make sure they're set to zero?"

"Yeah?" I didn't like the sound of this, especially since it was six-thirty and I hadn't drunk more than 10 percent of my Golden Arches java.

"Machine Number Two here is set to Nixon 183, McGovern 0."

"What?"

"I talked to the election judge and she claims that it was from the absentees. But the absentees are not counted until the polling closes, right?"

"That's my understanding, but even so, it defies logic that we wouldn't get at least one vote." Then again, getting one vote in Whittier would have rated as a moral victory.

I started to go through the pile of paper on my desk to find the number of our election-day attorney.

"And this is one of the college precincts," Tommy added.

"I'll call the campaign attorney. I'll have him call you. You stall voting with that machine until he talks to the judge. What's your number?"

He gave me the number of the phone booth in the church that was serving as a polling place.

I hung up and called the central L.A. campaign headquarters.

The attorney immediately saw the urgency of the issue. "I need to call this fellow Johnson at the precinct. But we will need a law enforcement officer to go over and confirm the count so that we have another witness. Ideally, a member of the local police. Call the Whittier Police Department to report the irregularity."

"You want me to call the Whittier Police Department? Uhh . . . I don't . . . think . . . that's such a good idea. I think someone local should do it. Someone who lives there."

"Maybe, but there's no time. The polls open in fifteen minutes. We need to get a cop, ideally with a camera, over there immediately. I'll call Johnson. You call the cops. Talk in fifteen minutes."

I had hoped Bowermaster would arrive by 6:30—he'd make the call. But aside from me and my bad coffee, the office was empty. I called information, got the number for the Whittier PD, and dialed.

"Whittier Police. Officer Palmer speaking."

"Yes, yes. Officer Palmer. I am calling to report election irregularities and possible fraud at Whittier election Precinct 103. Apparently, the machines are not set to zero for all candidates, as required by law."

"What do you mean? What are you talking about?"

"The voting machines at Precinct 103 need to be at zero for all candidates before the voting begins. But machine Number Two is set to Nixon 183, McGovern 0."

"Slow down. Who is this? And where is this? What's this about?"

"Whittier 103. Near the campus."

"And your name, please."

"Uhh . . . huh?"

"Your name, please."

"Rick Ri . . ." I coughed over the second syllable of my last name.

"Didn't catch that."

"Rick Ri . . ." This time I cleared my throat.

"Listen, son. Can you just tell me your last name?"

"Ridder. Rick Ridder. R-I-D-D . . ."

"I don't need you to spell it."

"Sorry."

"Say, don't I know you from somewhere?"

"Uhh . . . let's just say we've met before."

"You're the kid I pulled over. Victor Ridder is the name on your driver's license, right?"

"Right. But now I need you or someone to go down and see that they reset the counter on machine Number Two at Precinct 103 before the polls open, which they're supposed to do in five minutes!"

By this time, I was speaking as fast as I'd been driving six hours earlier.

"Slow down, son. You want us to do what?"

"Make sure the count is set to zero in polling booth Number Two in Whittier voting precinct 103, which is just off the Whittier College campus. "

"I still don't understand what this is all about, but we'll send someone down this morning to check it out."

"No, you've got to do it now! Before they start voting."

"Listen, kid. I cut you a big break earlier. Don't push me on this. We'll get down there."

The second after he hung up, the other line lit up. I answered. It was the attorney.

"I spoke with the election judge. After I threatened a Temporary Restraining Order and told her the cops are coming down—they are coming, right?—she backed down and said she would reset the counter. Not a very cooperative person. She acted as if it was her civic duty to set the counter at 183 for Nixon."

"I'm not sure when the cops will get there. They weren't very responsive to my claims."

"As long as they get down there soon. Let me know if there's any more craziness."

He hung up and I didn't hear anything further until about 6 p.m., when Tommy called to tell me the police finally arrived and were following up on some voter-fraud accusation from the morning. They left upon hearing from the precinct election judge that "Everything was fixed."

By that time, the results from the East Coast were in and, for all I knew, the McGovern count on machine Number Two was still zero. In any event, I think I can safely say that 183 possibly fraudulent votes in Whittier, California, hometown of President Richard M. Nixon, did not have a material effect on the 1972 presidential election.

• • •

In the fall of 1973, I was a college student in Middlebury, Vermont.

It was a Wednesday night like any other college Wednesday night, the night when the following weekend's debauchery is two long days away and the hangover from the liberties of the weekend prior has finally subsided. I had been at the library, having been privy to, but not a participant in, a sexual encounter in the stacks holding the *Congressional Record*. I wasn't sure of the precise extent of this bibliocoupling, but from all the huffing and puffing and competing cries of, "We shouldn't be doing this here" and "Nobody will see us—who the hell reads the *Congressional Record*?" it was clear that the library stacks were a source of more than academic research.

Upon returning to my dorm room, I found a note taped to the door in my roommate's script: "Call Paul Summitt. Call collect. Call first thing in the morning. CApital-2-6894. Area code 202. Washington, D.C."

"CA-2"? I bit my lip, remembering something from the McGovern campaign: CApital-2 was a Senate number. But who was Paul Summitt? I racked my brain, going through faces and names the way sophomore guys go through the freshman facebook looking for the new hot girls.

Nothing. Nada. Zip. Zero.

Wait. Maybe it was Paul Sullivan, my boss during the McGovern campaign in Oregon and California. The Hawaiian Hammer, the king of the unannounced drop-in, Torquemada in a flowered shirt. My roommate might have screwed up the message—as was his tendency.

Sullivan must be in Washington. Now, why was he calling me?

I awoke the next morning and headed to the dorm floor phone to place the collect call. "Select Committee. May I help you?"

I dropped the receiver. I picked it back up.

The telephone operator spoke in the nasal tone they spend hours teaching at the operator academy: "We have a collect call for a Mr. Paul Sullivan from a Mr. Victor "Rick" Ridder. Will he accept the call?"

"I'm sorry, but there is no Paul Sullivan here."

So, Sullivan hadn't left the beaches of Waikiki after all.

I spoke up. "How about Paul . . . Summitt?"

"Mr. Summitt is interviewing a witness right now. May I take a message?"

Interviewing a witness.

I took a deep breath. "Yes. Uhh . . . tell Mr. Summitt that Mr. Victor Ridder returned his call."

"I'll do that, Mr. Ridder. Good-bye."

"Wait. Don't go."

"Yes, Mr. Ridder?"

"What select committee is this?"

"This is the Senate Select Committee on Presidential Campaign Activities."

She hung up while I mumbled, "That's what I was afraid of."

The Watergate Committee. Senator Sam Ervin's star chamber. What could the Watergate Committee want from me? I was clean. I was honest. I'd never had a brush with the law.

Wait. Whittier. "McGovern for President."

A harmless prank. Or . . . was it a dirty trick that had gotten the attention of the feds? We'd defaced the sign welcoming Americans to the hometown of their president. The cop had said he wasn't going to report us if we removed our handiwork.

I needed to think and think fast. *Everybody in politics pulls pranks,* I told myself. Wait—that sentiment was the manifestation of the Watergate mentality in me! I was sinking to Republican levels of moral turpitude.

But, I'm a Democrat. Maybe they just want to question me on some other case. Yeah, that must be it. But what?

Time for my history class, featuring a lecture on Warren Harding's Teapot Dome scandal. Every time the professor mentioned the word *prison,* my hands shook. The clink. The hoosegow. The pen. Do they have Curtis, too? Could he have blabbed that it was my idea?

The class ended. "Hey man," said my friend Charley, "during class you looked like you had just been sentenced to six months on the rack. What's the matter with you, anyway?"

Charley stared into my eyes. I stared back. I tried to blink. My eyelids weren't working. "Well," I said, "I suppose somebody's got to know."

"What happened? You get called to the dean's office? Your parents pulling the plug on you?"

"I got a call from the Watergate Committee."

"Ridder! The Watergate Committee! Wow! I thought there was something desperate about you."

Charley kept shouting. Other members of the class encircled us.

"I didn't do anything," I said, not that I was sure of it.

"Let's get out of here," I said to Charley. We pushed our way through the crowd and headed to the dorms.

We kept walking. Charley kept talking. "Ervin doesn't call you up for nothing. You must be in it real big. Just what were you doing back there for McGovern?"

"It wasn't Ervin," I said. "It was a guy called Paul Summitt."

"What did he say?"

"I haven't talked with him yet. I have to call him back."

"When?"

"Right now."

"Oh, good. I want to watch this."

"This isn't a spectator sport."

"Oh, come on. You're going to need a witness."

I was in the soup already—what did I have to lose?

"All right, Charley boy. Let's go."

We walked up to my room without speaking. I was trying to come up with something to say to Summitt—some language that would enable me to hold on to a speck of my dignity. *Stay on message*—yeah, that's it. That's what Westwood would tell me: just keep repeating the message. But what's my message? I didn't do it? I was just the driver?

Charley was no doubt hoping for disaster, something to stare at the way you can't take your eyes off a wreck at the side of the road.

My hands were shaking again. I felt the first beads of sweat on my forehead. I put the dime in the slot and waited for the operator to answer.

Charley watched. "Ridder, you look like you just flunked out of school and now you have to tell your parents you're comin' home."

The phone rang and I told the operator I was making a collect call. A male voice came on the line. "Operator, we'll accept the call. Mr. Ridder?"

I answered in my most dignified voice—an octave below normal. "Yes. Mr. Summitt?"

"Yes, this is Paul Summitt. Mr. Ridder, before we begin—you do know who we are, don't you?"

"Uhh, yeah, yeah," I stuttered. "You're the, uh, Watergate Committee, right?"

"Yes, that is correct. Mr. Ridder. Have you told anyone about this phone call?"

I looked at Charley who still had a silly grin on his face. "Yeah, my friend Charley. Charley Snowden."

"That's fine, Mr. Ridder, and I'm sure that other friends will know. But the content of this discussion will be confidential. It must remain between you and me, Mr. Ridder—and, of course, the committee. Is that clear?"

"Is this on the record?" I asked.

"Yes, anything you say could be used in the ongoing investigation of the Select Committee. But only you and I and the committee will know about it for now."

It was on the record, but no one knew except Summitt. In other words, I could disappear—and no one would ever find out what had been said or what Turkish prison cell I'd been thrown into until Summitt's notes found their way to the National Archives in the next millennium.

"Now, Mr. Ridder, is there anybody with you at this time?"

I looked at Charley, whose look of glee at my distress had been tempered by paranoia at the mention of his name. So I mentioned it again. "Yes," I said, "Charley is here. Charley Snowden. S-N-O-W—"

"I don't need you to spell it, Mr. Ridder. We're not interested in this Charley—"

"Snowden."

"Would you ask Mr. Snowden to leave the room?"

"Actually, I don't have a phone in my room. This is the dorm phone."

"No one can be there. No one can hear our conversation, Mr. Ridder. There have been too many leaks associated with this investigation already. We can't afford any more."

*My witness—gone.*

"Okay. Hang on a second." I cupped my hand over the receiver and leaned down to Charley. "Charley, man, you've gotta split."

"What the hell for?"

"Security, man, security."

Charley didn't budge.

"Leaks, man. This stuff is confidential."

"Yeah, and who am I going to leak it to? The college newspaper? Tell him I'm your lawyer. I am in pre-law."

"Charley, man, I can't *begin* this thing by lying. Besides, if you're my lawyer, I'd better pack my bags for Leavenworth right now."

He scowled. "All right, I'll go, but only if you promise to tell me everything—and I mean everything—afterward."

"He's gone, Mr. Summitt."

"Well then, Mr. Ridder. Let's begin, shall we?"

As though I had a choice.

"Mr. Ridder, you worked on the McGovern campaign, is that correct?"

173

"That is correct."

*Just answer the questions*, I told myself. *Never elaborate.* I'd heard that on some cop show.

"Mr. Ridder, you worked security at the Doral Hotel during the 1972 Democratic Convention in Miami, is that correct?"

"Yes, that is correct."

"You worked on the sixteenth floor of that hotel?"

"Right."

"What were your responsibilities on the sixteenth floor, Mr. Ridder?"

"My primary job was to make sure that nobody without a blue or red button made it past me—unless of course, he or she was pretty well known."

"Mr. Ridder, a blue or red button?"

"Yes, they were security badges. Someone with a blue button could go anywhere. A red button restricted you to the sixteenth floor."

"I see. Mr. Ridder, what other duties did you have?"

"I answered phones in the Boiler Room. It was the political operations room."

"Oh. Very well, Mr. Ridder. What was on the seventeenth floor?"

"The seventeenth floor? The senator and his top aides."

"That would be Senator McGovern, is that correct?"

*Damn, he is literal.*

"Yes, that's correct," I sighed.

"Mr. Ridder, did you have access to that floor?"

"Not really. I was a red button. But I did make it up there a few times to clear individuals through to the seventeenth floor."

"Very well, Mr. Ridder. Is there anything else you wish to say concerning your duties?"

"No." *Never elaborate.*

So far no mention of the Whittier signs. No doubt everything to this point was intended to lower my guard.

"Mr. Ridder, does the name Michael McMinoway mean anything to you?"

"Let me see. Michael Mac . . . what?"

"McMinoway."

"Can't say as I know him, although it does sound familiar."

"Familiar?"

"Maybe I saw it in the press."

"Yes, that is possible. Anything more?"

"Wait a minute," I said, and snapped my fingers. *McMinoway*. I did know that name. This third degree wasn't about vandalism in California. It was about espionage. "Was he that spy?"

"I'm asking the questions, Mr. Ridder."

"Sorry."

"Mr. Ridder. Are you sure you don't remember a McMinoway working on the sixteenth floor as a security agent?"

"I don't remember. Maybe. Could you tell me where he's from?"

"Excuse me?"

"Well, you see, sir, I'm terrible with names, but I can always remember people by where they're from."

"I'm not sure what he would have told you as to his place of residence. But let me give you a description. About five-ten, one-sixty, darkish complexion, black hair."

"Okay. I think I remember a guy that fits the description."

"So you now think you do remember a McMinoway?"

"*A* McMinoway? Yes. Now that we've discussed it, I do remember *a* McMinoway."

"Mr. Ridder, what were his duties on the sixteenth floor?"

"He was a button checker, but he didn't have access to the Boiler Room."

"He didn't? Why not?"

"Only a couple of people were supposed to go in. And certainly not this guy. This guy was strange."

"Strange? What do you mean, strange?"

"He kept trying to get into the Boiler Room, even after I told him he wasn't supposed to."

"Yes?"

"Yes. He tried to get upstairs, too."

"To the seventeenth floor?"

"Right."

"Hmm."

This interrogator was playing his cards close to the vest. But I could tell that his level of interest had just shot up the way the mercury in a room rose when the gym rats saw the women's ski team show up for their workout.

"How long did you work with him?" he asked.

"Well . . . I guess he started on Sunday afternoon . . . and I demoted him to the third floor on Monday."

"Why would you do that, Mr. Ridder?"

"Like I said, he was acting strange. And then Gene Pokorney, who ran the McGovern primary campaigns in Wisconsin and Texas, said he thought the guy worked for the secretary of state of Texas, who was opposed to McGovern."

"Mr. Rid—"

"That's when I thought . . ."

"Mr. Rid—"

". . . that this guy might be a Humphrey spy. So on Monday—"

"Before we get into any of this, Mr. Ridder, are you sure that this guy was McMinoway?"

"I think so."

"Mr. Ridder, you have leveled some pretty high charges against this man. This man could be charged with a felony. You should be certain of his name. "

"Felony?"

"Now, are you absolutely sure that the man you are speaking of is McMinoway?"

"Well, umm . . ."

And then I remembered. The damning detail.

"Mr. Summitt, did this guy have short curly hair—I mean, *really* short, curly hair?"

He sighed again. No, the last sigh had never ended; it just continued. "Could you hold on a moment, Mr. Ridder? I'll see if we have *anything* more."

He put me on hold. I could only speculate as to what he was saying to his compatriots. Clearly, I was mixed up in something dangerous.

"Mr. Ridder, he did have short black hair at the time."

"Then it was him! I knew it!"

"Mr. Ridder, why the hair?"

"It was too short. It was a dead giveaway. Nobody in the McGovern campaign had short hair. And I mean nobody. And, he wore a tie. None of the staff wore ties in Miami in August. It was a regimental tie, striped, like he'd bought it at the Brooks Brothers Prep Shop. Dead giveaway."

"You could tell all this from a tie?"

"Sure could. The other thing was that McMinoway wore a white shirt. Not even the senator wore white shirts. This McMinoway didn't look like a McGovern person. Didn't act like a McGovern person."

"Let's begin again. Saturday morning, Mr. Ridder. What were you doing? And how, if at all, was McMinoway involved?"

"Saturday was simply setting up the security table, distributing the red and blue buttons. Getting to know people."

"Did you meet McMinoway on Saturday?"

"I think I first saw him on Sunday afternoon."

"Good. What happened on Sunday?"

"Not much. I had my crew of people with me."

"Your crew? At age nineteen, you had a 'crew'?"

"How did you know my age?"

"Campaign records. Your crew?"

He knew more about me than I knew. I had to be very careful.

"Yes, I did have a crew," I said.

"How had you gotten those people together?"

"Friends, mostly, although some were assigned to me."

"Okay. On Sunday, did you notice anything about McMinoway?"

"Not much. His short hair, his white shirt, maybe that he was from California. Not much else."

"Why California?"

"All the weirdos in the McGovern campaign came from California."

"Did you ever find out if he *was* from California?" Summitt asked.

"Yeah. I asked for his references in the campaign and he gave me only California organizers from the primary."

"Did you pick him for the job?"

"Hell, no! He wormed his way into the position."

"Could you be more specific, Mr. Ridder?"

"Political campaigns are full of leeches—you know, people who tag along."

*Freeloaders, clueless activists, political wannabes, and a few neverweres.*

"I went to get some coffee and when I returned, he was working. We were always short of personnel. You've got to remember that it was a twenty-four-hour operation. He probably slid in with the rest of the characters. He seemed to be acquainted with the methods we were using."

"Okay. Sunday. Five p.m. Mr. McMinoway was there. What, other than his original appearance, made you think he might be a spy?"

"Occasionally, we got messages for the seventeenth floor. You had to go up a flight of stairs to the Secret Service. It was a pain in the ass to go upstairs—but McMinoway seemed to volunteer all the time to take messages there. I've never seen anything like it. He was always trying to go to the seventeenth floor."

"That's where McGovern and his top aides were, right?"

"Right."

"Okay, Mr. Ridder. Now: Monday. What was it that caused you to fire him?"

"I didn't fire him. I just demoted him down to the third floor."

"If you knew he was a spy, why didn't you fire him right off?"

"I *thought* he was a spy. I didn't say that I was absolutely *certain* he was a spy. I figured, either way, if he worked security downstairs, it would be safe. There wasn't anything important on the third floor. Hell, if nothing else, he could stuff envelopes."

"I see. Mr. Ridder. Now, were there any other reasons why you . . . demoted him?"

"He was still always trying to get into the Boiler Room. I simply couldn't have him under my command."

"Your command?"

"I *was* chief of security for the sixteenth floor." I was standing by my story.

"One last question, Mr. Ridder. Is there any possibility that Mr. McMinoway could have watched television with George McGovern at any time during the convention?"

"Maybe that's what he was doing upstairs. . . . But no, I don't think the Service would have let him stay up there for more than a minute."

"So you don't think that it's possible that he watched television with George McGovern at any time during the convention?"

"Hang on . . . yeah. Yeah! Tuesday night, the senator came down from the seventeenth floor to congratulate everybody in the Boiler Room and he stayed and watched TV with us. McMinoway was probably there."

"Mr. Ridder, when did you just say McGovern came down?"

"To the best of my recollection, it was Tuesday. Yeah, Tuesday he came down to watch George Wallace with us."

"Mr. Ridder, I thought you had demoted McMinoway *Monday* afternoon. Why was he on the sixteenth floor on Tuesday night?"

Snagged. This guy was nothing if not tenacious. Now I was caught, ensnared in my web of hazy remembrances.

"I don't know," I said, slightly panicked. "Maybe he wasn't there. Maybe I fired him Wednesday. I don't recollect . . ."

"Mr. Ridder, I need to know what day you demoted him."

"I *think* it was Monday."

"Mr. Ridder, this is important. Can't you try to recollect?"

"I don't know."

"By 'I don't know,' are you asserting that you're certain that you *can't* recollect?"

"Uhh . . ."

"Or, alternatively, are you saying that you don't know if you *can* recollect?"

"I'm not . . ."

"It's an important difference, Mr. Ridder."

I was nodding silently, but for the moment no words would come.

"Mr. Ridder, I feel that I should warn you: you have leveled some pretty serious charges against this man. You seem to remember some odd things: his clothes, his hair length, that he was always running upstairs. But, Mr. Ridder, you don't remember what day you fired him?"

"I'm trying to remember."

I wiped the sweat off my forehead—I felt like a one-man monsoon.

"Mr. Ridder, I hope you recollect fast."

"Listen, I was really tired that night and . . ."

"Mr. Ridder, let me be perfectly clear. What you have said in our conversation could be used in a Senate hearing. Let me repeat: a Senate hearing. You could be called to testify. And let me tell you, Mr. Ridder, that no United States senator is going to let you get by if you say that you were tired."

"Maybe I did fire him on Wednesday. I don't know."

I was floundering. What was the worse they could hang on me? Some kind of perjury? Memory failure? Could I land in federal prison? No beer for eighteen months to four years.

"Mr. Ridder, Wednesday is two days' difference from Monday, as per your original story. Can you account for that discrepancy?"

"I'm not sure . . ."

"Mr. Ridder, is there any reason that you might have fired Mr. McMinoway on Monday, as opposed to Wednesday?"

"Let me think. Hmm. Monday. Well, at that point, we were just trying to go into the California challenge, and . . ."

"The California challenge?

"This was a challenge by Hubert Humphrey to McGovern's taking all the delegates in California."

"Okay, Mr. Ridder. Let's go back to Monday."

"Monday, yeah. On Monday, we were dealing with the California challenge."

"Okay. Continue."

"I think that I might have wanted him out of there so that he wouldn't hear our plans."

"But if that was Monday, why was he on the sixteenth floor on Tuesday, watching television with Senator McGovern?"

"Maybe he wasn't there. I don't know. I can't say."

"Mr. Ridder, I'm going to need more than that."

"I'm not certain what day. I'm not . . . I'm not John Dean, you know."

"Mr. Ridder, did you demote McMinoway on Monday or on Wednesday?"

"I don't know!" I shouted.

"Mr. Ridder, I should warn you that you will probably be subpoenaed to appear before the Senate Select Committee on Presidential Campaign Activities, where you will testify under oath. Let me tell you right now that Mr. Sam Dash, the committee's majority counsel, doesn't look lightly on people with poor memories."

This investigator was trying some cheap intimidation tactic on me, less crude than a cop's nightstick to the ribs, but no less effective.

"But, I . . . I didn't do anything. . . . Did I?"

"You have made serious allegations of political espionage. I suggest you have things together soon."

"But, I don't know what happened."

"Mr. Ridder, you claimed you did earlier." Summitt paused. "Mr. Ridder, let me leave you with this. In the next few days, I suggest that you refresh your memory on the events that occurred between July 8, 1972, and July 11, 1972. Is that clear?"

"Yeah. You bet. Anything you want."

"Very good. Now, Mr. Ridder, where will you be for the next couple of days?"

"I'm going to visit my sister in Boston."

"Do you have a number where we might be able to reach you? We may need you in Washington on Monday. It is good that you will be in Boston. It will be easier for you to get down here."

I gave him the number.

"Mr. Ridder, I need not remind you that this conversation is strictly confidential. The committee appreciates your cooperation, Mr. Ridder. We will be in touch. Have a good day."

He hung up.

I returned to my room and put on a record of Janis Joplin singing "Ball and Chain." I fell onto my bed. Charley walked in, smiling.

"Well, man, so you talked to the feds. What happened?"

"I can't tell you."

"What do you mean, you can't tell me?"

"Top secret. Confidential."

"But I'm your best friend."

"No, Charley."

"Aw, come on. One little secret?"

"Forget it."

I left for Boston immediately, cutting Criminal Sociology 102. It was comforting driving the four hours—no phones, no pesky friends. Just me and my memory.

By Sunday, I was certain I had demoted McMinoway on the Wednesday of the Convention. That meant I could answer the question of why he was with McGovern on Tuesday night. But was it the truth?

When I returned to school late Sunday afternoon, there were two notes on my door. One said to call Charley immediately. The other said to call Summitt immediately. I called Summitt. The number on the note turned out to be his direct line.

"Mr. Ridder, Sam Dash and the Committee have decided that we will not need your testimony on Tuesday, so you will not be subpoenaed. The committee did not find you to be a sufficiently credible witness."

"What? Not credible? Everything I told you happened. I'd swear to it, just to lock up that little spying Humphrey bastard." The weekend away had given me a new assertiveness.

"Mr. Ridder, we were willing to go with the haircut, the tie, the shirt, the Texas connection—incidentally he has no Texas connection—and all the rest, as evidence for why you thought he was a spy, but it's your actions in California that had everyone rethinking your credibility."

"The McGovern posters? On the 'Welcome to Whittier Hometown of President Nixon' signs? The cop said he wouldn't put it on my record!"

"What are you talking about? A report in a file in California says that you charged that there was voter fraud in Whittier. One hundred and eighty-three for Nixon. Zero for McGovern. That's not remotely credible. Even if they were trying to steal the election, no one would have set a machine at one hundred eighty-three to zero. They would give McGovern at least ten to cover their tracks. It's not even remotely believable. Fred Thompson would be all over this. You are just not credible. I gotta go. Have a good evening, Mr. Ridder, and remember that this is all confidential."

He hung up. I dialed Charley and told him to meet me in my room. He came right over.

"So, you headed to DC? Are you their next victim?"

I shook my head. "I am not a credible witness. "

"You're not? So you're not in trouble?"

"I can't talk about it. But no."

"Well, that's too bad, I guess."

I noticed that he was holding an envelope in his hand.

"Hey Charley, what's that?"

"Oh, yeah, it's for you. I picked it up at your mailbox. It's from the dean's office."

He handed me the envelope. I opened it.

"It's from the dean's office all right," I said.

"What's it about?"

"They want anyone who has knowledge of sex in the library the other night to come forward." I paused, looked at Charley and said, "I signed in to the library that night."

"Do you know anything about that? Sex in the library. Wow!"

"I know nothing. Nothing," I said, crumpling the letter and tossing it into the trash bin next to my desk.

• • •

Michael McMinoway appeared before the Watergate Committee the next day to discuss his role as a spy for the Nixon and Humphrey campaigns, although in Miami he was working strictly for Nixon.

• • •

Only six weeks before election day in 1992, my candidate, Rep. Ben Nighthorse Campbell, had been leading by more than twenty points in his U.S. Senate race against Terry Considine, his Republican opponent. But at that point, two weeks before the polls opened, his lead had shrunk to less than five points.

The campaign consulting team held a conference call to determine our next move. We could respond to our opponent's charge that our candidate had missed congressional votes by pointing out that our opponent had a worse absentee record in the Colorado State Senate than our candidate did in the U.S. House. Or we could present to the taxpaying voters of Colorado the evidence that our opponent had failed to pay property taxes on one of his business investments for three years.

The polling showed that the response ad on attendance was the most effective (voters hate hypocrisy), but only as long as voters were hearing from our opposition about our candidate's attendance record. Why? Because voters don't remember what a candidate's ad said for more than three days. So, if we came on with our response, and their attack was *not* still on the air, our bombshell would be a dud.

As I headed down I-25 listening to the conference call, it was clear that our team of wizened campaign consultants was flummoxed. Should we run the hypocrisy ad in the hope that the opposition would stick with that attack, or should we hit the other campaign on the property tax issue? It was 5:30 p.m. and our media consultant, Joe Slade White, needed to know what we were going to do by 10:30 that night so the ad could be produced and delivered to the stations by noon the next day.

After serious back and forth, our pollster, Mark Mellman, suggested we take a break, think about it, and reconvene at ten that evening for a decision. We agreed.

At 6 p.m. I walked into a TV studio to produce a TV ad on stopping the Spring Bear Hunt in Colorado, an initiative placed on the 1992 Colorado ballot by animal-rights groups to halt the hunting of bears in the Spring, after hibernation. We could only afford three hours of studio time, so our editing session was to be short.

About halfway through the session, I was pacing back and forth cogitating more about the Senate race than baby bears when I saw a small stack of white papers next to the production console. Always curious, I walked over, picked them up, and glanced at them.

They were TV spot scripts. They were our Senate opponent's TV scripts. They were scripts of TV spots that had been produced in this studio immediately before our editing session.

I quickly stuffed them into my briefcase. Then I saw the wastepaper basket, brimming with similar white sheets of paper.

When the studio engineer stepped out of the room for a phone call, Larry Bulling, who was working on the bears account with me, performed a mini dumpster-diving activity. In among the Coke cans and Snickers wrappers, we found more evidence of the direction our opponents were headed.

On the ten o'clock conference call, I let the debate among the team go for a couple of minutes before saying, "I know precisely what they are going to do."

"And how do you know what they're going to do?" Mark Mellman asked.

I described our fortuitous discovery, then read them the scripts we'd found on the console and in the trash. They further detailed Ben Nighthorse Campbell's absenteeism.

The campaign responded with a very fine TV spot on the distance Terry Considine traveled to work at the Colorado State Capitol—six miles—and the distance Ben Nighthorse Campbell traveled to work at the U.S. Capitol—1,900 miles—and who had the worse attendance record: Terry Considine.

Our numbers moved back upwards four days later. We followed with the property tax hit, and—game over. We won.

A week after the election, the local newspapers sponsored a bipartisan election recap luncheon where Joannie, my partner, told the story about finding the scripts. She ended her comments before a stunned Republican campaign team with the words, "You know, you Republicans should learn the benefits of recycling."

# RULE #17

# NOBODY LIKES OUTSIDERS
# (FROM WASHINGTON, D.C., OR ANYWHERE ELSE).

What is the one sentence I hear most as a political operative? "We don't do it like that here." That's the reflex reply of anyone who wants to demonstrate territorial hegemony.

I once returned from an overseas trip to a precinct meeting to plan the get-out-the-vote effort in my neighborhood. One of my neighbors asked me to recommend a course of action because I was a professional in politics. I stood up and described a program that had been implemented elsewhere in my state. Before I could finish, I was told by another of my neighbors, "Well that's fine for north of the park, but we don't do that here south of the park."

I sat down, knowing the park to which he referred was one block by one block in size.

The best way to circumvent that line of attack is to ask first, "How do you do it here?" That question motivates everyone to give their best advice and you are then able to fashion the precise plan you'd initially prepared, but using their own words, ideas, and conventions. It's called *buy-in*.

That's ideal. Many times, it's better to hide and let your clients (who are local) carry the plan as their own. This may mean staying completely out of sight and not letting anyone, including senior members of the campaign or party, know that you're there.

A client of mine in Sydney, Australia, asked me to remain secreted either in my hotel room or in a specific area in the headquarters over a six-week period. This was to ensure that friends, the opposition, and the press, did not recognize me on the streets of Sydney. Further, they never had me speak with the actual client, the premier of New South Wales, so that he could claim deniability when he was asked about "hiring an American consultant."

On another occasion, I was about to board a flight to Sydney to help in a campaign to make Australia a republic—by kicking out the Queen—when my cellphone rang. I answered. It was the Australian client.

"Where are you?" a breathless voice asked across the international phone lines.

"I'm in Denver, boarding a flight on my way to Sydney. Be there in fourteen hours," I said.

"Oh, thank God. Don't get on that plane. A reporter is claiming there's an American in Sydney now, helping the Republic movement, which will make everyone believe we want an American-style presidency."

"What? That makes no—"

"Don't come. I now have complete deniability. I will call later." He hung up.

I never did fly to Sydney for that particular cause, but I did give some advice over the phone. They lost.

Even if you are operating *sub rosa*, whenever an outsider comes into town—whether from across the state or across an ocean—people get suspicious. In some part, it is because they are afraid that the new operative does not understand the culture, the traditions, the geography, or the local sports. They may also be afraid that the outside operative will highlight the campaign's deficiencies, to everyone's chagrin.

This apprehensiveness seems to be particularly acute when the outsider comes from Washington. Such consultants are met with anticipation and dread. Everyone knows it will be a learning experience, but no one knows who will be the beneficiary of the lessons.

• • •

In May of 1972, I was the first McGovern national staffer dispatched to New Mexico to meet with the McGovern state chair, assess the campaign, and stay on the ground to assist the chair until the national state coordinator arrived in two weeks.

At the Albuquerque airport, I was met by a volunteer in his mid-twenties who drove me in his VW bus to the McGovern headquarters near the

University of New Mexico. The HQ was in a Victorian-period home with natural wood throughout. McGovern and antiwar posters adorned the walls.

I felt comfortable. These were my kind of people. This was my kind of operation—a western version of Madison, Wisconsin, in 1972.

I was ushered into the office of the New Mexico state chair, where a smallish man with dark hair and a mustache sat behind a very large antique desk. I came in smiling, with my hand extended in greeting. "Good to meet you, Mr. Sanders," I said.

He did not move from the seat. He did not smile. He did not extend his arm. He simply asked, "Who sent you?"

I knew, from my 10,000 miles of roadwork, not to say, "I'm here from Washington." So, I answered with the truth, sort of.

"I came from the western regional office in Salt Lake."

"Salt Lake. So Westwood sent you?" he asked, referring to the McGovern national co-chair, Jean Westwood, who worked out of Salt Lake.

"Yes, Jean asked me to come down."

"Why?"

"Why? Uh, because she thought I could help the campaign here."

"By doing what?"

"Whatever needs to be done. I could help design a field program like the one we had in Oregon. I could work the phones. I could even go up to the Navajo reservation. I speak some Navajo."

I didn't tell Mr. Sanders that the sum total of my Navajo lexicon was twenty words.

Then he said some words that I, in the vastness of my many months in the business of politics, had already heard dozens of times as I entered a state: "We don't like outsiders here."

"I know, I know. I've been in nine states for McGovern, and initially everyone says that. But—"

"But nothing. We're different here."

"I realize that. I will be utterly inconspicuous. I understand that you don't want a story about outside organizers."

"You don't understand. We don't like outsiders here. I don't like outsiders here."

"I understand. I won't be a problem. I went to high school in Arizona and have been through New Mexico often."

As I spoke I looked for a place to sit down. I didn't find one.

"I don't care if your great grandfather was a Navajo chief and your great grandmother was Georgia O'Keeffe. You won't work here. Just get on the plane and go back to Utah. We don't need you, we don't want you. We don't like outsiders here."

"I'm sure there is something I could help with," I said. "Phone banks? Door-to door? I've supervised canvasses all over the country."

"I will tell you one more time, kid. We don't like outsiders here."

"Is there another headquarters, say, in Santa Fe, where I could go work? I don't have to be here in Albuquerque." I was beginning to sweat.

Sanders stood up. His right hand moved toward the top drawer of the desk—I thought he was going to pull out a pad and pencil to write down the address of the Santa Fe office.

Instead of a pad and pencil, he pulled out a large revolver. Pointing at my head, he repeated, "You don't understand. We don't like outsiders here."

I had faced a café owner in West Yellowstone, Wyoming, who literally threw me out of his establishment for my McGovern button, and a pickup truck driver who thought it sport to run me off a road in Idaho for my antiwar bumper-sticker. Political opponents exercising their right to free speech had called me all manner of epithets. But I had yet to encounter a political ally so forthrightly exercising his rights under the Second Amendment.

If this was some form of hazing rite, I had no desire to join the fraternity.

"Could I use the phone?" I asked.

"Sure. Who you calling?"

"Barbara McKenzie," I answered, naming the national western regional director, who was in Washington, DC.

"I knew you were from Washington."

"No, no," I said, my voice quivering, my knees knocking. "It's just that I know that Westwood, who sent me here, is not in Salt Lake at the moment."

I dialed. He continued pointing the gun. I was lucky. Barbara picked up on the first ring.

"Barbara, it's Rick. I'm here in New Mexico."

"Great to hear from you. How's it going there?"

"Great. In fact, it's going so well that they don't need me here."

I am sure that Sanders could hear the voice at the other end say, "What do you mean they don't need you there?"

"They've got it all under control. And—"

"You just got there, for chrissakes! We can't fly you there and pull you out right away."

"I know, I know. But I just got word that there's . . . um . . . a crisis in Utah . . . which . . . um . . . I have to attend to. Really, everything is good here. Really. Really good."

"What goddamn crisis? Nobody has called me from Utah. Besides, Westwood will handle it."

"That's just what I was saying to the chairman here—that Westwood is out of town and I have to go back. I'll call you from Utah."

"But . . ."

I hung up. I informed the New Mexico chairman of the crisis in Utah.

"Yes, they need me back there right away. Good thing I'm not needed here."

He thanked me for dropping by, returned the revolver to the drawer, and shouted at the volunteer to drive me back to the airport in the VW bus.

At the airport, I headed to a phone booth and called McKenzie collect. "What the hell is going on?" she demanded. "You better *not* be at an airport. I will be very disappointed with you if you are. That last phone call—what's going on with you? Have you been drinking? Are you stoned? We sent you there to get the state under control and—"

"He had a gun. Pointed at me."

"What kind of gun?"

"I am not sure of the manufacturer, but it could have been a Colt 45 for all I know. Or a 357 Magnum. Or a German Luger. Or a Smith and Wesson. What the hell do I know about guns? I'm a nice, nonviolent person. I only know that it was a gun of some kind and it was pointed at my head and that he was telling me to leave the state because, as he said, 'We don't like outsiders here.'"

"Was the gun loaded?"

"How the hell should I know? I just know I didn't want to find out."

"Where are you now?"

"At the airport. Where do you want me to go?"

"Utah, I guess."

"I'll take polygamists over gun nuts anytime."

Barbara sighed. "My mistake. We should have sent someone from New Mexico. It's different there."

• • •

For some reason, among Washington-based campaign consultants and candidates, attempting to appeal to the Colorado conservation and environmental communities initiates political malpractice on a grand scale.

There was the U.S. Senate candidate whose media consultant (from Washington) insisted that he demonstrate his commitment to wilderness in Colorado and his own outdoor heritage by donning snowshoes in a television spot. The spot was beautifully shot on a bluebird day with deep snow and snow-capped surrounding peaks. Looking into the camera, the candidate tromped through snow, professing his concern for Colorado's quality of life and the preservation of its natural beauty.

Lovely. Except it was clear that he had never worn snowshoes before. His movements made him look more like a grape-stomper than a practiced mountaineer. Why was he having so much trouble? It turned out that he had the snowshoes on the wrong feet.

Few people noticed—except the very people to whom he was attempting to appeal—the outdoor community. His numbers dropped, but eventually he won a Senate seat. I am told he did not wear snowshoes to his swearing in.

Then there was the Republican U.S. Senate candidate in Colorado whose DC-based consultants included a spectacular photo of a mountain in one of his TV spots while the candidate proclaimed his commitment to Colorado's environment. Unfortunately, his Democratic opponent and his opponent's campaign manager had both climbed the depicted mountain. It was Mt. McKinley—in Alaska, not Colorado. The Republican candidate pulled the ad but the damage had been done. He lost.

Candidates are not the only ones who have such profound geographic myopia. One of the major environmental groups in the U.S., in supporting a candidate and his efforts to make a Colorado canyon a National Monument, produced a TV spot featuring a canyon in Utah. When I called the political director in Washington to point out that they had the wrong canyon in the wrong state and that they should change the ad, his comment was, "No one else has complained. You are the only one. They are all the same out there, right? If we change it, then we're admitting a mistake. Can't do that."

The candidate lost.

# RULE #18

# INTERNATIONAL CAMPAIGNS ARE LIKE ALL OTHER CAMPAIGNS—ALL SCREWED UP.

For American consultants, the only difference between working domestically and working on international campaigns is that when you're abroad, finding a solution to a campaign crisis is hampered by language, protocol, time zones, cultural peccadilloes, and personal security. Accordingly, I have developed a few standard expectations for international engagement.

## 1. NEVER EXPECT ENGLISH TO BE ENGLISH.

Some catch phrases of American politics translate smoothly into slogans usable in the UK or Australia. For instance, "More cops on the street!" becomes "More bobbies on the beat!" "Deadbeats on welfare" becomes "Bums on the dole." But sometimes, the translations are less successful.

I first went to the UK to learn more about door-to-door campaigning. In a nation where television advertising is largely banned, the political parties, particularly the Liberal Democrats, are known for the effectiveness of their door-to-door operations as a means of communicating with voters. Through an old Gary Hart campaign colleague, I received an invitation to witness the Lib Dem canvass program for a by-election in North Yorkshire. I went, watched, and found the party's work extraordinary in its methodological rigor and attention to detail—but something was missing.

Upon returning to the States, I wrote a note to the Lib Dems' campaign management team. "Your door-to-door operations are very strong," I told them, "but you don't make use of the telephone, another powerful vehicle of communications." They wrote back and asked if my telephone-savvy business partner, who was also my wife, could write a manual on the use of the telephone in campaigns in general and in get-out-the-vote efforts in particular.

This was our first big international gig. We put our heads together and came up with a wonderful book, distilling everything we knew about the political applications of Alexander Graham Bell's invention. We were excited. This book would be a big marketing tool; it would give us the cachet we needed to break into the international political marketplace. We planned to put it on the coffee table in our office reception area and give a copy to every potential client. This manual would effectively highlight our capabilities and enhance our credibility.

We copied it to a floppy disk and sent it to London, where the Lib Dems would print it. About six weeks later, a box arrived. We ripped the package open, eager to see our handiwork in print, and there it was, the title emblazoned on the front cover: *A Guide to Knocking Up with Telephones*, by Rick Ridder and Joannie Braden.

Huh . . . okay. We had successfully written a phone-sex manual.

The book was a big hit with the Lib Dems. It never saw the top of our coffee table.

## 2. ENGLISH DOESN'T ALWAYS TRANSLATE TO OTHER LANGUAGES, EITHER . . . OR, WHAT DO YOU MEAN I CAN'T SAY THAT?

Message and language are culturally bound. In other words, if you don't understand the language, the message may become incomprehensible.

I landed in Barcelona with a fifty-slide PowerPoint presentation as the centerpiece of my message and polling presentation. I felt good. We had worked with the client on a poll conducted in the Catalan language, and I felt certain we had nailed the message of the campaign. The key to victory was well detailed and presented, in English, in the PowerPoint.

Fifteen members of the campaign staff and party elders gathered in a university classroom. Each of the fourteen males was seated with his arms folded across his chest. The lone woman stood, hands on hips, at the back of the room.

"This campaign is about leadership," I began. "This campaign is about *new* leadership for Cataluña." Then I began clicking through each of the fifty slides—every one with data supporting the New Leadership message.

At Slide 15, a man raised his hand. It was the North American-educated campaign manager—no doubt wanting to note the brilliance of my concept.

"Yes?" I said.

"Rick, Rick, there is a problem."

Confident in my presentation, I knew that whatever the problem was, it had to be trivial.

"What is that problem?" I asked.

"There is no word in Catalan for leadership."

"Uhh . . . what?"

"In Catalan, we have no word for leadership. And the word closest to your concept of leadership has a negative connotation. It says a person is an arrogant bully."

So I was calling for New Arrogant Bullying. Since Franco had been dead twenty-three years by that time and wasn't running for office, I realized I'd chosen the wrong slogan.

"But, but . . . your team did the translation from the Catalan to English," I said. "And you used the word leadership."

"Yes, yes, that it is true, Rick. But, that was shorthand for a group of words and phrases we tested that might add up to leadership in English."

The room was silent as I looked at my computer screen to determine how many slides of the remaining thirty-five had "leadership" on them. Twenty-five did. I skimmed though the remaining slides, turned off the projector, and waited for the campaign team to dissect the presentation and me.

The first response came from a man who observed, "You know, we do have a Catalan word for 'new.'"

## 3. MAKE SURE TO COLOR INSIDE THE LINES. OR PICK THE RIGHT TREE.

Ah, you say, in foreign countries, elections are enviably more sane than American ones. They are sober affairs in which voters spend weeks educating themselves on the foreign and domestic policy positions of each candidate and party.

Not necessarily.

In most major democracies, colors define parties. Conservative or moderate parties often sport blue. Social liberals, such as the Liberal Democrats of Great Britain, are identified by yellow. Social Democrats in Europe go for red, along with the image of a rose.

In less developed nations, which lack universal literacy, colors are even more critical to party identification. Few South Africans do not recognize the green and black representing Nelson Mandela's Freedom Party.

In New Guinea, the situation is more complicated. In the early nineties, I flew with Bill Hamilton, a leading American political pollster, to Sydney, Australia, where we met with Robert Darlington, who represented the governing party of Papua New Guinea. Over a few "flat whites"— Australia's version of a latte—Darlington said, "I'd like you to help with our re-election campaign."

"We'd be happy to," Bill replied. "What do you want us to do?"

"I need a poll, and quickly. We don't know if our message is resonating, particularly with voters in the upcountry areas."

I was pleased that the first thing he said wasn't, "We need to know if we are ahead or behind." Darlington had his priorities right.

"Sure, we can do this," I said, as Bill raised a skeptical eyebrow. "Tell us a bit about your country."

"Approximately 20 percent of the population lives in the Port Moresby area, and the rest are pretty much scattered. Some citizens reside in a few small towns, but mostly they live in villages of 500 to 1,000 people."

"Okay," I said. "The total population is about five million. So four million are scattered?" I was proud to show that I hadn't flunked sixth-grade math.

"Yes," said Darlington. "They are what we call 'upcountry.'"

"There are roads and highways that reach them, yes?" I said.

"Some roads, yes, but much of the access is by canoe or skiff."

I reached for the next trick in my bag. "No problem. We'll do most of the interviewing by telephone.

"No," said Darlington, in that way-too-British cheery tone of voice. "You can't do that. Less than 15 percent of the population has access to phone service, and they all live in Port Moresby."

Bill was beginning to dissect the intricacies of the problem. "So we are going to have to send our interviewers by canoe to interview the voters face to face."

"Yes," said our host.

"What is the primary language?" I asked. "I'm assuming it's English, because Papua New Guinea, was once ruled by Australia."

"English *is* one of our official languages, but there are more than 800 different languages and dialects spoken. The primary one is Tok Pisin, a sort of pidgin English that is spoken by about 25 percent of our citizens."

"That's not so bad," I said.

"Nearly all of those speakers live in Port Moresby."

"And you said you wanted to poll the upcountry folks," Bill replied.

"Precisely."

"And they speak 799 different languages."

"Correct."

"You're losing me," said Bill. "How will we communicate with these citizens? How will we know how to test their candidate preference? How can we test their acceptance of your message if we have to do it in 800 languages?"

"Trees."

Bill and I both leaned across the table toward our host.

"Trees?" we said in unison.

"Yes. Every political party in Papua New Guinea is associated with a type of tree. A specific species of palm tree might be associated with a conservative party, a coconut tree with a social democratic party, or a banyan tree with the local tribal party. Everyone knows which tree belongs to which party. It's very simple. Candidates place their posters on a specific type of tree to indicate the party with which they are associated."

"How many parties are there?" I asked.

"Ten major parties, but more than seventy small regional and tribal parties."

Again, my math skills were up to the task. "So . . . we will need to be able to identify more than eighty varieties of tree?"

"Ridder," said Bill, "you know anything about forestry?"

"Lots. When I'm in Vermont in late winter, I can tell the difference between an oak and a maple. The maples are the ones with buckets attached."

Bill very cordially turned to Darlington and thanked him for his time, saying, "We will get back to you shortly."

We left. I caught up with Bill a few minutes later at the hotel bar where he was nursing a martini. "So," I said, "what do you think? A little different, huh?"

"A little different? I've been doing this for more than twenty-five years, and this is the first time someone has asked me to conduct a survey in 800 different languages, in an area where there are no phones and no roads, where transportation is by canoe, and where we have to know the party affiliation of trees. Plus, we don't know how much this government has offended the folks upcountry—maybe it's enough that some people might communicate their unfavorable opinion with spears, poison darts, and head shrinking. Every dissatisfied voter could mean an interviewer finds himself in the soup—literally. Do you have any idea what that would do to our Workers' Comp rates?"

"Not to mention how much we would have to pay for interviewer inoculations: typhoid. Malaria. Beriberi," I added.

"This is not for me, Ridder. No 800 languages, no trees, no canoes, no thank you."

He returned to his martini. I stared at my beer. "So," he finally asked, "do you plan on overseeing the field elements of this survey?"

"Hell, no. I have three children."

"Then I suggest we decline the opportunity."

"Good idea."

I called Mr. Darlington to decline the account. I referred him to a deeply loathed Republican competitor.

## 4. PICK THE RIGHT LIBRARY OR THE RIGHT LIBRARIANS.

Before you take on a campaign, whether it's for an initiative, a referendum, or a candidate, you have to do some research. Today, most campaigns conduct exhaustive background research on their issues or candidates to determine what's hidden in the small type or in the college records. As former Nixon and Reagan speechwriter Ken Khachigian put it, "All politics begins in a library." He was right, but the key is to pick the right library and the right librarians.

• • •

A friend of mine once characterized political campaigns in Venezuela as "the longest-lasting floating crap game of all time." Political operations in the early 1990s were marked by a comical lack of management structure, a stunning disregard for credible research, and an almost total reliance on campaign insiders for strategy and tactical advice. Otherwise, they were the model of efficiency.

Joseph Napolitan, the *eminence grise* of international political consulting, brought me in to help him with a particular situation in this foreign country in 1993. "We have a party primary in Venezuela," he told me, "but unlike any previous party primary, we won't be able to use television or radio. Some new party rule. We'll have to do it all by mail and . . . and I don't know what else. I want you and Rich Schlackman to go to Venezuela. Work together to devise a targeting and mail plan."

I met Rich Schlackman, one of America's leading Democratic direct-mail consultants, at the Miami airport for the flight to Caracas. On the plane, I learned that he did not speak a word of Spanish and that we would have to rely initially on my Spanish, learned in high school twenty-plus years previously. No problem, I thought, as long as it was in a place with *cerveza*.

Once we arrived, however, we learned that we would have an interpreter, the U.S.-educated attorney Luis Sanchez. Luis was surprised to learn of our assignment. "You are here to do what?"

"Napolitan sent us down to plan a targeted mail program," Rich said.

"Ah, mail. Yes. Let's talk about that with the rest of the campaign team." Luis walked us into a conference room where four elegantly attired older men sat smoking cigarettes as they discussed the campaign. After we introduced ourselves through our interpreter and sat down, one of the dapper smokers said in Spanish, "So Joe told you to come down? How can we help?"

I smiled, nodded, and began, "*Queremos* . . . uh, *hacer . . . correo. Si, correo.*" Fortunately, Luis stepped in and spared us all from the pain of listening to more of my Spanish. I assume that what he was said roughly corresponded to, "They're here to help us use mail to communicate to the voters."

Whatever Luis said, the smoker at the end of the table nodded and, through Luis, said, "This will not be a problem." Then he asked how much mail we wanted to send.

"Two to three million pieces," Rich said, "assuming each potential primary voter is to receive three pieces of mail." The old man nodded again, then said that he would invite the Venezuelan postmaster general to meet with us that same afternoon.

Rich and I were duly impressed. Luis, however, who was standing well behind the table, was violently shaking his head.

The smoking old man at the end of the table wasn't finished. "Where are you going to get the addresses for these people?" he asked.

"I work with computer databases to select and sort addresses for political mailings," I said, glad for the chance to exhibit my credentials. "I am here to determine if there are computerized lists that we might use."

The old man started to nod his head when one of the others began talking in broken English. "No problem. No problem. The government has a list of every voter in Venezuela. Twenty million names."

"Really? Is it on paper? Or is it computerized?"

"*Sí, sí*. All on computer."

"What's in the file? Does it include name, address, age, party registration?"

"I will call over to the president's office and they will give the details," said the old man at the end of the table, who then stood up and walked to a room next door.

I could hear him making the call. Two minutes after leaving, he returned with a fax in his hand. "Is this what you were looking for?" He handed me the fax. It detailed the file layout of a national voter file.

"Wow," I said. "This is amazing. They have name, address, age, gender, and even party affiliation and vote history. This is great! We rarely get a file in the states with this kind of data. Seventeen million records. So how do we get this file? How much does it cost?"

"I talk to the president. There will be no charge. Tomorrow afternoon will be okay?"

"*Sí, sí*. That would be wonderful," I said.

As Rich and I walked toward the elevator with Luis I asked him, "Why were you shaking your head just now?"

He checked the interior of the elevator to make sure we were alone. "There is no postal service in Venezuela. When I have to send legal documents, I use FedEx."

"So?" Rich said. "You use FedEx to send stuff to the States. What does that prove?"

Luis shook his head. "No. I use FedEx to send stuff across Caracas. The messengers are highly irresponsible and there is no mail system, so I send the letter via FedEx. It goes to Memphis, then comes back to Caracas. That's the only way to be sure that papers are delivered."

"Let me get this straight," I said. "The letter starts in Caracas."

"Right."

"Then it goes to Memphis to a FedEx distribution center. "

"Right."

"Then it comes back to Caracas."

"That is correct."

"And this is the most efficient way of sending documents across town?"

"Exactly."

"I dunno," Rich said. "Let's see what the postmaster general says this afternoon."

After a lunch of Venezuela's national dish, beef, we returned to the conference room with the four members of the campaign strategy team. Soon the postmaster general arrived. A large man with dark, slicked-back hair and olive skin, he was as perfectly dressed as all the other men we'd seen, he listened carefully as Luis translated Rich's description of his mail plan.

"We plan to send two to three million pieces of mail over three weeks," Rich said, "to universes of five-hundred thousand to one million households. Most households will get three pieces of mail. Some will get four."

"No problem," the postmaster general assured us.

"How long will it take for a piece of mail to be delivered?"

"Three days at the most."

"Really? From Caracas to Maracaibo, it takes only three days for a piece of mail to be delivered?"

"Sometimes only two days."

"And how much should we budget per piece—not a letter, but something like this?" Rich pulled out an eleven-by-seventeen one-fold sample of campaign literature—standard size in the U.S. for political mailings.

Luis translated the general's answer: "He says, 'For three million mail pieces we can make a deal. In U.S. currency, eight cents per piece.'"

Satisfied with the price, we agreed to return the next day to pick up the computer tapes with the voter files. As Rich and I left the meeting, Luis was close on our heels. He looked right and left to make sure we were alone, then said, "It's bullshit. You can't send a postcard from Angel Falls and hope that it will ever reach its destination—even if you mail it to someone who lives ten feet from the Falls."

Rich was undaunted. "Luis, the *postmaster general* just told us he could handle three million pieces and that they would arrive in three days. He should know, shouldn't he? At that cost of postage, we can print close to four million with the budget they've got. Let's go have a drink and work this out."

Luis shook his head. The three of us headed to a bar and enjoyed the national drink of Venezuela: Scotch whisky. At that time, per capita, Venezuelans drank more Scotch than any nationality outside of Scotland.

As we received our drinks, Luis pressed his case again. "Not possible. Not going to happen. No way. They can't deliver *three* pieces of mail. Never mind three *million*."

"So why would he say that he *could* deliver the mail when he *can't*?" Rich asked.

"It's cultural. Venezuelans do not want to admit that they can't do something. Look, have you noticed all the newsstands with hundreds of magazines? Newsstands wouldn't exist if the magazines could be delivered to your home."

Rich looked perplexed, then got an idea. "What if we write a letter from the candidate. Mail it to 200 friends of the campaign and ask in the letter that they simply call campaign headquarters when they get it. We could even put money in it as an incentive—say, five dollars."

"Money in it? Bad idea. It will be stolen for sure, and the letter will be trashed." Earlier in the day Luis had told us to take off our watches before leaving the hotel to avoid certain theft. I was beginning to sense a theme. "But the 200 letters? Okay, try it if you don't believe me. Go crazy with it." Luis took a deep breath, shook his head, then ordered one more whiskycito (scotch on the rocks).

The next day, we presented the mail-test suggestion to the campaign team. All agreed it was a good idea except the guy who had called the postmaster general.

We quickly went ahead and wrote the letter, developed a list of 200 friends, and tracked down their addresses—mostly by having the staff call them. I should have seen the need to call most of these "friends" as an ominous sign. But I figured that everyone complains about the post office. Mail gets lost, the price of stamps keeps going up, and the lines to send a package keep getting longer. But the job gets done. *It's the same everywhere. Isn't it?*

We dropped the 200 letters at the post office late that evening and gave specific instructions as to how the campaign should track the phone calls from the mail recipients. We wanted to learn when each person received the letter, which city he or she lived in, and if the letter arrived unopened. Before we left for the airport the next morning we were presented with two large reels of tape with the Venezuela voter file on them

Back in the States, I FedExed the computer tapes to Voter Contact Services, one of the nation's major voter file vendors, and awaited their report. It came three days later in a call from Dennis Dill, the firm's lead programmer. "I've just finished auditing that Venezuelan file for you," he announced.

"Yeah, well?"

"They sent more than seventeen million records, all right. But only thirty thousand are complete. We have name, address, date of birth, gender, party affiliation, and vote history on only thirty thousand of the seventeen million."

"Still, we must have millions with at least name, address, and party affiliation. Since it's a primary, we only need people from the party."

"Way ahead of you. I selected all those with any party affiliation and with a name and address."

"And?"

"Fifty-one thousand names."

"You're telling me that there are only fifty-one thousand names with a complete name and address for anyone with any party affiliation?"

"You got it. But first, let's take the larger problem. Take this fellow here, Juan."

"Okay, Juan. What's his last name?" I asked.

"No last name."

"Just Juan."

"Yep, just Juan. But he does have an address."

"Well, that should be all we need. What's Juan's address?"

"*Bajo de la tienda.*"

"*Bajo de la tienda.* There. *Bajo de la* . . . wait. That means 'below the store.' Below what store? What street? What city?"

"Don't know. Juan is his name. *Bajo de la tienda* is his address. No last name. No street. No city. No state. No party. No date of birth. No vote history. I presume he's male but there is no gender on him, either. We got maybe a hundred thousand with complete names and addresses—tops. The rest are crap."

I hung up and dialed Rich. Rich had just gotten off the phone with Venezuela: after four days in the mail, the campaign had received one phone call acknowledging receipt of our letter. It was from the old man who had called the postmaster general. Ten days later we had another two.

We're still waiting for the other 197.

## 5. THERE WILL BE NO EASY ENTERING, EXITING, OR EXISTING.

James Bond's archenemy, SMERSH, must have recruited the guy who followed me for three days in Ukraine. He wore a navy pea coat, leather gloves, and black work boots, and he was tall enough to play power forward in the NBA. Everywhere I went, he stood fifty yards away. I checked with my client to make sure he had not paid for bodyguard services; I was assured that such services would be supplied only on my request and would be paid for out of my fee. I had made no such request.

Upon departing my Kiev hotel at 5 a.m. to head to the airport, I saw him standing fifty yards from the hotel door, smoking a cigarette. I almost went over to tell him that he was risking esophageal cancer but realized I didn't speak his language. I also doubted he would appreciate the advice.

This guy was far more cordial than the border security men I encountered in Malta. They detained me for ninety minutes, trying to determine the nature of my business in their country. I explained to them that I was a businessman who conducted surveys, or polls, of the Maltese public. "Of course, you understand that my clients' names are confidential," I added. Actually, they didn't understand that, or much of anything else, given their limited knowledge of English and my reciprocal ignorance of Maltese. Our conversation, such as it was, took place while they unpacked my suitcase and briefcase. Strangely, they never checked my coat pockets, where the floppy disk with the polling presentation for the opposition party would have been found. Nor did they comment on my Clinton-Gore tee shirt, my Dean for America sweatshirt, or my well-worn Gary Hart baseball cap. I get much of my haberdashery from my clients.

I have entered countries as a businessman, a tourist, a photographer, and a baseball scout, all in order to avoid identification as a purveyor of tools to overthrow (democratically, of course) a country's current government. I have even entered countries and left within an hour.

I was in Buenos Aires when I got a call from a consultant in Colombia inquiring if I was interested in working on a Colombian presidential race. I expressed my interest and noted that my flight the next day stopped in Bogotá on its way to the States. I told her I could meet with her and the candidate, then fly home a day later.

"Perfect," she said. "We'll have someone waiting for you just past customs, in the arrivals hall. He'll take you to the Hyatt where we'll meet with the client."

Perfect, indeed. What a stroke of luck. Out of nowhere, a new account. I disembarked in Bogotá, got my passport stamped by immigration, went through the baggage claim and customs, then looked for someone holding a sign saying "Ridder." No one in the arrivals hall. Okay, there must be someone out on the main concourse. No one. Well, then, outside. No one. I walked back inside. No one.

I walked outside again to find a taxi to take me to the Hyatt Hotel. No taxis. I stood outside for ten minutes. No taxis. Checked the arrivals hall again. No one. Tried to call the consultant. No answer.

I went up to the ticket counter and found that my seat was still available on the flight that had brought me to Colombia and was headed back to the States. I got a boarding pass, went through immigration, bought some whole-bean Colombian coffee, and settled back into seat 14D.

I got a hold of the consultant three days later by telephone. When I asked why there had been no one to meet me as agreed, she said, "They were kidnapping Americans that day, so we didn't think it was a good idea to pick you up."

Suddenly the account didn't seem like such a boon. I declined the business.

# RULE #19

# KNOW TECHNOLOGY AND THE TOOLS OF COMMUNICATION.

There is nothing better than finding a new technology that truly works for campaign communications. The printing press, the telephone, the word processor, radio, television, and certainly Google and Twitter have brought about monumental change and benefits to political campaigns. But I suggest that the most important technological advancement for a political campaign is the tape recorder. With the tape recorder, campaign operatives no longer relied upon the notes of journalists or, worse, the memory of a candidate to learn the truth of what the candidate or the opposition actually said.

Notwithstanding Rose Mary Woods and savvy tape editors, the tape recorder both reduced and increased the frequency of "He said what?" moments in campaigns because it provided an accurate rendition of spoken words.

The subsequent advent of television and film simply added the visual element of "He did what?" to the audience's ability to determine the veracity of the behavior.

• • •

In early 2003, having just become manager of Howard Dean's presidential campaign, I was sitting in my office responding to the deluge of emails that now accompany modern campaigns when a young staffer, Zephyr Teachout, came running into my office. "Rick, Rick! Howard just blogged! He is the first presidential candidate to blog!"

"Oh, you mean clogged," I responded. "I didn't know Howard knew how to clog." I may not be a practitioner of traditional dancing, but I know of the steps. Kind of. And I wan't overly surprised that a Vermonter such as Howard Dean might have practiced a rural folk dance form such as clogging.

"No! He BLOGGED!" she repeated.

"Oh, blogged. Blogged. Of course. Yeah. Sure. Blogged. . . . Blogged?"

She shook her head with her eyes closed. "Its short for *Web Log*. *Blog*."

I drew a deep breath and said, "Yeah, that's great. So, Howard is the first presidential candidate to . . . blog?"

"Yes."

Zephyr exited, still shaking her head at the troglodyte who was her boss. A few minutes later, Dean stepped into my office.

"I hear you blogged," I said, tossing off my newfound technical term.

"I . . . blogged?"

"Yes. That's what Zephyr just told me."

"All I did was type something out about my Iraq position and respond to the Powell deal at the UN."

"Well, apparently you blogged."

So that was the beginning of presidential campaign blogging—a new form of communication with a traditional purpose—telling the world the candidate's position on an important issue. Tweeting would come next—blogging in just 140 characters.

Later that night, I talked to Joseph Napolitan who admitted that he didn't know how to "blog" but that he understood its purpose. Then he laughed and repeated his favorite mantra, "All campaigns are different. All campaigns are the same."

• • •

The Liberal Democrats had scored a major victory with the performance of their party leader, Nick Clegg, at the first televised debated among prime minister candidates in British history. All the major TV and newspaper instant polls had declared him the winner and pundits were marveling at his performance.

Although I had helped with Clegg's debate prep, I had then been banished back to Colorado; the Lib Dem management wanted to make sure the press knew of no American consultants associated with the campaign. I watched the debate in the comfort of my Denver office, on BBC America.

With the first release of the instant polling, I sent a congratulatory message to the Lib Dem team and recommended that the various poll results be posted to the front page of the web site with the headline "Clegg Wins Debate."

One hour post-debate: I looked at the website. The party manifesto was still prominently displayed, all 10,000 words of it, with a picture of the unveiling of the manifesto from four days earlier. There was no mention of the debate poll results. They must be busy, I thought. They will switch it. They must know that forty million British voters want information on the new hot politician, and that many of them will go to the Lib Dem website. They'll fix it.

Two hours post-debate: website unchanged. Had they forgotten everything I told them about instant response? I sent another email, telling them that not only were they not communicating their victory, but that there was no "Donate Now" button on the front page or a place to capture an email address.

Three hours post-debate: website unchanged. It was time to use the phone and tell the client to change the website pronto! Busy signals. My call didn't even go to voice mail. There must have been something wrong with the international lines.

Four hours post-debate: website unchanged. Both the Conservative and Labour party websites were trumpeting tidbits of positive spin from the debate, their donation buttons front and center. It was 1:30 a.m. in the UK. I sent a text message. No reply. I waited until the morning. I was sure that by the time I woke up in Colorado, the site would be updated.

Seventeen hours post-debate: website unchanged. In my morning emails, the campaign told me, "We are getting to that."

Twenty hours post-debate: website unchanged. I reached the campaign director by phone. I pointed out that the website still had the manifesto featured. "Yes. We are getting to that," I was told. "We have been fighting the Twitter wars. All our staff is on Twitter, responding to what is on Twitter," he replied.

"Let me get this right. Fifteen million Brits have home Internet. At least that many have it at work. How many have Twitter? Maybe three million?"

"Yes, but we need to respond. Besides, the newspapers have all the news anyway."

"But can a supporter give money, sign up as a volunteer, or learn our story from the newspaper?"

"Hmm, I see. Good point. We'll get to it," said the campaign director in a decidedly British fashion.

Twenty-four hours post-debate: website unchanged.

Thirty-six hours post-debate: website changed with the addition of articles twenty-four hours old. But there was no Donate button front and center or immediate email-capturing capability, and the manifesto was still prominently displayed.

During the next five days, Nick Clegg was more popular than Winston Churchill during World War II, according to the oldest survey research firm in the UK. But the website never captured the names or the money that would have built upon this newfound success. Opportunity lost.

• • •

I was asked to go to Arizona for Hillary Clinton for President in early December 2007, as a campaign consultant; I later became state director. Before I left, one of our firm's very talented researchers, who was also an ardent Obama supporter, walked into my office and said to me, "You know, you're going to get killed in Arizona. Obama has four times the Facebook likes in Arizona that Clinton does."

"Facebook? Have you looked at the average age of a primary voter in Arizona?" *Facebook*, to the sixty-and-older voters in Arizona at the time, would have called to mind a picture book of college freshmen they received more than forty years prior. Note that this was in 2008.

"Yeah, but Obama will be able to mobilize thousands of volunteers through Facebook and easily communicate with them."

"Clinton will be able to communicate with primary voters. It's called *mail*, as in *snail* and *e*."

"What?" said our researcher. "Old people don't email! The penetration level is much lower than that of younger voters."

"Not among primary voters in Arizona. Remember, old people have grandchildren. They love photos of their grandchildren. And to get those photos quickly and easily, they use email. And they read their snail mail."

Hillary easily won Arizona, effectively using both forms of mail.

• • •

Upon my departure from the Dean for President campaign in April 2003, I was allowed to keep my Blackberry—at the time, the newest PDA technology for receiving calls and email—for a few weeks. Then the finality of my resignation was complete.

Sending my Blackberry back to the headquarters in Vermont, I inserted the following ditty in the box.

### Silenced Communications
(apologies to Edgar Allan Poe)

Once upon a midday dreary, while I pondered, weak and weary,
Over many a quaint and curious volume of forgotten campaign lore,
While I nodded, nearly napping, suddenly there came a buzzing,
As of something arriving, arriving at my PDA's door.
"Tis some email," I muttered, "arriving at my PDA's door—
Only this, and nothing more."

Deep into daylight peering, long I stood there wondering, questioning,
Pondering of hundreds of messages no mortal ever dared respond to before.
"Surely," said I, "surely there is something in my email in-box."
"Let me see then, what threat there is, and this mystery explore;
This I whispered, and an echo murmured back the word "Nevermore."
Merely this, and nothing more.

Click here, I opened the message, when, with a flirt and a flutter,
In there was a statement from a friend of the days of yore;
Not the least diplomatic was he; only a few words from Vermont had he
Those few words, as if his position in those words, did bore
All he wrote, "Your Blackberry nevermore."
This it is and nothing more.

But now my Blackberry, sitting lonely on my placid desk, expresses only
That one word, as if its soul in that one word did outpour.
Nothing further that was uttered—not another email before it is shuttered.
Till I scarcely more than muttered, "other PDAs have flown before—
On the morrow it will leave me, as my electronic toys have flown before."
Quoth the Blackberry "Nevermore."

# RULE #20

# DON'T FORGET THE CHUM!

Even when a campaign starts out with a powerful rationale, such as stopping a war, bringing people together, or otherwise saving the world, before long the cause will take a backseat to what we call the chum—the posters, yard signs, and bumper stickers; the pens, pencils, and erasers; the lapel pins, refrigerator magnets, and coffee mugs; the T-shirts, sweatshirts, and workshirts; the dog collars and bobble-head dolls; the iPhones and iPad covers, and a host of various other *tchotchkes*. The chum is supposed to be the spice to perk up the stew; it's not supposed to be the meat. But sometimes the chum becomes the beef while the issues are demoted to the oregano you can barely taste because it's been sitting in your kitchen cabinet since the days of William Howard Taft. (I'll bet he made one fabulous bobble-head doll.)

More staff and candidate hours are consumed, and more internal dissension is provoked, by the nature of the chum—the design of the posters, the color of the bumper stickers, the fabric used in the T-shirts ("I certainly wouldn't ask anyone I know to wear a cotton-poly blend! Those shirts are made with fossil fuels!"), where the hats are made, the manufacturer of the buttons—than by anything else.

"What about the coffee mug? Twelve-ounce? Twenty-ounce? White? Green? Black? Thoughts? Opinions? Arguments? The floor is open. Oh, and could someone write the speech we're giving this Friday on the economy? Put one of the interns on it—the senior staff are all busy choosing pictures for the magnets."

The average voter couldn't care less about chum. I may be going out on a limb here, but my considered judgment is that John Q. does not wake up in the middle of the night to announce, "Damn it, I've made up my mind to vote for Congressman Blutarski. Why? Because he gave my wife an emery board! And not just any emery board—an emery board that was exactly the right size, shape, weight, color, and level of abrasiveness. Her nails are important to her, and therefore they're important to me. Congressman Blutarski understands that."

But woe betide the campaign adviser who fails to ensure that the emery board's size, shape, weight, color, and level of abrasiveness are exactly as Congressman and Mrs. Blutarski ordered them. After all, a nuclear weapon is just a means of killing ten million people. But an emery board? That's something on which history might turn.

I've seen campaigns use all manner of gimmicks and toys.

There was the candidate for Colorado State House who passed out screwdrivers embossed with the words "Charles Lilley. A handy man around the House." He lost.

Then there was the candidate in a college town who passed out Frisbees printed with the words, "I will take flight for you! Barett for City Council." The flighty Mr. Barrett forgot that most college students neither vote in city council elections nor seek political advice from Frisbees. He lost, too.

There have been good choices. In 1984, then-congressman Tim Wirth's campaign staff fashioned a lapel pin to resemble an Allen (hex) wrench, to symbolize the Pentagon's $9,600 expenditure on an item that costs thirty cents in the local hardware store. The lapel pin became a symbol of his fight against government waste and a bloated military budget. Soon, even the local TV anchors were wearing them on the evening news. He won. I won't say the chum made the difference for Wirth, but if someone handed you an item valued by Uncle Sam at nearly ten grand, wouldn't you vote for him?

Bumper stickers are a particular favorite of activists. My mother once told me that the Mondale for President campaign was a disgrace because bumper stickers were unavailable in her state of Virginia. I told her that perhaps the Mondale campaign was distributing bumper stickers only in those states where he had an inkling of winning (which turned out to be, um, few). After she accused me of buying into a strategy that forgot Democrats in the non-targeted states, I quickly promised to use my connections to get her one from Ohio, so the back of her car would not be bereft of a demonstration of her support.

One of my first encounters with a campaign consultant came when I was working as a field operative in the McGovern campaign. This hardened veteran, not associated with the campaign, told me one evening over too many glasses of Jack Daniel's, "The reason McGovern's losing is that his bumper sticker doesn't have an American flag on it. The more liberal the candidate, the larger the flag needs to be on the bumper sticker."

This sounded like good advice so I passed it on to my superiors. Given the result of the election, I am guessing they ignored it.

In a later campaign, the same consultant applied his magic formula, but to little effect. On his order, the campaign paid for the printing and distribution of thousands of oversized bumper stickers and yard signs festooned with his candidate's name next to an oversized depiction of Old Glory. One day, four weeks before the election, he turned on the TV to find out that ten years earlier his candidate had been arrested—three times— while taking part in anti-American demonstrations in Holland.

You know those giant flags that fly over car dealerships on the highway? The ones as big as Rhode Island? Even flags the size of Alaska couldn't have saved that guy. He lost.

For candidates, decisions about chum are intensely personal. As such, they also tend to be intensely bad. Just because someone can press the flesh or give a speech, there is no reason to believe that he or she has the eye of a graphic designer. One candidate insisted that her yard signs be printed not just in baby blue but in a light shade of baby blue: a *baby* shade of baby blue. We tried to dissuade her, we appealed to her common sense—and when that didn't work, we summoned up our most commanding voices: We know what we are talking about!

"But I've always wanted my yard signs in baby blue. It's my favorite color!"

She ordered the signs in baby blue. When they came back from the printer, they were unreadable, as we'd predicted, in daylight or dark.

Need I add that she lost?

Some candidates love animals. There was the woman running for school board whose logo was a giraffe eating leaves from a tall tree. Her slogan: "We need to reach for the top." Every yard sign had the image of the giraffe. I tried to explain to her that people don't elect giraffes to school boards.

She doubled her order of the signs. She lost.

• • •

In the 1980s, Larry Zebratti was running for county commissioner in rural Wyoming. I drove up from Denver in mid-summer. I was excited. He was one of my first clients and, despite the overwhelming GOP majority in the county, I felt certain that with solid strategy and adequate resources, John had a chance.

We held our first meeting at a diner, where Larry laid out his campaign plan.

"I've got the locations for yard signs and the billboard all picked out. A friend has designed the yard signs and the buttons. I told her exactly what I wanted."

He pulled out a sheet of paper on which were printed reproductions of the yard signs and billboard. "Our colors are black and white; the background is black-and-white stripes. And, of course, there's a picture of a zebra, with the words ZEBRATTI FOR COMMISSIONER, across the center. What do you think? Good stuff, huh?"

Seeing how pleased he was with himself, I tried to go slowly. "Black and white. Pretty stark, don't you think?"

"You betcha. People will see it and remember my name."

I pressed on. "The zebra—what does that symbolize? You're not running for football referee."

"Ha! You're funny. People will remember my name. Zebra, Zebratti. Get it?"

"Um, yeah. I get it. Um, look, Larry, generally a symbol expresses some sort of values. What does a zebra say to people?"

"I don't know, but by November, they will know my name."

We moved on to a discussion of rural issues, paid the check, then adjourned to his home for a beer. Stepping through the doorway, I became fully aware of Larry's commitment to his theme. The entire house was done up in a zebra motif. The walls: black-and-white striped wallpaper. The couch: black upholstery with white pillows. The bedspreads: black-and-white striped. The lamp stands: little zebras. The rug: zebra stripes. Little zebra figurines. A big stuffed zebra. Pictures of zebras on the walls.

Campaigns are about contrast, I always tell my clients. Create a contrast, both positive and negative, so that voters come to the conclusion to choose your candidate. But this was . . . extreme. Okay, I thought, the tender approach didn't work, time for some tough love.

"Larry, don't you think this black-and-white zebra thing is a bit out of control?"

"No."

"All right. Your personal life is up to you. Zebras, black-and-white—chairs, tables, dishes, socks. Go for it. But in the campaign, let's try to tell the voters who you are and what you are fighting for. Soooo, how does black-and-white tell the voters why you're running?"

"It shows them I'm decisive and independent."

"Okay. And it does this how?"

"If I use gray, then I'm wishy-washy, in the middle, bland, blah. Cold mashed potatoes. Warm beer. Tepid tea. If I use red, then they'll think I'm either a Commie or a Republican. That's the beauty of black-and-white. Black and white, right and wrong, distinctive. *And*, it gives me—what is it you politicos say?—name recognition. Neat, huh?"

"Yeah, neat. Sure is. But let's explore some other colors that might not be so, um, stark. Yellow and brown, for example, which are the state colors. Or maybe green, or . . ."

"Green? I'd lose right away. Green? You want me to use *green*? The voters would think I was some hippie tree-hugger. This is Wyoming, my friend, not Vermont. It's John Wayne, not Robert Redford. It's red meat, not mushroom quiche. *Green? Green!* I can't believe the state party sent you all the way from Denver to give me such rotten advice. Green. Have you ever actually worked on a campaign west of the Mississippi before?"

He stuck with the black and white. I drove home. He lost.

• • •

It is not as if battles over colors and logos are confined to campaigns for school board, city council, or county commission. Every candidate for the United States Senate, it seems, has a friend who's a semiprofessional graphic designer and knows precisely the image that will vault him or her to the halls of power. "You *must* use my friend to design the logo," the candidate will demand. "He's been at the forefront of corporate branding. He does 'graphic positioning,' I think he calls it, for at least a dozen major corporations."

Upon further inquiry, those "major corporations" turn out to be coffee shops, yoga studios, and car washes.

For a candidate named Stanton, I listened to one of these graphic masterminds explain how his logo design, which intertwined the S and the T, was "symbolic of Stanton's ability to integrate all Americans, creating a flow of energy much like the harmonic balance of yin and yang."

The political director of the campaign quickly ended the designer's involvement in the campaign, saying, "Fuck this shit. There are fewer Chinese in this state than there are African-Americans in Vermont. I ain't gonna worry about the Yins and Yangs. Christ, I can't even get decent kung pao chicken around here."

Stanton lost.

Ah, but *presidential* campaigns are different, you say. People seeking to be the leader of the Free World, you contend, acknowledge that without competent graphic design, all that we hold dear is at risk.

Um, not necessarily. The 1984 Gary Hart for President campaign selected a delightful logo. It was dark blue with metallic silver lettering— very contemporary—but it came with a problem. The designer, who lived in Phoenix, was so determined to make the logo look "high tech" that he created his own font.

Remember, this took place before every laptop computer was home to half a million fonts. Projects had to be sent to professional print shops, which worked with a wide array of standard fonts. Of course the shops didn't stock the one fabricated by the artisan from Arizona, so anytime the campaign needed to have something printed with the official logo— letterhead, envelopes, posters, coffee mugs, key chains, lapel pins, etc., etc., etc., in other words, every damn item we ordered—we had to have it produced in Phoenix. In the days before email, with FedEx just getting started, this was a problem, especially for organizers in New Hampshire and Maine.

• • •

At the beginning of 2003, when I first came on as campaign manager of the Howard Dean for President campaign, the leadership had already selected a logo. It was blue with yellow lettering, in a funky, barely readable font that resembled a first grader's initial attempt at the alphabet.

Call me unimaginative, call me old school, but a first grader's hand scrawl is not exactly presidential. I took up the subject with Dean's chief of staff,

Patricia. I trod carefully. Perhaps the design had been her idea. Perhaps she considered it her shining contribution to the well-being of the human race. Maybe it had been a part of a campaign voter engagement effort: "Design the Dean campaign logo and win lunch with Howard Dean." This was the winner—picked by her.

"Say," I said, trying to be nonchalant, "I was just wondering. How did we end up with this logo?"

"You don't like it?" she shot back.

"It is not that I don't like it, it's just that, to me it looks not, um, completely presidential."

"We've been using it for six months and no one has complained until you."

"I understand," I said. "But, um . . . well, who designed it?"

"The people doing our website."

"You mean, the guys who do those sites for New England prep schools?" I asked.

"Right. Howard's brother found them."

"So that explains the logo's look."

"What do you mean? It looks good."

"It looks like it's for someone running for school board."

"What's wrong with that? The name of the font happens to be 'Chalkboard.' I think it looks very grassroots and very Vermont."

"Yeah, but we have a candidate who is running for president of the United States, not school board or king of Burlington's Ben & Jerry's Day Parade."

The look on her face told me that she didn't appreciate my humor. Nonetheless, I persisted. "I'm going to get some other concepts designed."

My assistant, Courtney O'Donnell, worked her New York advertising contacts to come up with a "branding and logo expert." Before the "expert" went too far, I made sure he had never set foot in a yoga studio. He assured me that he hated yoga.

Five days later, fourteen treatments of a Dean for America logo arrived in my email. All were red, white, and blue. Some had flags. All were readable. All looked as though the font had not been produced by a six-year-old. Or a seven-year-old. In fact, not by any child at all. I was pleased. I began showing them around the office and soon the staff had narrowed the choices to three. I sent a PDF of those three to the campaign's media consultant, Steve McMahon.

"I like 'em," Steve told me when I called. "They're good. I can use them in the TV spots. But have you checked with Patricia and Howard?"

"I told Patricia that I was seeking alternatives to our current logo because I don't find it presidential."

"You told her that?"

"I did."

I knew it. Did she design it herself and tell the website guys to use it?

"She picked it out, personally, despite our objections," said Steve, who had worked with Dean for years. "She is absolutely committed to it. Not sure why—maybe because Howard likes it. If Howard likes it, Patricia likes it. And he likes it because it's his brother who found the web guys who designed it."

"Candidates and family. Can't live with 'em, can't lock 'em up in dungeons until the election is over."

"Let's give the new ones a try anyway," Steve said, in a voice heavy with futility.

The following day, Howard and Patricia returned from the road. Before I had a chance to arrange a meeting, Patricia popped her head into my office. "Howard doesn't want to change the logo."

The old preemptive strike—she'd gotten to him before I could.

"You talked to him about this?" I said.

"Yes. He doesn't want to change it."

"Let's discuss it. Get Howard in here. I'll get Steve on the phone."

"Okay, but he doesn't want to change it," she said as she walked away.

Right. He doesn't want to change it. Got it. A few moments later, Howard dropped into my office, ostensibly to discuss a scheduling snafu. Then he brought up the logo.

"I understand you want to change the logo," Howard said.

"Yes, I do. The current one is not presidential."

"Patricia doesn't like the changes. Let's get her in here and Steve on the phone, and let's talk about it. Let me see the changes."

Maybe there was hope for the new logo after all. Maybe this candidate really was different from all other candidates.

I showed him the various options; he pointed at one with a flag in the background. "I like that one. We're running an antiwar campaign, so we ought to have the flag."

Progress! Patricia showed up, Steve got on the line, and the conversation began. Howard liked the flag logo; Steve said we needed something "with a bit more class than the current logo." I again used the word *presidential—* hoping that it would push one of Howard's buttons. I mean, what presidential candidate doesn't want to look "presidential"?

But Patricia had Howard's buttons catalogued and memorized— particularly his pecuniary proclivities. "We will have to redo everything," she said. "Letterhead, brochures, bumper stickers—everything. It will cost us *thousands* just for the printing."

I could see Howard flinch at the sound of the word *thousands*. So she used it again: "And who knows how many *thousands* we'll have to pay the graphic designers." (*Flinch.*) "And *thousands* to redo the website." (*Flinch.*)

"Thousands?" Howard shouted. "I had no idea it would cost *thousands*."

"Wait a minute," I said. "We can phase in the logo as we reprint materials. The website is being redesigned anyway. The graphic designers are doing it for free, to add it to their portfolio. The cost will be minimal."

But Howard, who takes immense pride in his parsimonious (more commonly known as "ultra-cheapo") nature, was lost in the notion that it was going to cost *thousands* to make the switch.

"Thousands! We can't afford to change it now. Maybe in a few months we'll look at it again."

In other words, the whole idea was being buried.

Steve, who had been quiet during the whole conversation, put the final shovelful of dirt into the grave. "We ought to change it, but let's do it for the general election."

"Yes," said Patricia, "let's change it for the general." Maybe it was just me, but I sensed a certain gloating in her voice.

Let's review the chronology. This scene took place in January 2003. The primaries would begin in January 2004. If we won the nomination, the general-election campaign would start some time during the spring or summer of that year, meaning we'd have to live with the very-grassroots-and-very-Vermont "chalkboard" font for the next year-and-a-half.

In case you're wondering how the logo was revised after Howard won the nomination, let me inform you that it wasn't because he didn't.

After the meeting adjourned, I called Courtney, who called the branding expert to thank him for his efforts. The expert had a few choice words for Courtney about the Dean for American campaign staff: he questioned our intelligence as well as our parentage.

But we barely noticed the insult, because by then we were immersed in meetings over our next crucial decision: what to put in the gift bags for Democratic National Committee members at their winter meeting. Should it be Vermont maple syrup or Vermont cheddar cheese?

. . .

On that warm, sunny June day in Barcelona, in the summer of 1999, after finishing my morning *cortado* and *pan con tomate*, I walked into the headquarters of Maragall for Generalitat de Cataluña. Pascual Maragall was running for governor, more or less, of the province of Cataluña.

The Maragall campaign's director of fundraising, Enrique Alverez, greeted me. A stylish dresser whose features are Iberian to the core—long, dark hair, combed back; tanned face; sharp, blue eyes—Enrique grabbed my arm and started to pull me back into the street. He was talking *muy rapido*—in English.

"Rick, you must come and see. We took your advice from your last visit."

I got all puffed up because clients rarely appreciate my genius. They pay for my advice—sometimes—but generally don't take it. "Really? " I asked. "What did you do?"

"Well," said Enrique as he unlocked the door to the Maragall headquarters' adjoining storefront, "you know how you suggested that we give our big contributors a little something to distinguish themselves?"

"Yes, yes, like a lapel pin. Or a poster. So, you did that?"

"Yes, but look at how we have improved on it."

With that, he opened the door and turned on the lights, revealing an A-to-Z Maragall emporium. There were posters, hats, scarves, buttons, stickers, ribbons, T-shirts, mouse pads, pencils, pens, refrigerator magnets, banners, yard signs, kitchen towels, coffee cups, and yet-to-be-unpacked boxes containing who knew what kind of other chum. Each piece was in the campaign colors: yellow and red.

The items were laid out on various tables, the posters hung on the walls. Enrique, the impresario of this spectacular display, was clearly proud.

"This is good, yes? We give these items away to contributors and volunteers."

"Yeah. This is, um, a little bit more, um, extensive than a lapel pin."

"Ah, yes, Rick, it certainly is. Have you seen these?" Enrique reached into a large cardboard box filled with items wrapped in plastic. "You remember last time you were here, you told us about how a friend once mailed—what do you call them? Potholders? *Sí*, potholders—he once mailed potholders to voters?"

"So I did."

On my previous visit, I had told Enrique that fifteen years earlier, Ross Bates, a California mail consultant, mailed small potholders with the candidate's name imprinted on them to households of young single males. "Do you know of any single guy under thirty-five who has a potholder?" the consultant said. "This is something the voter will use. And every time he does, he'll see the candidate's name."

Enrique started unwrapping one of the items he'd pulled from the box—an oven mitt. "Nobody in Cataluña uses potholders, but we do use kitchen mitts."

He threw me the mitt, which was a large and thick and long enough to extend to the middle of your forearm. Sure enough, the candidate's name, along with the full-color yellow and red logo, was printed all over it. "How many do you think we will need for the campaign? I ordered five hundred—do you think that's enough?"

"Darn, I left the statistics for use of kitchen mitts in Cataluña back at the hotel," I blurted, still in shock at the way my suggestion of a lapel pin had produced this Filene's Basement of campaign crapola. I picked up a Maragall stress ball and squeezed. "Okay. How many donors do you think we'll have? And how many might want a kitchen mitt as opposed to some of the other goodies?"

"We have maybe 1,000 individual donors."

"Okay. It's probably safe to say that maybe half of our donors will want kitchen mitts. Then five hundred of these babies will be enough for our donors."

Another box then caught my eye—full of large items in campaign yellow. I picked one out of the box. "What's this?" I said.

"A raincoat."

I examined it—yes, I was holding in my hand an official Maragall raincoat. It was made of yellow rubber and resembled what a New England fisherman preparing for a Nor'easter would wear. I had never seen rain in Barcelona during previous visits.

"Does it rain much in Barcelona?" I asked.

"Oh, no. We have more than 300 days of sunshine a year."

"That's what I thought. The rain in Spain falls mainly on the plain, right?"

"On the plain?"

"Yes, the *rain in Spain stays mainly on the pla-ain. By George, I think she's got it.*"

He looked at me blankly as I ended my foray into musical theater.

"Never mind, Enrique. No rain, right, got it. Soooo . . . why the boxful of raincoats?"

"Collector's item. Something special for people to wear when it rains."

I'm not a meteorologist, but before I had left home I did a bit of research to learn what clothes I needed to bring. I found that a raincoat in Barcelona in June is as useful as a summer jacket in Moscow in February.

"Isn't summer the dry season?"

Again, this was June. Election day was in October. Between now and then: sunshine and more sunshine.

"Yes, but my friend, that's the *beauty* of it. That's what will make the coats so special when it *does* rain. All these people prepared with their Maragall raincoats. Genius, *si?*"

"Uh, *si*. Yeah. Great."

I sighed, then looked around the Maragall warehouse once more. Something was missing. "Where are the lapel pins?"

"Really? We don't need lapel pins when we have hats, ribbons, T-shirts, mouse pads, kitchen mitts, raincoats, coffee cups, shot glasses, coasters, rain hats, laptop protection sleeves, bumper-stickers, logo-labeled bottled water—everything."

"Right. Okay. I'll see you in a bit. Good work. Yeah. Okay."

I headed next door to campaign headquarters where the campaign manager accosted me and started jabbing his index finger into my chest.

"Did you see (*jab*) what you started (*jab*) with that stupid idea (*jab*) of a lapel pin, Ridder? (*jab, jab*) We will be very (*jab*) careful about taking your (*jab*) advice (*jab*) from (*jab*) now (*jab*) on (*jab*)."

. . .

The activist stood shaking his head. He was a seemingly full-time campaign volunteer whose auto's backend was festooned with bumper stickers from failed candidates of yore. Why was he unhappy?

Take a guess. Okay. Probably he was unhappy because the campaign in question, for a seat in the United States Senate, had not spent any money on television. You can't win without lots of TV advertising.

Actually, the campaign had spent $5 million on TV.

Then it must have been because there was no direct mail. Everyone knows that direct mail is the key to political success. Keep those mailboxes good and stuffed.

No, the campaign had sent eight pieces to nearly every targeted voter in the state.

Then he must have been unhappy because, despite the commercials on every channel every five minutes and the four-color oversized postcards shoved into every mailbox in the state, the candidate lost.

No, the candidate won.

Then he must be upset at the margin, which was razor-thin, when a decent campaign would have made it comfortable. What kind of mandate do you get from a micro-win?

No, the guy won by 20 percentage points.

Well, then . . . what was the goddam problem?

"It wasn't a real campaign," said the activist, "because nobody was on the corner of University and First doing Honk-and-Waves at seven in the morning."

Honk-and-Waves are a common feature of campaigns in my home state of Colorado. The truly dedicated candidate will occupy high-traffic street corners at rush hour to wave campaign signs to the ongoing traffic, in the hope that drivers will indicate support by honking their horn. (Come to think of it, the practice should be called Wave-and-Honk. Is it misnamed simply because Honk-and-Wave sounds better? Or because the people who do Honk-and-Waves tend to be confused by chronology, cause-and-effect, and reality?)

As many as forty activists may assemble on a single corner to wave signs in the final days before an election. Of course, much jostling for prime waving positions takes place between the supporters of rival campaigns. Bad behavior sometimes breaks out: destruction of signs, physical abuse, and the shouting of foul-mouthed epithets of such variety that they provoke political-consultant envy with their gutter-level erudition.

Strangely, the worst transgressions of the law take place during primary battles—family feuds have nothing on the bitterness that can break out during an intraparty battle between two candidates who agree on almost everything. Signs are not just destroyed; they are burned. If the signs have a stake attached to them (to make for easier waving), expect the stake to be wielded as a lance or bludgeon. One Honk-and-Waver was rushed to the hospital after he was pushed into oncoming traffic by opposing H-and-W'ers who claimed rights to the corner because they had been standing there for a month before the other side appeared on the scene.

Normal people don't stand on street corners at zero-dark-thirty waving signs for political candidates. Well-adjusted people don't find personal affirmation in the honking of horns by complete strangers who may well be beeping not because Candidate X speaks to their ideals of justice and patriotism but because a Hummer just cut into their lane without a turn signal. Psychologically stable people don't engage in mortal turf wars over who has the right to a particular patch of sidewalk from which they can endanger the lives of commuters whose attention should be on the road, not on a gaggle of poorly groomed enthusiasts seeking to distract them.

Upon participating in a Honk-and-Wave, my good friend the noted Swedish political consultant Bo Krogvig observed, "Just who in the hell do they think they're persuading? If I were a driver, I would question the sanity of a candidate whose supporters think this is an effective way to convince anyone to vote for anyone or anything."

While activists are obsessed with Honk-and-Waves, candidates themselves focus on a different item as the one most essential to the progress of all that is good in the world: yard signs. Many a campaign manager has been fired for failing to distribute yard signs either in sufficient quantity or with enough speed, or to the right locations.

To avoid free agency in campaign management here are a few guidelines: The first rule of yard-sign distribution is to put three outside the candidate's home. The second rule is to line the route to his or her office and campaign headquarters. The third dictum: stick half a dozen outside the opponent's headquarters. The fourth: plaster the street where the opponent lives. And the fifth: give a handful to the most vocal activists in the campaign.

Simple, easy, effective. Do yard signs, maintain employment.

I never paid much attention to yard signs until the early 1990s, when I was asked to conduct a campaign training session for the Democratic members of the Tennessee legislature.

The room where the training was held had a balcony attached to it. Through most of the two days of training, I discoursed on the finer elements of campaigning—message development, door-to-door contact, public speaking, policy points, and communications—with less than transfixed attention from my audience. A few members listened. A few more were polite enough to pretend to listen. Most, however, spent the time on the outside balcony, kibitzing, smoking, and enjoying the state's pride and joy: Jack Daniel's Tennessee Whiskey.

Near the end of the second day, I mentioned the words "yard signs." All of a sudden, the majority leader of the Tennessee State House of Representatives stood up, ran to the door leading to the balcony, and screamed, "Boys! Get in here now! He's gittin' to the good stuff. He's talkin' 'bout yard signs."

Over the next two hours, the balcony was empty as I answered one question after another about yard signs: big or small yard signs, plastic or paper yard signs, metal or wood yard signs; opponent's yard signs and friends' yard signs; down-ballot yard signs and up-ballot yard signs; the color of yard signs, the font of yard signs, the height of yard signs.

Toward the end of the session, having plowed through Yard Sign Tactics 101, I led my students into the lofty arcana we pros call Advanced Strategic Yardsignology. Are more than four yard signs at a four-way intersection overkill? Do you place yard signs in vacant lots? What about "talking yard signs" (where you change the yard sign's message during the course of the campaign)? When do you post yard signs in places other than yards—such as in homes or shop windows? When do you post yard signs? What do you do if a yard sign is vandalized? What's the best way to vandalize the other guy's yard sign? And then, for the doctoral program in Yardsignological Engineering: how do you implement ballot-order yard signs? (The truly committed activist displays a yard sign for every candidate he or she supports for every office, positioning the signs so they replicate the order of offices on the ballot.) What do you do when another candidate wants to share space on what we with decades of yard-sign experience call "split yard-signs"?

I could go on and on. And did. Ultimately, we entered the sublime world of rural candidates: field signs.

After I'd taken the last question, the speaker of the Tennessee State House of Representatives rose from his chair. "You know, Rick, many times during the last couple of days I thought we'd wasted our money bringing you in all the way from Colorado. But, by gosh, the last two hours were worth every dime we spent. Thank you."

You never know what's going to make 'em happy.

• • •

Immediately after Gary Hart won the 1984 New Hampshire primary, there was a major strategy powwow at his media consultant's office in Washington, D.C., to plan for Super Tuesday. In the chandeliered and oak-paneled surroundings, a bit more upscale than our headquarters in a former peep show and porn shop, the chief strategist announced, "We're going to Georgia and Alabama." Turning to the campaign's national field director—me; I got the job title because, due to reductions in force, we had no one else in the field department—he asked, "What do we have there?"

"We have a broad organization in Georgia, with fifty identified supporters in Atlanta and Macon, but we're a little weaker in Alabama, where we have only two names." I realized I was trying to make a mountain out of a mole. (It would be an exaggeration to say I had any size hill to work with.) "But we are on the ballot in both states."

The lead strategist looked at me with incredulity. "Holy shit, Ridder. I don't know how you're going to do it, but in three days you *will* make people think that there are more than fifty people in the State of Georgia who support Gary Hart for President of the United States."

"Three days?"

"That's right, because that's when Gary Hart will be in Atlanta."

The meeting ended late at night. I went back to the campaign HQ, racking my brain to come up with a way to turn 50 people into 15,000. How much cash would it take to bribe 15,000 Georgians? Since it's a right-to-work state and we don't have to deal with unions, which solidly support our primary opponent, Walter Mondale, can we do it on the cheap? Is there a secret slush fund we can tap into? Are Nixon's plumbers out of jail yet?

Then I remembered a phone call I'd received two months earlier. I went to my desk and rummaged through all my notes. There was the guy's name and phone number. He lived in Alabama.

I went home confident.

I called the next morning.

He answered, "Joe Wiley."

I knew nothing about Joe Wiley, other than that he was a Democrat, supported Hart, lived in a place with an Alabama area code, and had called a few months earlier with an offer to produce low-cost signs.

"Joe, Rick Ridder from the Hart campaign. You called a few months ago about printing some signs."

"Oh, yeah."

"I need those signs."

"Sure thing. When? Where? How many?"

"In two days. Atlanta, five thousand lining the route from the airport to every downtown hotel and to the capitol. Then, a day later, Macon, three thousand. Same deal, airport to downtown to City Hall."

"You're kidding."

"No, I'm not kidding. Can you do it?"

"Give me thirty minutes—I gotta call the printer and my boys. This will not be easy."

I assumed his "boys" to be his truck drivers, not a gang of street toughs who would leave a trail of broken kneecaps behind the trail of Hart for President yard signs.

For thirty minutes, I drummed on the desk. Grabbed coffee. Paced. Drummed some more. Drank the coffee. Paced some more.

Right on schedule, Joe called back. "I can do it. I've got a brochure so I will copy the colors, but what's the deal with that font?"

"Don't ask."

"I'll come up with a similar font. Send me $2000 now. I'll bill you $2,500 more when I finish."

"I gotta clear it with the money guys," I said, knowing this was not a trivial sum to the cash-starved campaign. After an hour of pleading, I finally convinced the campaign comptroller that we had no other way to show visibility in Georgia. It wasn't as though we had actual, you know, *supporters*.

I called Joe back to give him the okay and dropped a check in the mail.

I waited a day before I called for an update.

"How are we doing?"

"I sent the boys with the first truckload over to Atlanta about forty minutes ago. It'll take 'em a few hours, but it'll be all right."

I didn't believe him, but if he was lying there was not much I could do.

Four hours later, I received a call from one of our fifty Georgia supporters reporting that someone was putting up yard signs in downtown Atlanta and around the capitol. "They're made of really cheap cardboard," he complained. "And what the hell is wrong with the font?"

"Don't ask."

"But hey, it's still pretty cool."

Joe's guys finished the job. The payoff came when *The CBS Evening News* reported, with the yard signs in the background of the shot, "Hart appears to have an extensive organization in Georgia. There are signs everywhere from Atlanta to Macon."

# RULE #21

## BEWARE OF THE BEARS.

It is not as if bad things always happen in politics as a result of bears. It is just that you must take a judicious approach when enticing, referencing, or aiding bears.

• • •

In May 1972, my McGovern colleagues and I drove overnight and well into the next afternoon from Oregon to Salt Lake City. As we walked into the Salt Lake McGovern headquarters, Mary Ellen Simonson, Deputy Western States Director, greeted me with, "Ridder! Washington wants you in Billings tomorrow for a 10 a.m. meeting."

It was already 4 p.m. I was facing a four-hundred-mile, ten-hour drive. I started north to Big Sky Country.

Two cups of ten-cent coffee at Sambo's in Twin Falls, a can of Coke from a truck stop in Rexburg, and a Dodgers game on the radio from Los Angeles kept me awake until I found a pull-off from US-20 in Targhee National Forest, Wyoming, at about 11 p.m. It was a muddy road. There were splotches of snow around the bases of the pine trees, but I found a small clearing about a mile in. I got out of the Jeep and pulled my sleeping bag and a sleeping pad out of the back. The moon was bright, enabling me to see when I hung my ski parka, which was slightly wet from spilled Coke, on a tree branch fifteen feet away. I fell asleep under the western stars.

Some hours later—it was still dark—I awoke, feeling something light brush my nostrils. Opening my eyes, I noticed a feather drifting over them—so that's what was tickling my nose. I disregarded the two feathers—one on the nose, one over the eyes—as emanating from a small leak in my sleeping bag. When two more feathers drifted by, I wondered if I had inadvertently lain in some duck or goose nest. When a fifth and sixth floated down, I put on my glasses. There was nothing much on the ground but there was a snowstorm of feathers drifting down from above. I batted a few away and found the source of the blizzard—my parka. What had once been the Coke-soaked nylon of my ski jacket was now a jumble of strips of unrecognizable fabric, reaching toward the ground with feathers spewing forth.

Now the question: to remain perfectly still or get the fuck out of there?

I chose the latter. I leapt out of the sleeping bag and into the Jeep. Engine on. Lights on. Shift to first gear. Swing by to pick up the sleeping bag and my shoes. I took one look at the paw prints and determined that it wasn't Baby Bear or Mama Bear who'd indulged in the pause that refreshes, it was Big Ol' Papa Bear—and I was gone.

I arrived at the all-night café in West Yellowstone about an hour later; it must have been about 5 a.m. With my parka in tatters back in the forest, I donned my denim jacket and went inside. The waitress seemed to notice my edginess when I sat down at the counter.

"You okay?" she asked.

"Yeah, yeah. I'm okay." I wasn't, of course, but who am I to violate the sacred male obligation to insist upon being "okay" in the face of any injury short of amputation? Besides, I was campaign tough.

"Well, what can I get for you?" She stared at me. "You sure you're okay?"

"Yeah, yeah. I'm okay." I ordered the breakfast special.

As the waitress was heading to the counter to place the order, she swung back toward me. "Listen, if I were you, I'd take that McGovern button off your jacket."

"I wear that button everywhere. Don't worry about it. I'm okay."

"No, listen. The owner and manager here are . . . well, pretty scary on this stuff."

"Really, don't worry. I've worn this button in five states. In some very nasty places. I'm okay."

"No, really, these people . . . This is my summer job. I voted for McGovern in the Pennsylvania primary—that's where I go to college. When I mentioned his name last week, I was nearly fired."

"I'm okay. Don't worry. I'm okay."

Once she'd started back toward the counter, a large, older man with a checkered shirt walked along the counter, talking briefly with two other patrons a few feet away. He poured coffee into each of their cups, said a few words, and then came to me. He started to pour coffee into my cup, stopped, stared at my button, then said, "I don't serve communists. Get out."

"I'm not a communist."

"I won't have your type in my restaurant. Get out!" he shouted.

"Can't I eat my breakfast?"

He was bigger than I was—a lot bigger. "Out of here!" he shouted. "Now!"

I took a swig of coffee and decided that, having escaped one predator with my life earlier that night, I shouldn't stretch my luck with another. I left without asking for a takeout box.

At a quarter to ten I arrived at the Billings office building where the meeting was to take place. I cleaned up in the bathroom, then walked into the law firm hosting the gathering. The receptionist greeted me.

"Oh, they cancelled the meeting. No one thought you would be here by ten."

• • •

The Swedish focus group facility's observation room was crowded. There were three American consultants on one side with a simultaneous translator and five Swedish Social Democratic Party campaign team leaders on the other; they didn't need the translator. There was only minimal chatting among observers as they watched and listened to the twelve group participants behind the mirrored glass.

The moderator led the group through the basic questions: key issues, direction of country, and perception of the party leaders. Then the moderator asked another standard question: "Please, write down the animal that comes to mind that you most associate with the Swedish Social Democrats. In other words, if the Social Democrats were animals, what animal would they be?"

After a couple of minutes, the moderator asked a participant to read what she had written. She said, "bear." He asked another participant. He said, "bear." He then asked all those who had written *bear* to raise their hands. Ten out of the twelve did.

"Shit! They see us as bears," Bill Hamilton, the American pollster, exclaimed. "We got problems."

Another American consultant, Phil Noble, said, "They see us as mean marauders."

On the other side of the room, the Swedish team was high-fiving and smiling all around.

The Americans looked at the Swedes. The Swedes looked at the Americans.

Hamilton finally asked the Swedes, "Is there something we don't know here? Ten out of twelve just said, 'bear.' That is a mean, aggressive animal. You don't want to fool with them."

"Yes, ten of twelve said 'bear,'" said Bo Krogvig, the campaign manager, "but that is a warm, protective animal."

"So, is what we have here is perception problem? Grizzly versus mama bear?" asked Hamilton.

Krogvig laughed. "In Sweden, a bear has very positive characteristics. They are associated with motherhood and protection. This is very good for us."

The American consultants looked at one another.

"Who knew?" said Noble.

And they all lived happily thereafter, particularly when the Social Democrats took over Parliament a few months later.

• • •

We didn't have enough money for a real focus group. What little money the campaign had was earmarked for one TV spot airing over the last ten days of the campaign. So we gathered a few of our staff and friends around a conference table. The compensation for their insights was beer and access to a vegetable tray of carrots and celery with ranch-dressing dip.

I handed out the language of the Stop the Spring Bear Hunt ballot initiative that was on the November 1992 ballot, with a list of reasons why the initiative should pass. The list included rationales such as:

1. The shooting of mother bears in the spring leaves their cubs without their mothers;

2.  Bears are easier to kill in the spring because they lack the energy to run away after hibernating all winter; and

3.  Hunters use bait such as orange peels and jelly donuts to lure bears out of their dens to be shot immediately.

At first, the women in the group found the "leaving the cubs without their mothers" argument very persuasive. But then, the only person in the group who actually possessed a hunter's license became very agitated.

"It's, it's, it's . . . the jelly donuts!" he exclaimed. "I can't believe they would use jelly donuts. That's not sporting. That's not right."

There was an immediate chorus of, "Yeah. He's right. Jelly donuts. That's wrong."

Soon, the conversation devolved into every participant relating how they can't resist jelly donuts. Blueberry filled. Cream-filled. Apple-filled. It didn't matter what kind of jelly donuts; they were irresistible to humankind and therefore must be to bears.

We went into a TV studio later that week to produce the lone TV spot. We included film of baby bears with the mothers, baby bears without their mothers, mother bears without their babies, and a still photograph with a pile of oranges, donuts, and other bait, and a bear beginning to enjoy the fruits put forth.

The voiceover told the story of mother bears with their baby bears lured out of hibernation by hunters using special bait. The spot ended with the question, "Is it sporting to hunt mother bears by using jelly donuts to lure them out of hibernation? Vote Yes to Stop the Spring Bear Hunt."

The spot went up with ten days to go. Three days into airing it, our polling numbers started to rise, according to a TV channel's tracking polls. By election day we had moved ten points upward—and it's a rarity when a ballot initiative's support goes up during the course of a campaign. We won with over more than 70 percent of the vote.

At the election night party, one of the poll workers for the Stop the Spring Bear Hunt campaign came up to me and said, "Who thought of the jelly donuts? As I worked the polls, people were coming up to me and saying, 'I am voting "yes" on bears. Using jelly donuts—that's just unfair.'"

## RULE #22

# YOU NEVER KNOW WHAT
# YOUR CONTRIBUTION WILL BE.

Most campaign consultants dream of having a photograph with the president of the United States, with an inscription from the president saying, "My campaign consultant was the single reason that I won the election." Not the candidate. Not the voters. Not even the spouse of the president. It was the consultant. Only the consultant.

It doesn't happen. And it won't happen. Indeed, even a candidate for mosquito control board would never admit that his or her brilliant consultant was the reason for the victory. So, campaign consultants take solace in what little acknowledgement of their contributions to the betterment of the world and the human condition they may receive—however trivial it may be.

• • •

I got a call in February 1997 from Mark Grueskin, my longtime friend and the leading ballot initiative attorney in the state of Colorado. He quickly came to the point.

"I have a campaign for which you are eminently qualified. It is to legalize marijuana for medical use."

Even before he could tell me that the campaign would be modeled on a recent successful initiative in California and the upcoming Washington initiative, I informed him that our firm would welcome the opportunity to help relieve the pain suffered by a handful of Coloradans, thanks to the medicinal qualities of marijuana.

He asked if we could have a conference call the next day to discuss the particulars of the initiative: Who would be eligible for this particular medicinal relief? Who could sell it? And how much could a patient purchase or grow for personal use? I indicated we would be on the call.

The call started with the usual introductions. There was Mark, Luther Symons, and Joannie Braden from our firm, and myself. Also taking part were Bill Zimmerman and Dave Fratello, California-based consultants who had helped pass the California initiative and would coordinate with the funders.

Bill detailed the California situation: "In California patients are entitled to whatever amount is nececessary for their personal use. Of course they need a doctor's permission."

Mark jumped in. "That could be a lot of pot for a medical condition. I don't know if we can get that passed here. Too much."

"In Washington, they are proposing a maximum of fifteen plants," Luther interjected. "Even that seems way too much for Colorado."

"Fifteen plants is way too much," I said. "At my college in Vermont, John 'the Roach' Delanno had six plants growing on his dorm room windowsill, and even in the winter that seemed to provide enough whenever it was needed. The plants were pretty scrawny, for sure, but six seemed enough for a semester."

"The Roach Delanno Standard of six plants, huh? Fine with me," Mark announced, and continued. "Six and no more."

We all agreed on six for personal use, although in the end we allowed more than six plants granted under a severe medical necessity provision.

Fifteen years later, a number of other states have adopted the six-plant restriction for personal growth of medical marijuana. In 2012, Colorado took it to the next level, adopting the six-plant standard for the cultivation of recreational marijuana.

Moreover, the Roach Delanno Standard has had a broader impact.

• • •

In February of 2013, Joannie and I traveled to Uruguay, where we assisted grassroots groups and the Uruguayan government in legalizing marijuana. In our first meeting with the activists, I asked, "Will you have personal grow in the legislation? Can someone grow their own marijuana?"

One of the women activists simply said, "Oh yes. We modeled the proposal after Colorado's six-plant rule. It's the standard in the industry."

Joannie and I looked at each other, nodded, and muttered in unison, "The Roach Delanno Standard."

In December 2013, Uruguay became the first country in the world to legalize marijuana. The new law includes a provision for personal cultivation of up to six plants.

# A FEW MUSINGS AT THE END

I guess that helping to make marijuana legal is not as noteworthy as electing the president of the United States, though I do a have photo of a friend's marijuana plant that is seven feet high and four feet wide. I'm pretty sure it wouldn't have fit in my college dorm room, much less sat on the windowsill.

But the political consultant's job isn't always about helping elect a president or prime minister. Despite the odds against us and the incompetence we've encountered, our firm has helped elect seven heads of government, including a couple of successful U.S. presidents. Really though, it has been about making some positive incremental difference in the way people live their lives. I like to think we have done that and still do.

We know that the election of a single individual or political party or the furtherance of a cause will not necessarily put a chicken in every pot; however, just maybe we have succeeded in putting chicken fingers in a few of the right carry-out boxes.

• • •

In June 1994, I was sent to Macedonia by the National Democratic Institute (NDI) to conduct "Democracy Training" in small communities in the new nation.

We were driving to a town about two hours from Skopje, the nation's capital. Our driver was a member of a local community-organizing group that was sponsoring one of these democracy training workshops. The nation had recently split from the formerly communist Yugoslavia and was soon to conduct only the second "free" national elections in its short history.

We passed an old stone farmhouse that had clearly been well maintained. The brick was clean and the grass immediately around the home had recently been mowed, but the fields farther from the house were not tilled or otherwise tended. I stared at the austere farmhouse as we drove by and my gaze clearly caught the attention of the driver.

"It is the home of a family here," he said in a deep voice with a heavy accent. "They haven't lived there since 1943, when the Nazis took them away." He sighed. "Some of the old families maintain the house so that when they return, it will be in good condition."

We drove on.

The training was held in an old school classroom, with desks and a blackboard at the front. My talk was to be thirty minutes and cover the basics of democracy, how to vote, where to vote, and a bit about the formation of political parties. Then there would be Q&A, which was to last another thirty minutes.

At the end of the Q&A, when I announced "one more question," a man probably in his mid-eighties raised his hand and began to talk. The local organizer translated for me.

"He said, 'The problem is that all our politicians are crooks. We wanted them to build a dam to stop the flooding in our city and we paid them money for them to build the dam, and they took the money we paid, and never built the dam. And now we have no dam and no money. They are all crooks."

I asked him, " Do you know of people who are honest and not crooks?"

"Yes I do," he replied.

"Convince them to run for office so that you give people a choice between honest people and crooks," I concluded.

He looked me in the eye and said, simply, "You mean we can do that now?"

• • •

Marginal and dramatic changes in politcs often happen by quirks of fate or happenstance. Many times, campaign consultants take credit for brilliance in election strategy in situations where there is really no basis for claiming brilliance. Something lucky happens, or the circumstances highly favor the winning campaign. Sometimes, the winning campaign is simply not as bad as the opposition's—it's the "less worse" campaign.

Frequently though, the strategy, tactics, and technology don't make much of a difference if, in the end, the voters find the candidate insufferable. Bad candidates generally lose regardless of their political party. And even when they do win, they become lousy elected officials.

There are exceptions to this. Sometimes bad candidates are excellent legislators. Some politicians are incapable of communicating to the 400,000 people in their district or jurisdictions, but are masters of the insider politics of a body of roughly 400 elected officials, such as those in the U.S. Congress, a national parliament, or a state legislature.

Strangely, as a result of contemporary campaigns and outside monies, those elected officials who are able to work successfully inside their elected body may become more important in the coming years, because they are less suceptable to the pressures that are brought by campaign dollars.

The massive influx of outside money on U.S. campaigns has completely altered the influence a candidate has on his or her own campaign—including the message. In 2014, in Colorado's U.S. Senate race, the two candidate committees spent $35 million and over $65 million was spent by outside groups. Was that $65 million really spent detailing who and what the candidates were fighting for? Or, was it spent communicating the agenda of those who had the $65 million? Were the candidates and their campaigns simply vehicles in a demolition derby? Unfortunately, most winning candidates, in these circumstances don't have any idea why they won. Was it their message or the message of the independent organization?

Too often, campaigns now have no control over what voters see and hear about their own candidates. It is not just their opposition that is defining their candidacies, it is their friends, whose independent-expenditure campaigns may have an agenda that is not remotely reflective of the candidate's agenda or path to victory. We often see gun control advocates promoting a candidate's gun control positions, when the candidate would be better served if gun control were never made an issue.

Worse are allies who try to shoehorn their organizational message into the candidate's agenda with near-comic results. Think about a conservation organization airing *ad infinitum* a pro-abortion message. This occurred in a U.S. Senate race in 2014.

Amplifying this messaging conflict between outside groups and candidacies, is the highly targeted nature of today's political campaigns. Campaigns are tailoring messages and communications to *specific individuals*, using references unique to that person. Today, "all politics is customizable." Through technology, we have moved from promises of "a chicken in every pot" to "a chicken in your pot" to "a chicken in your pot—seasoned just the way you like." In a world of California customized closets, sleep-number beds, and build-your-own automobiles, it is no surprise that campaigns have followed suit. Taking the billions of bits of information available in the commercial world and applying that "big data" to campaign communications, a campaign can adapt its messaging to appeal to an individual, practically down to his or her fingerprint. For instance, by matching a voter's Internet cookies to an enriched voter file, a campaign professional can easily direct a specific online message about GMOs in baby food to a female who is thirty-five and sometimes—but not always—buys organic foods; has a household income over $70,000 a year; recently bought baby clothes; and lives in a specific area. This message is delivered as a pop-up or banner advertisement on only *her* computer, tablet, or smartphone.

Facebook can deliver campaign messages in newsfeeds to as few as twenty individuals at a time, based on specific demographics and usage behavior. So, your neighbor, who might be the same age and gender and have the same party affiliation as you, is receiving a very different candidate message from the same campaign because he "liked" a particular football team on Facebook and you did not.

As campaigns now appeal to each voter's specific issues, fears, wants, and desires through highly targeted messaging, they perpetuate the myth that, once in office, the candidate will do exactly what the individual voter wants. Yet, there is no way that any candidate or party can deliver on such precise expectations once the election is over.

Unlike the commercial world, big data allows customized communication *for* the voter but not *by* the voter. It is precisely this distinction that causes a dissonance in voter expectations. On the one hand, they are able to customize their phone, car, wardrobe, and—they are led to believe—political candidates. But this last impression is a myth.

This all puts greater pressure on those inside the decision-making body, who either no longer fear or hear the political cacophony, and are capable of legislative achievements. Often, these insiders are in safe legislative seats or are so personally popular that party associations are unimportant. They can focus on the political insitution to which they are elected and not be swayed by campaign and outside group pressures. They have a greater ability—if they so desire—to put aside ideological straitjackets to achieve some political success precisely because they will not be voted out of office. Further, they do not have to spend twenty hours a week fundraising to protect their seats, so they can focus on legislation.

I have been fortunate to work with some of these insiders and it is extremely frustrating, because they can and will break almost all of the rules.

For instance, I know one congressperson whose insanely erudite spouse is engaged in policy formulation. She no longer has any idea why she ran for office fifteen years ago, or why she should be re-elected now—other than that she is really really good at her job. She bases her campaigns on a strong coalition within a small geographic area, she is convinced that her encyclopedic knowledge of the process is the holy grail of political success, she spends little time raising money, and she demands that 3,000 yard signs be distributed one month before an election to guarantee victory. Her campaign efforts pretty much end with the yard sign distribution.

However, as an elected official in a safe seat with an uncanny comprehension of the needs of her legislative colleagues and the legislative process, she has made significant advances in health care for people with long-term injuries and disease. That ain't mere chicken fingers in a box.

Which all means that rules are there to be broken and perhaps should be broken, or adapted to a changing environment. Darwin was obviously thinking of political campaign management when he wrote *On the Origin of Species*; taking a static approach to political campaigns is a quick way to lose— and perhaps become extinct.

Remember, though—if you intend to break the rules, or the rules change, be mindful of the unintended consequences. You might actually find your candidate or cause to be successful.

Then what does anyone really know? Are there really any rules?

Happy trails!

# ACKNOWLEDGMENTS

This collection of stories and purported wisdom has been six years in the writing. There are few with whom I have spent much time over those years who have not contributed their insights and critiques. Indeed I have shared so many chapters and selections that my wife claims there will no one left to buy the book.

Joannie Braden has endured the brunt of this endeavor. She has suffered through the multiple drafts, the disappearance of her husband to coffee shops for extended periods of writing, and the too many times when I focused on the book, when it might have been better (and certainly more lucrative) to focus on current and future clients. At the same time, she always encouraged me to keep going. Most importantly, her suggestions and editorial contributions were always superb and significantly improved the stories and lessons. For all of this and so much more I am extraordinarily grateful.

Similarly my children, Alex, Nat and Jenn bore witness to the demands exacted through six years of my book-writing indulgence. I don't think I missed any births or marriages but certainly family dinners were delayed, transportation schedules altered, and a few runs together down snowy mountains missed as a result of this effort. It has never been easy for them and for this I am very appreciative.

I mention coffee shops because this book would never have been written without the comfort and caffeine of the Daz Bog at 17th and Downing or Satchel's and Buzz on 6th, both in Denver. The now defunct Steaming Bean in Steamboat kept me well jazzed during winter writing efforts.

Perhaps, though, the encouragement to write this book came as much from my friend Dan Gerstein, who acted as both cornerman and guidance counselor. He never shied from telling me of the trials of writing a book, nor did he ever say, "Forget about it." His wisdom and direction at all stages of this endeavor are much appreciated. Most importantly, Dan introduced me to talented individuals who served to make this book better.

In particular, Michael Takiff and David Groff were instrumental in the construct of this book. Michel took the raw copy of these stories and gave them life and rhythm. He talked me through the stories and then added language to give them more poignancy. David forced them into a structure and narrowed the stories to be less Homeric and more defined. He edited carefully to make sure that the lesson was well articulated and presented. They were the craftsman who totally refined an unfinished product. I owe a huge debt to both.

From them, it fell to the Radius Books gang to produce a final product. I could not have done this without them and copy editor extraordinaire Laura Ross.

Somewhere there is a member of the RBI staff of the past few years who did not have a hand in this endeavor. But I doubt it. Chrissie Nims, Lauren Stackpoole, Jessica Campbell Swanson and Michael Dabbs all spent numerous hours proof-reading the manuscripts. Niki Hawthorne, Bob Nelson, Adam Dunstone, Tyler Chafee, Craig Hughes, Callie Seymour and Faye Diamond gave significant input on exact dates, circumstances, and creative content. They were often the ones to say, "Remember when . . ." leading me to a lesson or a story. Faye, in particular, was not only tolerant of the commitment of staff time to this book, but let me know if there were needed elements or edits in the manuscript.

And then there were the interns and short-time staff who were dragged into fact checking and on-line searches. Keenan Duffey, Josh Patton, Jai Sutherland, Megan MacColl, Taylor Gibson, Cameron Bean, and Otilla Enica played a major role in the research endeavors as well as mitigating antiquated references.

Many friends and colleagues are part of the making of this book. I mention some—Hugo Haime, Mark Grueskin, Rich Schlackman, and Paul Sullivan—but there are many others who do not appear in these stories with whom I exchanged stories at bars and coffee shops around the globe. They are to be congratulated for suffering through those stories many of which, for good reason, never made it on these pages. This group includes just about every member of the International Association of Political Consultants (IAPC).

I would be remiss if I did not recognize the political parties and organizations with which I have been honored to work, as well as the political candidates who are, without exception, committed individuals and trying to better the human condition in the best way they know how. Many thanks to all of them for their efforts.

Finally, my Mother and Father contributed greatly to this endeavor—my Mother for introducing me to political campaigning at an early age, and my Father for encouraging me to follow my ambitions. I could not have had a career in politics, nor written this book, without them.

August, 2016
Coal Train Hill
Oak Creek, CO

**RICK RIDDER** is President and Co-Founder of RBI Strategies and Research, a former presidential campaign manager, and a senior consultant for six other presidential campaigns. Rick has consulted for numerous U.S. Congressional, gubernatorial, and state and local initiative campaigns. Internationally, he has worked in over 22 nations, including on the successful campaigns of five heads of state. His firm is one of the few to win Pollie Awards (the Oscars of the political industry) for creative efforts, technology applications, and management capabilities (International Consultant of the Year). Rick has also been recognized with the Award of Achievement from the Gleitsman Foundation for "commitment and leadership initiating social change." He has written for *Salon*, *Campaigns and Elections*, *Australian Financial Review*, *RealClear Politics*, and *The Denver Post*. He has appeared on *The Daily Show*, all major US networks, the BBC, Australian Broadcasting, and a number of other foreign broadcast networks.

Rick holds a B.A. from Middlebury College and an M.S. from Boston University, and is an adjunct professor at the University of Denver's Korbel School of International Studies. He lives in Denver, Colorado, with his wife and business partner, Joannie Braden.